CSI:

CRIME SCENE INVESTIGATION™

DEMON HOUSE

Collins • Rodriguez • Wood

TITAN BOOKS

CSI: CRIME SCENE INVESTIGATION

Created by Anthony E. Zuiker

Licensed to IDW by CBS Consumer Products

"Demon House"

ISBN 1 84023 936 0

Written by **Max Allan Collins**

Forensics Research/Plot Assist by **Matthew V. Clemens**

Pencils & Inks by **Gabriel Rodriguez**

Colours by **Fran Gamboa**

Painted Artwork by **Ashley Wood**

Lettered by **Robbie Robbins**

Edited by **Jeff Mariotte**

Design by **Robbie Robbins**

Published by
Titan Books
A division of Titan Publishing Group Ltd.
144 Southwark St
London SE1 0UP

First edition: September 2004

10 9 8 7 6 5 4 3 2 1

A CIP catalogue record for this title is available from the British Library.

Printed in Italy.

Also available from Titan Books:
CSI: Crime Scene Investigation – Serial (ISBN: 1 84023 771 6)
CSI: Crime Scene Investigation – Bad Rap (ISBN: 1 84023 799 6)

What did you think of this book? We love to hear from our
readers. Please email us at: readerfeedback@titanemail.com,
or write to us at the above address.

You can also visit us at **www.titanbooks.com**

IDW

$3.99

issue #1

CSI:

CRIME SCENE INVESTIGATION.

Demon House

chapter one

Fright Night

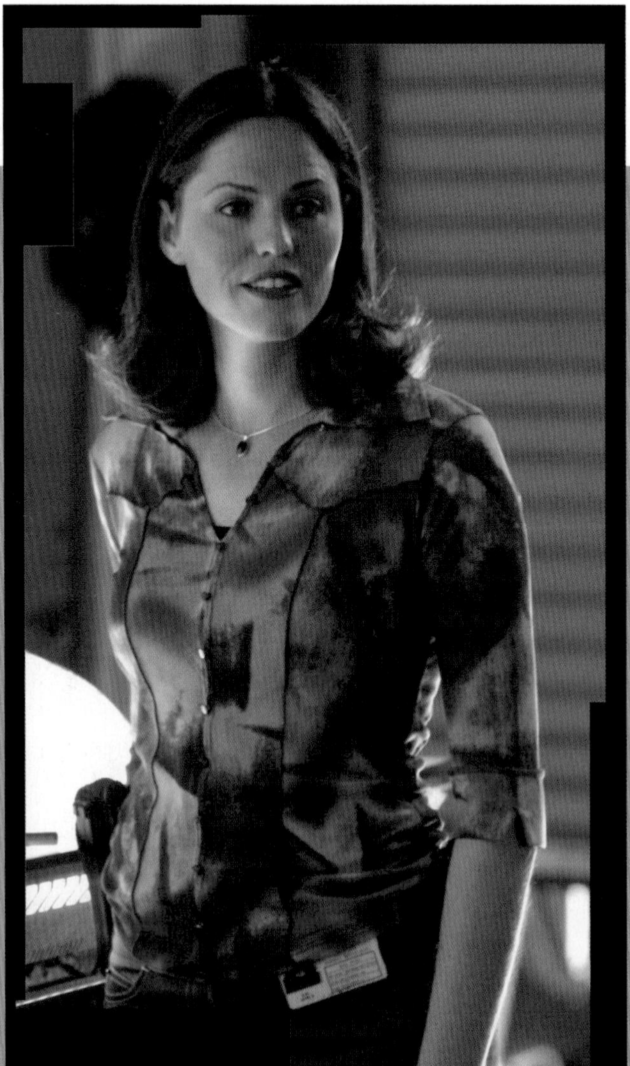

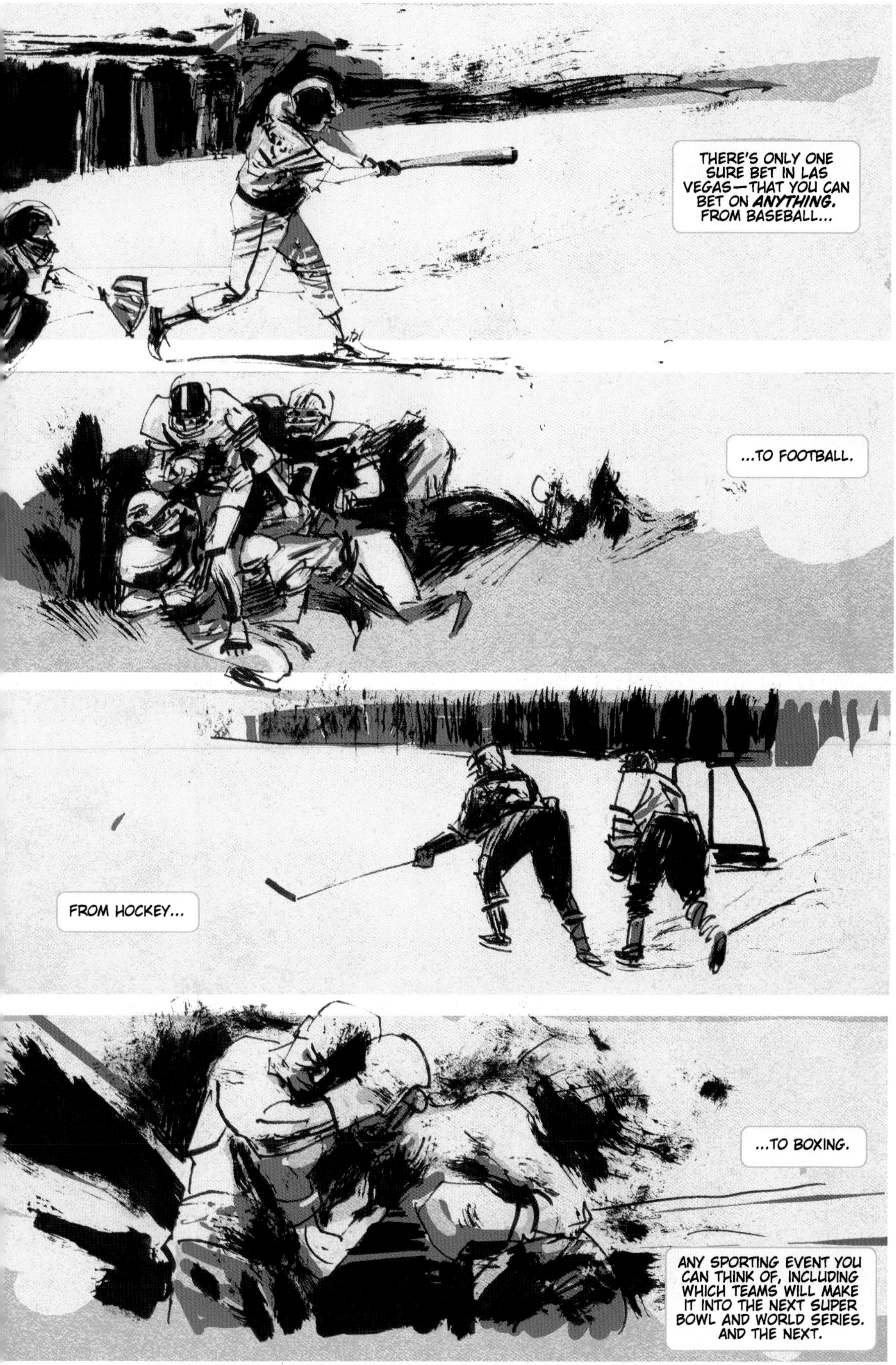
THERE'S ONLY ONE SURE BET IN LAS VEGAS—THAT YOU CAN BET ON *ANYTHING.* FROM BASEBALL...
...TO FOOTBALL.
FROM HOCKEY...
...TO BOXING.
ANY SPORTING EVENT YOU CAN THINK OF, INCLUDING WHICH TEAMS WILL MAKE IT INTO THE NEXT SUPER BOWL AND WORLD SERIES. AND THE NEXT.

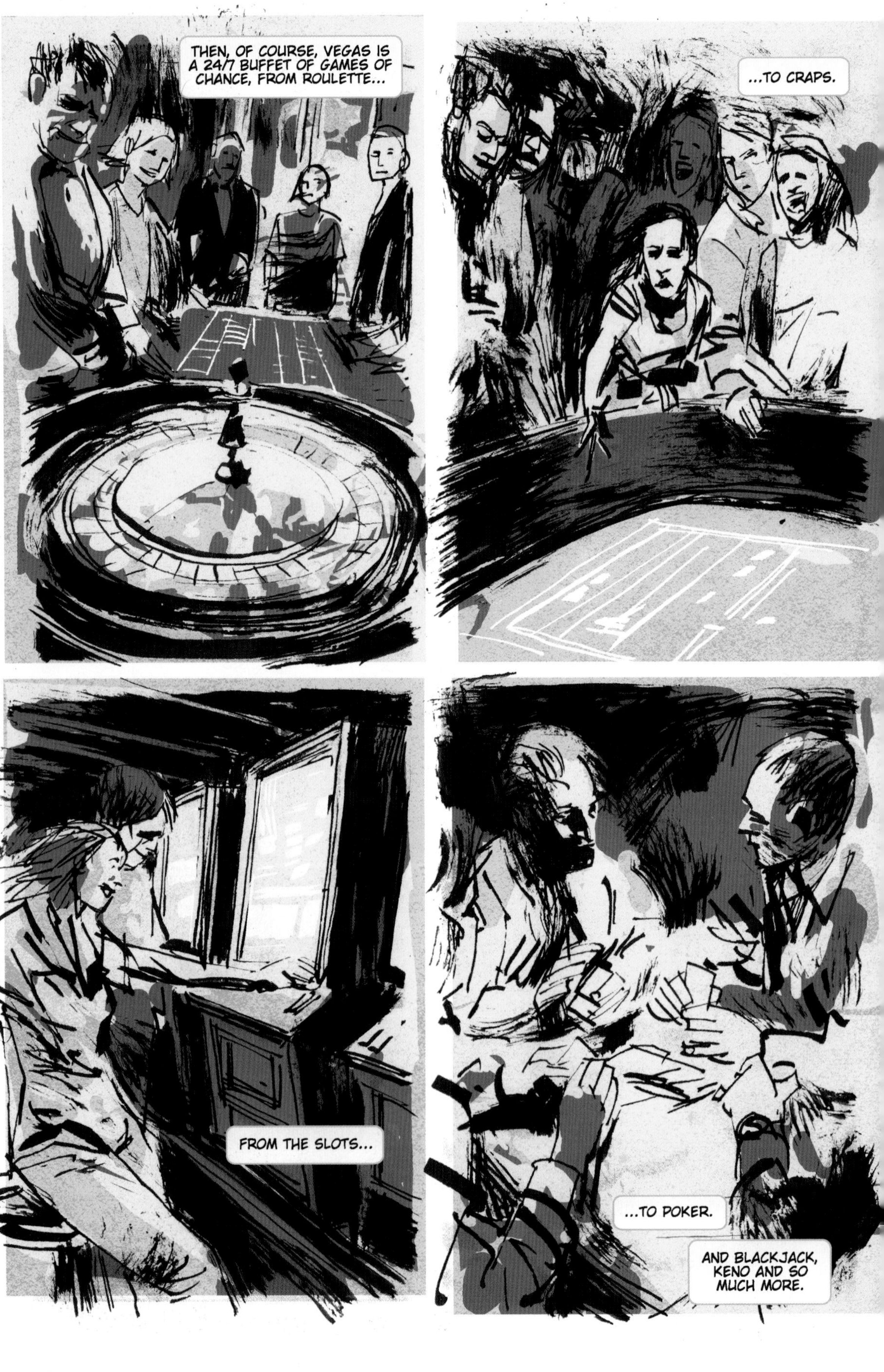
THEN, OF COURSE, VEGAS IS A 24/7 BUFFET OF GAMES OF CHANCE, FROM ROULETTE...
...TO CRAPS.
FROM THE SLOTS...
...TO POKER.
AND BLACKJACK, KENO AND SO MUCH MORE.

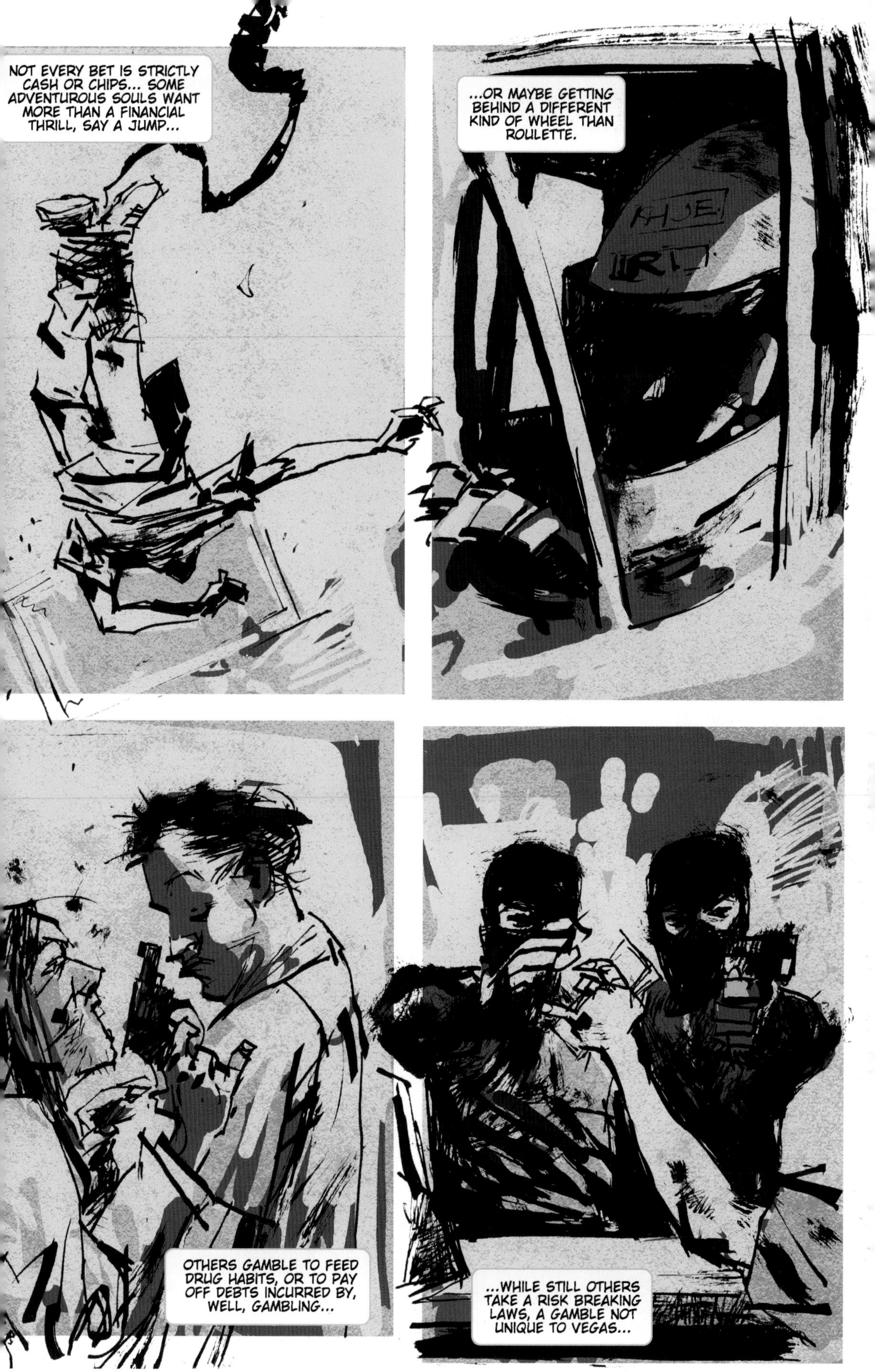
NOT EVERY BET IS STRICTLY CASH OR CHIPS... SOME ADVENTUROUS SOULS WANT MORE THAN A FINANCIAL THRILL, SAY A JUMP...
...OR MAYBE GETTING BEHIND A DIFFERENT KIND OF WHEEL THAN ROULETTE.
OTHERS GAMBLE TO FEED DRUG HABITS, OR TO PAY OFF DEBTS INCURRED BY, WELL, GAMBLING...
...WHILE STILL OTHERS TAKE A RISK BREAKING LAWS, A GAMBLE NOT UNIQUE TO VEGAS...

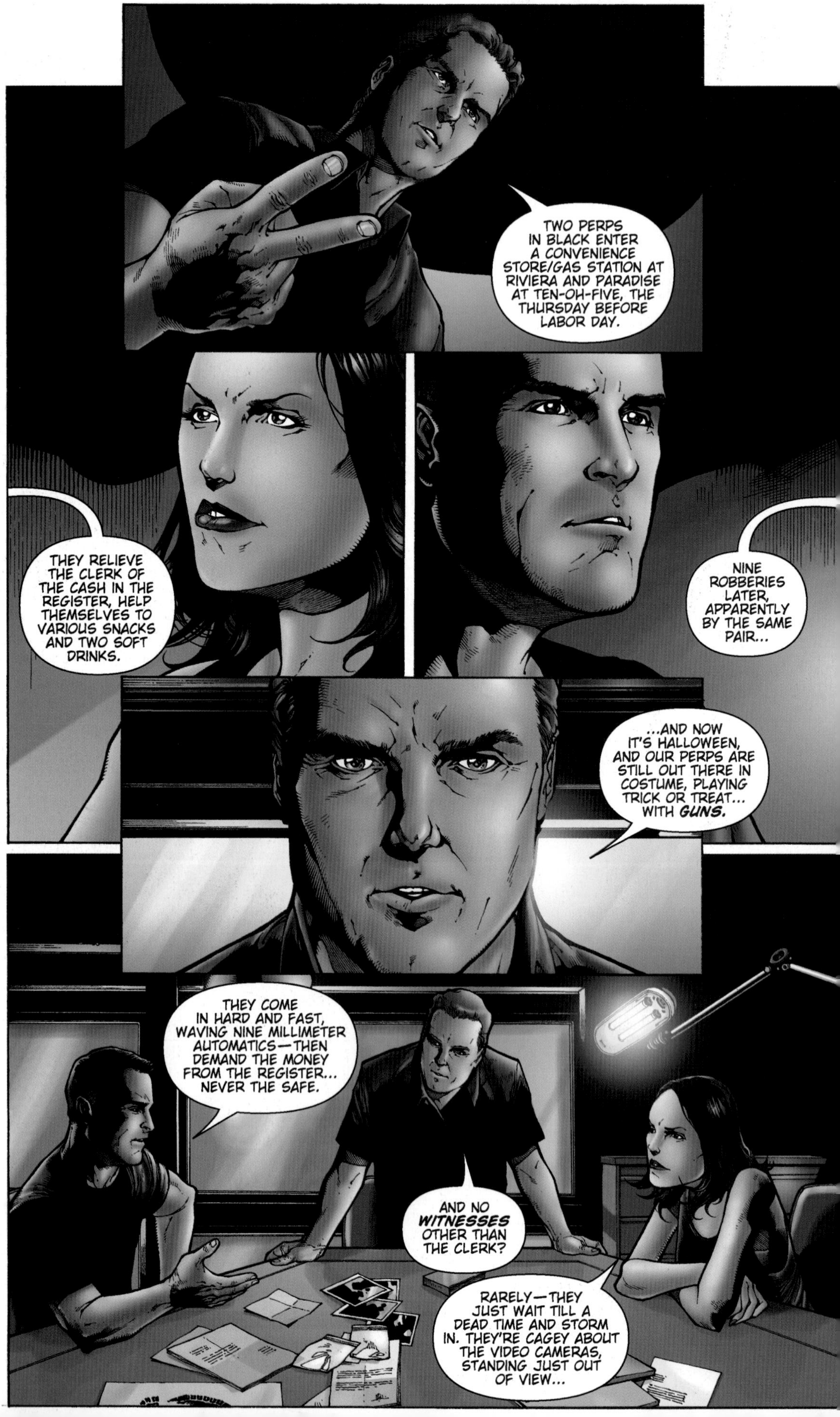
TWO PERPS IN BLACK ENTER A CONVENIENCE STORE/GAS STATION AT RIVIERA AND PARADISE AT TEN-OH-FIVE, THE THURSDAY BEFORE LABOR DAY.
THEY RELIEVE THE CLERK OF THE CASH IN THE REGISTER, HELP THEMSELVES TO VARIOUS SNACKS AND TWO SOFT DRINKS.
NINE ROBBERIES LATER, APPARENTLY BY THE SAME PAIR...
...AND NOW IT'S HALLOWEEN, AND OUR PERPS ARE STILL OUT THERE IN COSTUME, PLAYING TRICK OR TREAT... WITH GUNS.
THEY COME IN HARD AND FAST, WAVING NINE MILLIMETER AUTOMATICS—THEN DEMAND THE MONEY FROM THE REGISTER... NEVER THE SAFE.
AND NO WITNESSES OTHER THAN THE CLERK?
RARELY—THEY JUST WAIT TILL A DEAD TIME AND STORM IN. THEY'RE CAGEY ABOUT THE VIDEO CAMERAS, STANDING JUST OUT OF VIEW...

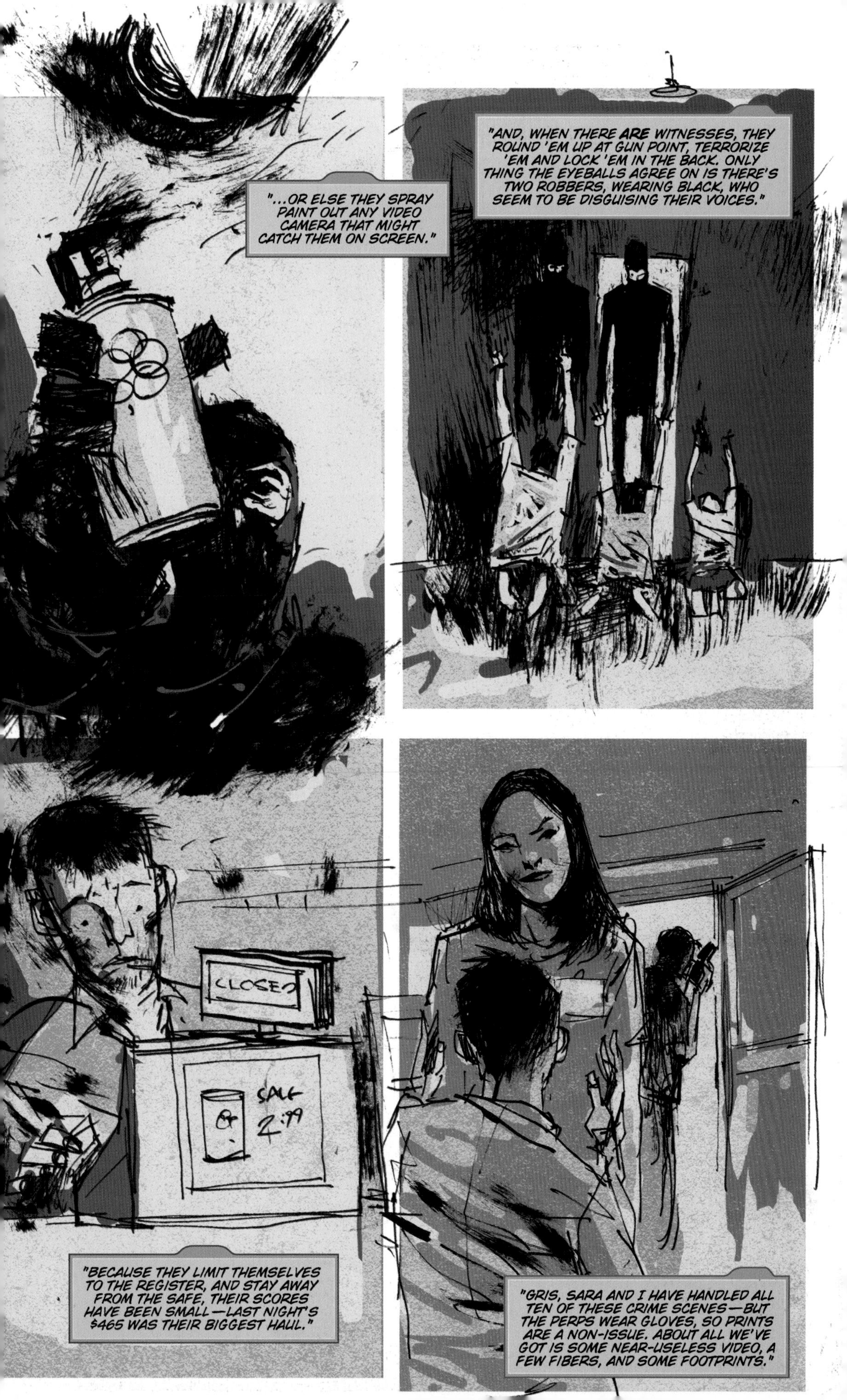
"...OR ELSE THEY SPRAY PAINT OUT ANY VIDEO CAMERA THAT MIGHT CATCH THEM ON SCREEN."
"AND, WHEN THERE ARE WITNESSES, THEY ROUND 'EM UP AT GUN POINT, TERRORIZE 'EM AND LOCK 'EM IN THE BACK. ONLY THING THE EYEBALLS AGREE ON IS THERE'S TWO ROBBERS, WEARING BLACK, WHO SEEM TO BE DISGUISING THEIR VOICES."
CLOSED
SALE
2.99
"BECAUSE THEY LIMIT THEMSELVES TO THE REGISTER, AND STAY AWAY FROM THE SAFE, THEIR SCORES HAVE BEEN SMALL—LAST NIGHT'S $465 WAS THEIR BIGGEST HAUL."
"GRIS, SARA AND I HAVE HANDLED ALL TEN OF THESE CRIME SCENES—BUT THE PERPS WEAR GLOVES, SO PRINTS ARE A NON-ISSUE. ABOUT ALL WE'VE GOT IS SOME NEAR-USELESS VIDEO, A FEW FIBERS, AND SOME FOOTPRINTS."

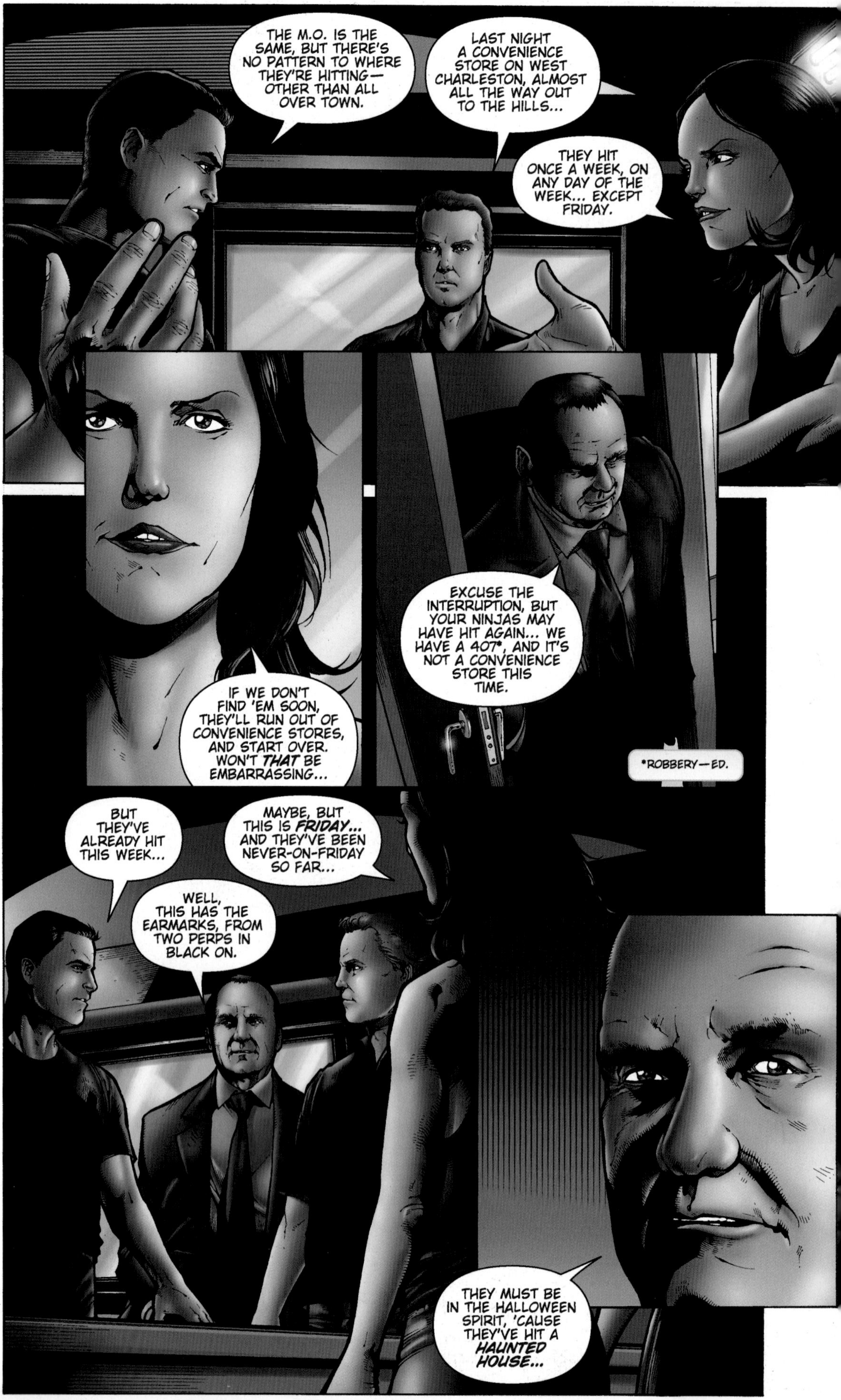
THE M.O. IS THE SAME, BUT THERE'S NO PATTERN TO WHERE THEY'RE HITTING— OTHER THAN ALL OVER TOWN.
LAST NIGHT A CONVENIENCE STORE ON WEST CHARLESTON, ALMOST ALL THE WAY OUT TO THE HILLS...
THEY HIT ONCE A WEEK, ON ANY DAY OF THE WEEK... EXCEPT FRIDAY.
IF WE DON'T FIND 'EM SOON, THEY'LL RUN OUT OF CONVENIENCE STORES, AND START OVER. WON'T *THAT* BE EMBARRASSING...
EXCUSE THE INTERRUPTION, BUT YOUR NINJAS MAY HAVE HIT AGAIN... WE HAVE A 407*, AND IT'S NOT A CONVENIENCE STORE THIS TIME.
*ROBBERY—ED.
BUT THEY'VE ALREADY HIT THIS WEEK...
MAYBE, BUT THIS IS *FRIDAY*... AND THEY'VE BEEN NEVER-ON-FRIDAY SO FAR...
WELL, THIS HAS THE EARMARKS, FROM TWO PERPS IN BLACK ON.
THEY MUST BE IN THE HALLOWEEN SPIRIT, 'CAUSE THEY'VE HIT A *HAUNTED HOUSE*...

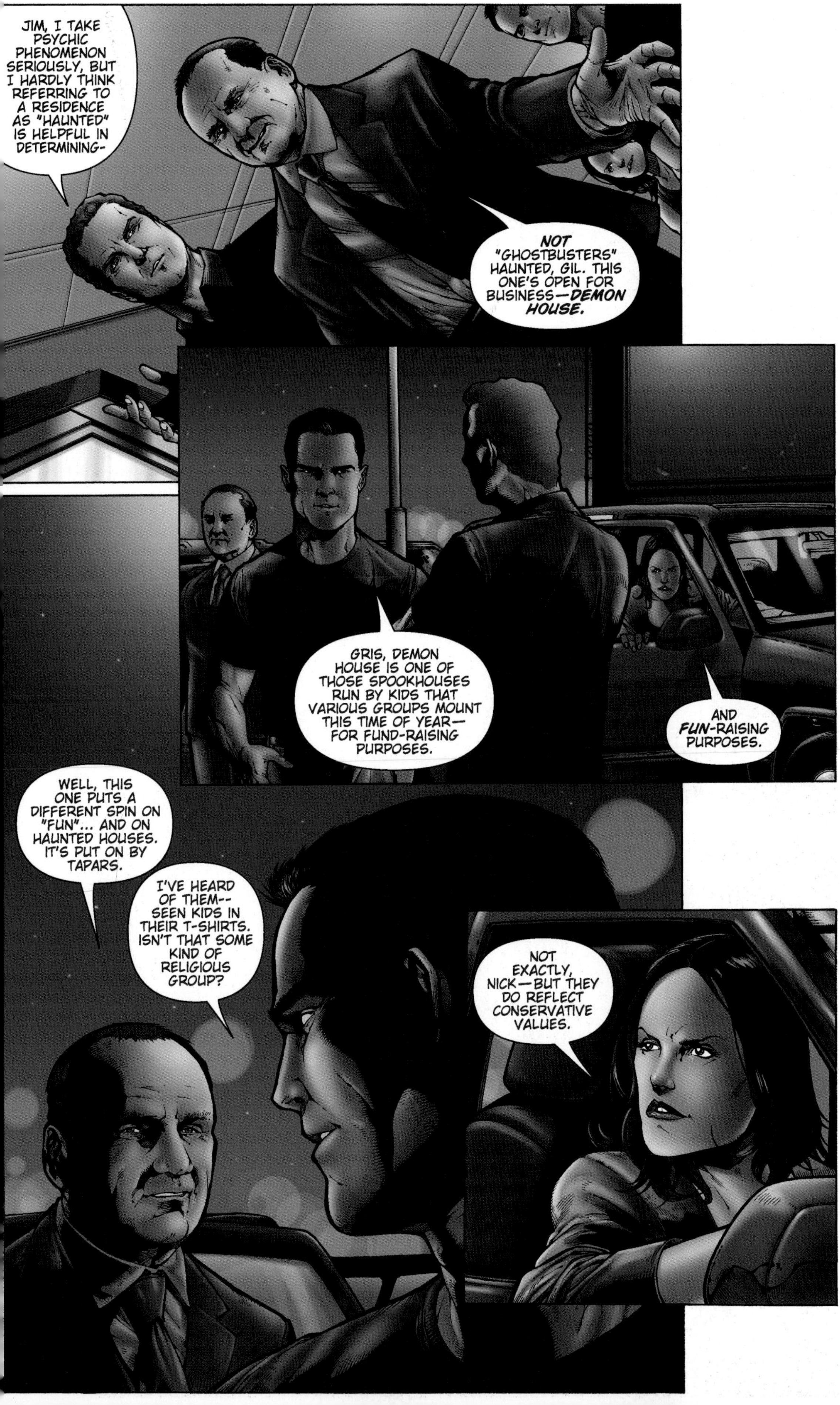
JIM, I TAKE PSYCHIC PHENOMENON SERIOUSLY, BUT I HARDLY THINK REFERRING TO A RESIDENCE AS "HAUNTED" IS HELPFUL IN DETERMINING-
NOT "GHOSTBUSTERS" HAUNTED, GIL. THIS ONE'S OPEN FOR BUSINESS—DEMON HOUSE.
GRIS, DEMON HOUSE IS ONE OF THOSE SPOOKHOUSES RUN BY KIDS THAT VARIOUS GROUPS MOUNT THIS TIME OF YEAR—FOR FUND-RAISING PURPOSES.
AND FUN-RAISING PURPOSES.
WELL, THIS ONE PUTS A DIFFERENT SPIN ON "FUN"... AND ON HAUNTED HOUSES. IT'S PUT ON BY TAPARS.
I'VE HEARD OF THEM--SEEN KIDS IN THEIR T-SHIRTS. ISN'T THAT SOME KIND OF RELIGIOUS GROUP?
NOT EXACTLY, NICK—BUT THEY DO REFLECT CONSERVATIVE VALUES.

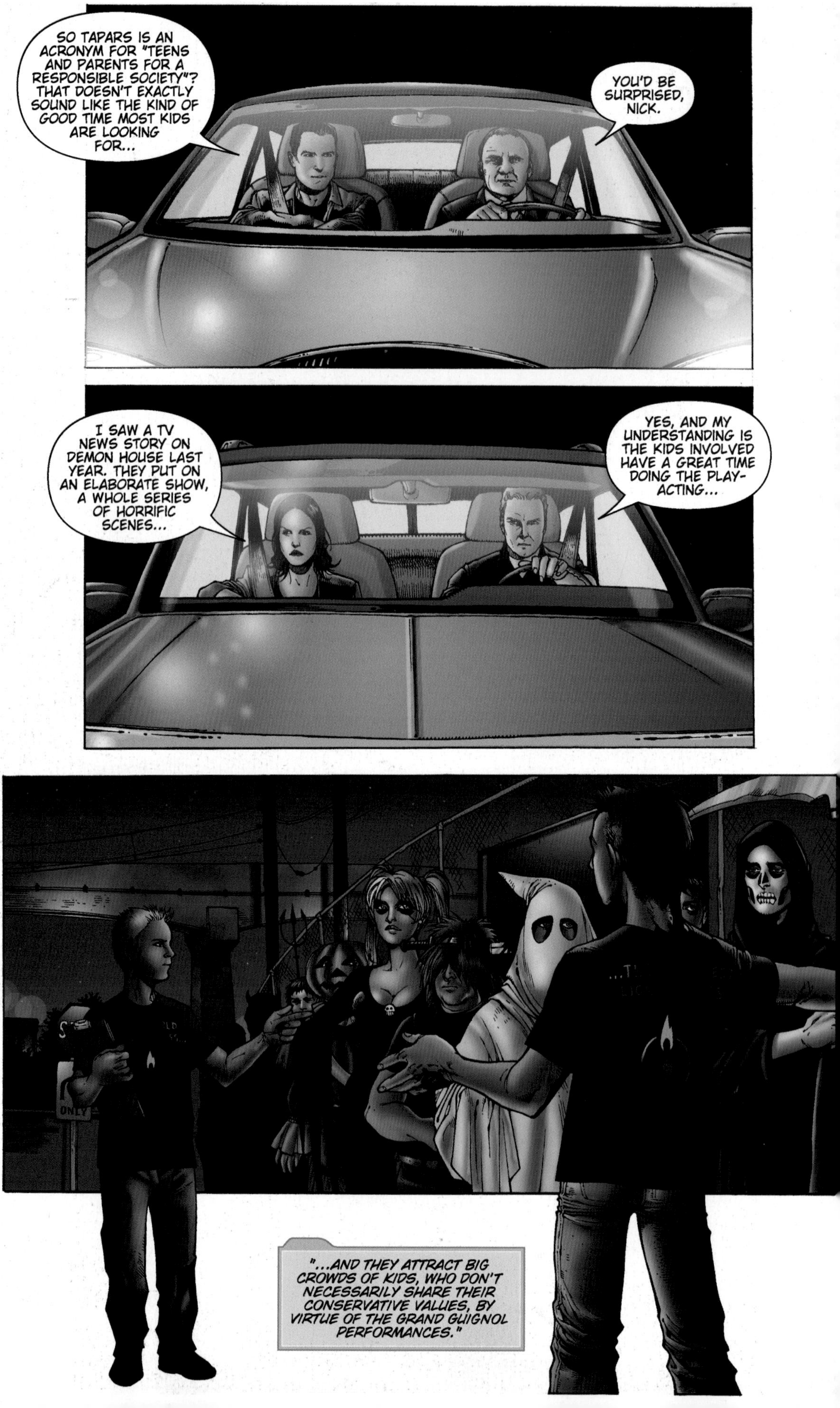
SO TAPARS IS AN ACRONYM FOR "TEENS AND PARENTS FOR A RESPONSIBLE SOCIETY"? THAT DOESN'T EXACTLY SOUND LIKE THE KIND OF GOOD TIME MOST KIDS ARE LOOKING FOR...
YOU'D BE SURPRISED, NICK.
I SAW A TV NEWS STORY ON DEMON HOUSE LAST YEAR. THEY PUT ON AN ELABORATE SHOW, A WHOLE SERIES OF HORRIFIC SCENES...
YES, AND MY UNDERSTANDING IS THE KIDS INVOLVED HAVE A GREAT TIME DOING THE PLAY-ACTING...
"...AND THEY ATTRACT BIG CROWDS OF KIDS, WHO DON'T NECESSARILY SHARE THEIR CONSERVATIVE VALUES, BY VIRTUE OF THE GRAND GUIGNOL PERFORMANCES."

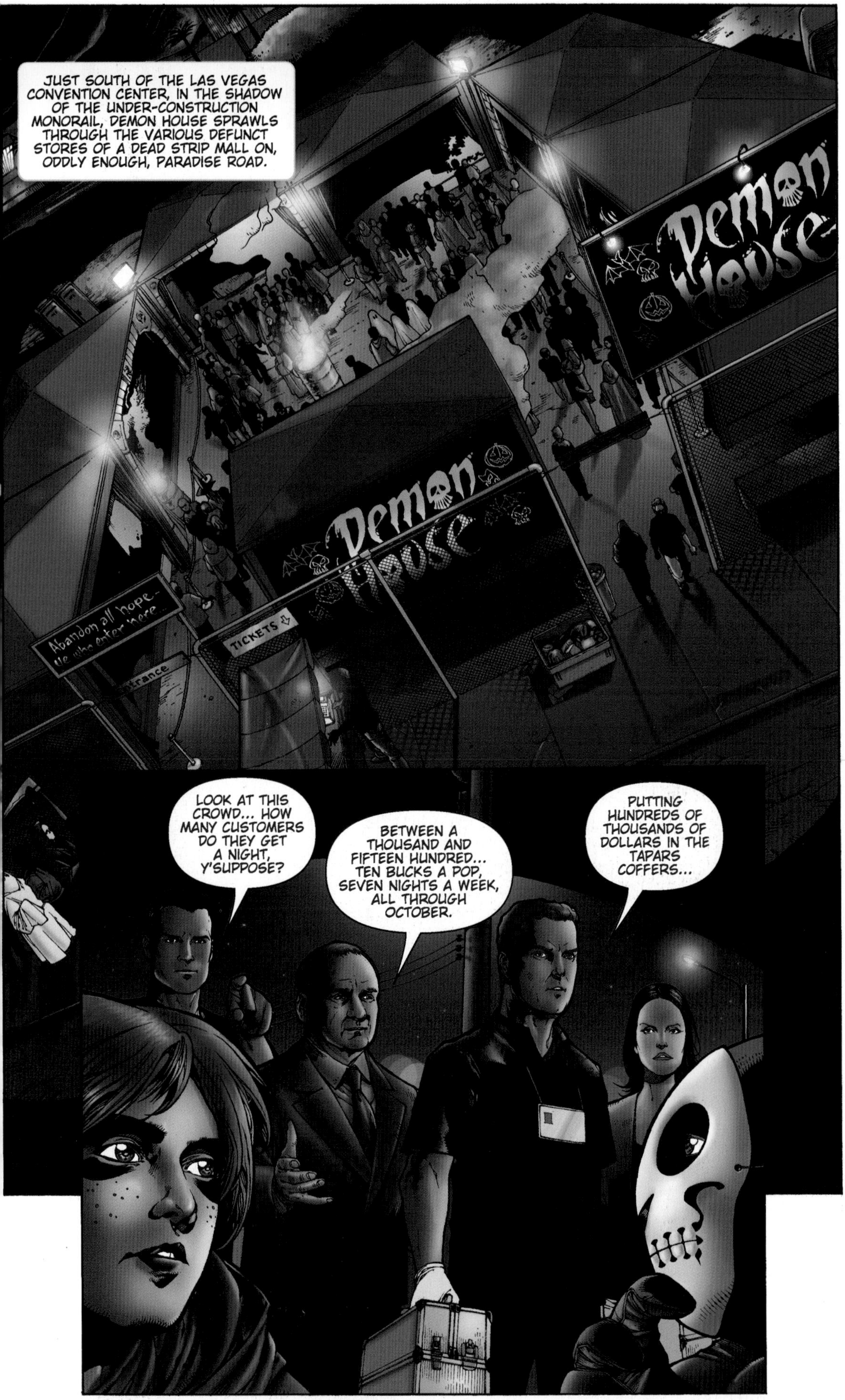
JUST SOUTH OF THE LAS VEGAS CONVENTION CENTER, IN THE SHADOW OF THE UNDER-CONSTRUCTION MONORAIL, DEMON HOUSE SPRAWLS THROUGH THE VARIOUS DEFUNCT STORES OF A DEAD STRIP MALL ON, ODDLY ENOUGH, PARADISE ROAD.
Demon House
Demon House
Abandon all hope— ye who enter here...
TICKETS
LOOK AT THIS CROWD... HOW MANY CUSTOMERS DO THEY GET A NIGHT, Y'SUPPOSE?
BETWEEN A THOUSAND AND FIFTEEN HUNDRED... TEN BUCKS A POP, SEVEN NIGHTS A WEEK, ALL THROUGH OCTOBER.
PUTTING HUNDREDS OF THOUSANDS OF DOLLARS IN THE TAPARS COFFERS...

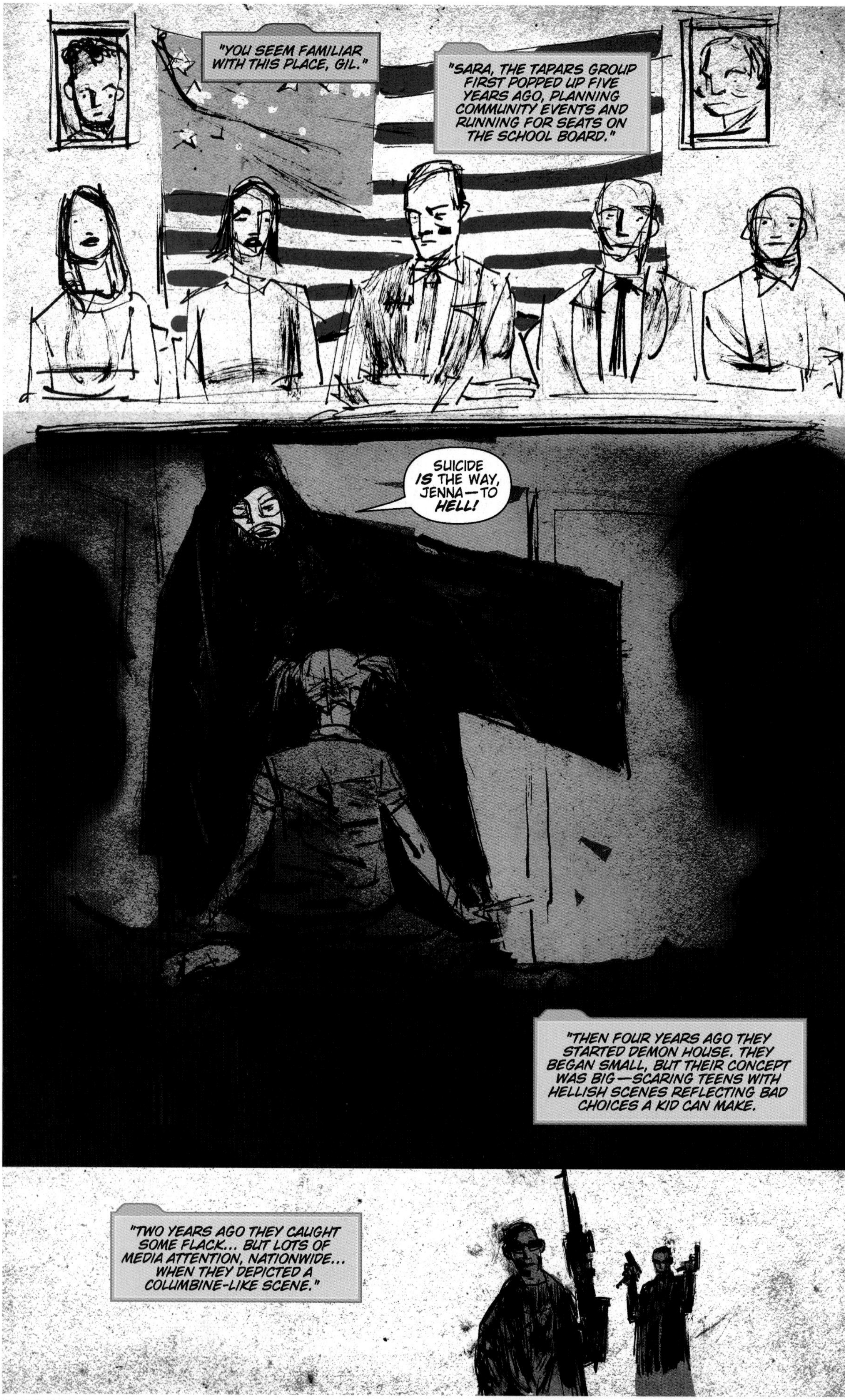
"YOU SEEM FAMILIAR WITH THIS PLACE, GIL."
"SARA, THE TAPARS GROUP FIRST POPPED UP FIVE YEARS AGO, PLANNING COMMUNITY EVENTS AND RUNNING FOR SEATS ON THE SCHOOL BOARD."
SUICIDE *IS* THE WAY, JENNA—TO *HELL!*
"THEN FOUR YEARS AGO THEY STARTED DEMON HOUSE. THEY BEGAN SMALL, BUT THEIR CONCEPT WAS BIG—SCARING TEENS WITH HELLISH SCENES REFLECTING BAD CHOICES A KID CAN MAKE.
"TWO YEARS AGO THEY CAUGHT SOME FLACK... BUT LOTS OF MEDIA ATTENTION, NATIONWIDE... WHEN THEY DEPICTED A COLUMBINE-LIKE SCENE."

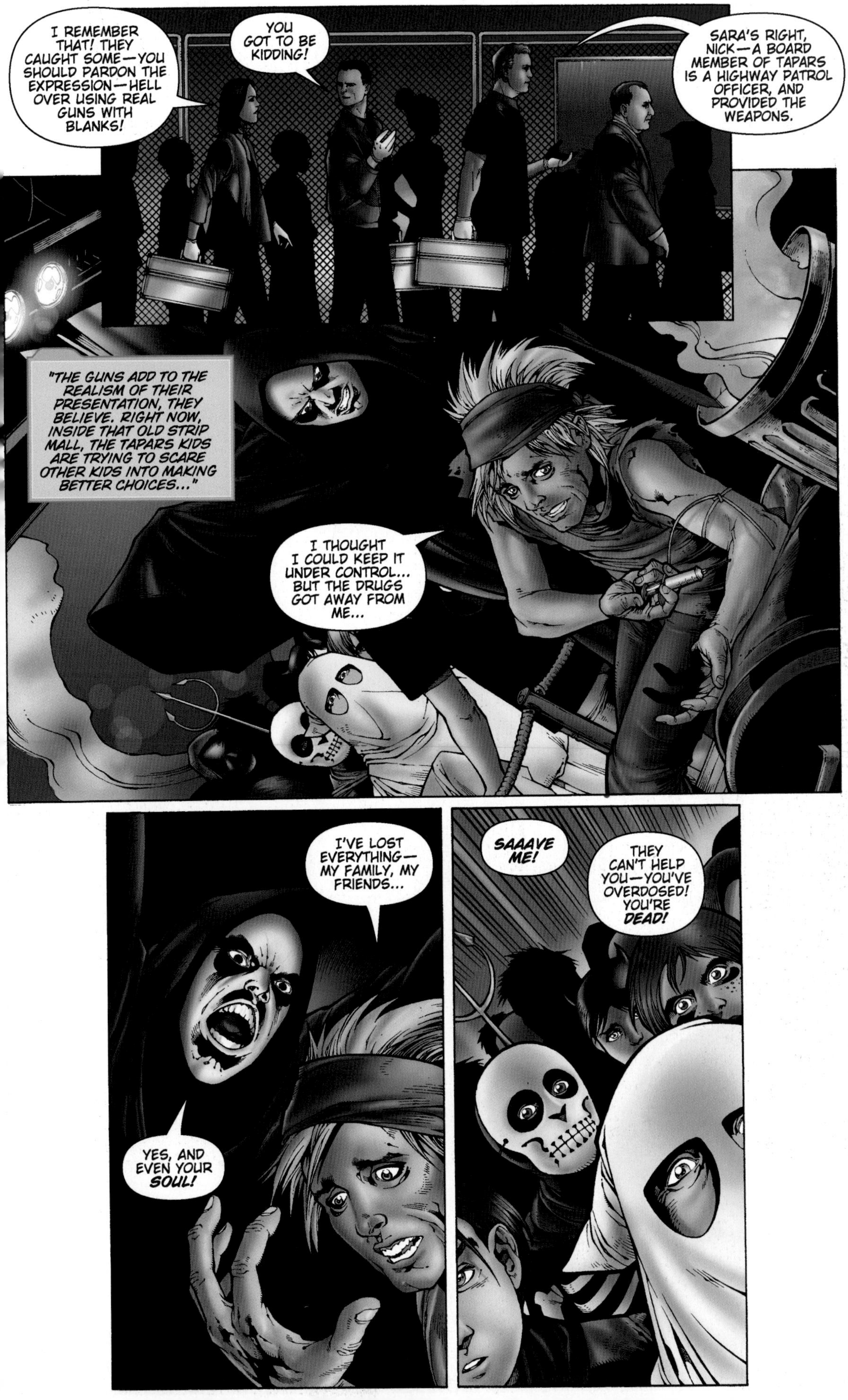
I REMEMBER THAT! THEY CAUGHT SOME—YOU SHOULD PARDON THE EXPRESSION—HELL OVER USING REAL GUNS WITH BLANKS!
YOU GOT TO BE KIDDING!
SARA'S RIGHT, NICK—A BOARD MEMBER OF TAPARS IS A HIGHWAY PATROL OFFICER, AND PROVIDED THE WEAPONS.
"THE GUNS ADD TO THE REALISM OF THEIR PRESENTATION, THEY BELIEVE. RIGHT NOW, INSIDE THAT OLD STRIP MALL, THE TAPARS KIDS ARE TRYING TO SCARE OTHER KIDS INTO MAKING BETTER CHOICES..."
I THOUGHT I COULD KEEP IT UNDER CONTROL... BUT THE DRUGS GOT AWAY FROM ME...
I'VE LOST EVERYTHING—MY FAMILY, MY FRIENDS...
YES, AND EVEN YOUR SOUL!
SAAAVE ME!
THEY CAN'T HELP YOU—YOU'VE OVERDOSED! YOU'RE DEAD!

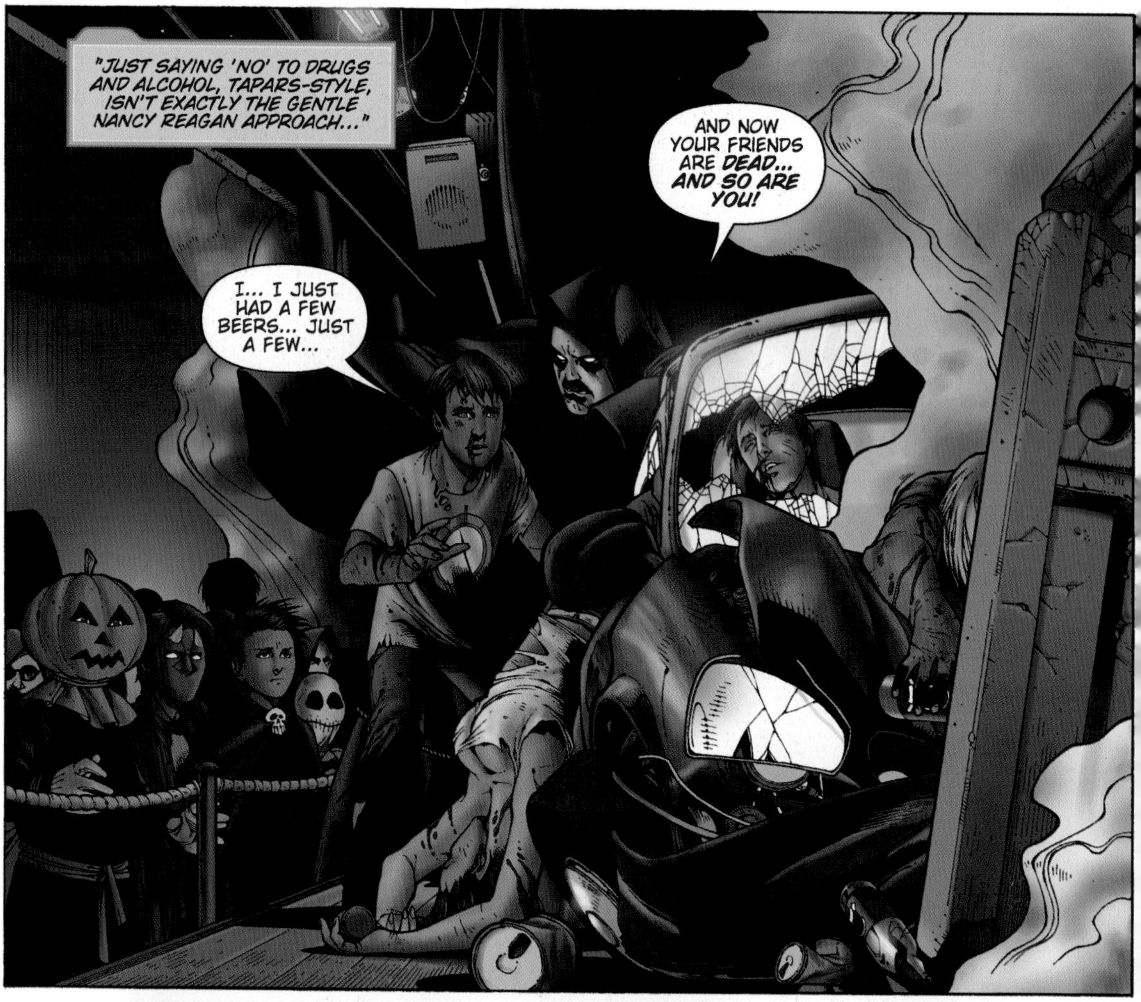
"JUST SAYING 'NO' TO DRUGS AND ALCOHOL, TAPARS-STYLE, ISN'T EXACTLY THE GENTLE NANCY REAGAN APPROACH..."
I... I JUST HAD A FEW BEERS... JUST A FEW...
AND NOW YOUR FRIENDS ARE DEAD... AND SO ARE YOU!

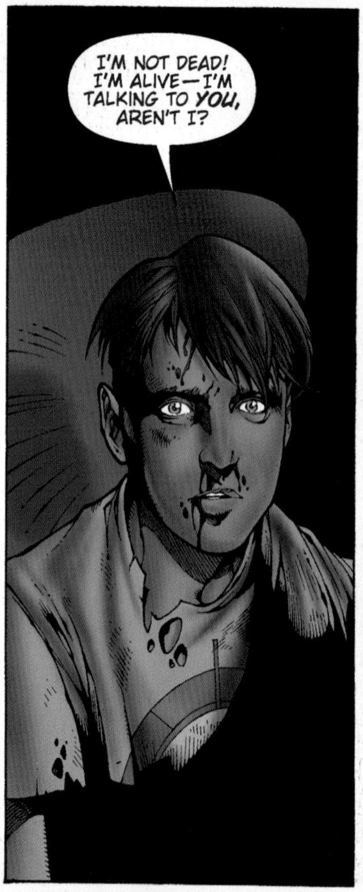
I'M NOT DEAD! I'M ALIVE—I'M TALKING TO YOU, AREN'T I?

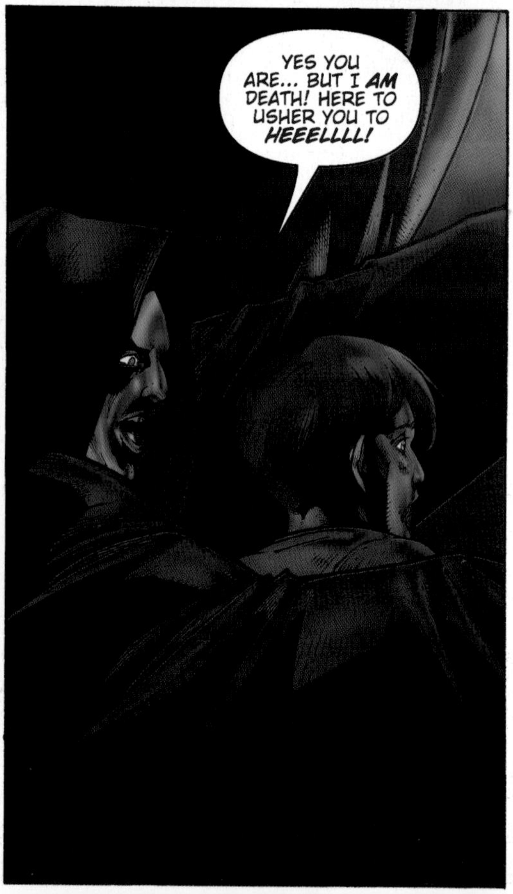
YES YOU ARE... BUT I AM DEATH! HERE TO USHER YOU TO HEEELLLL!

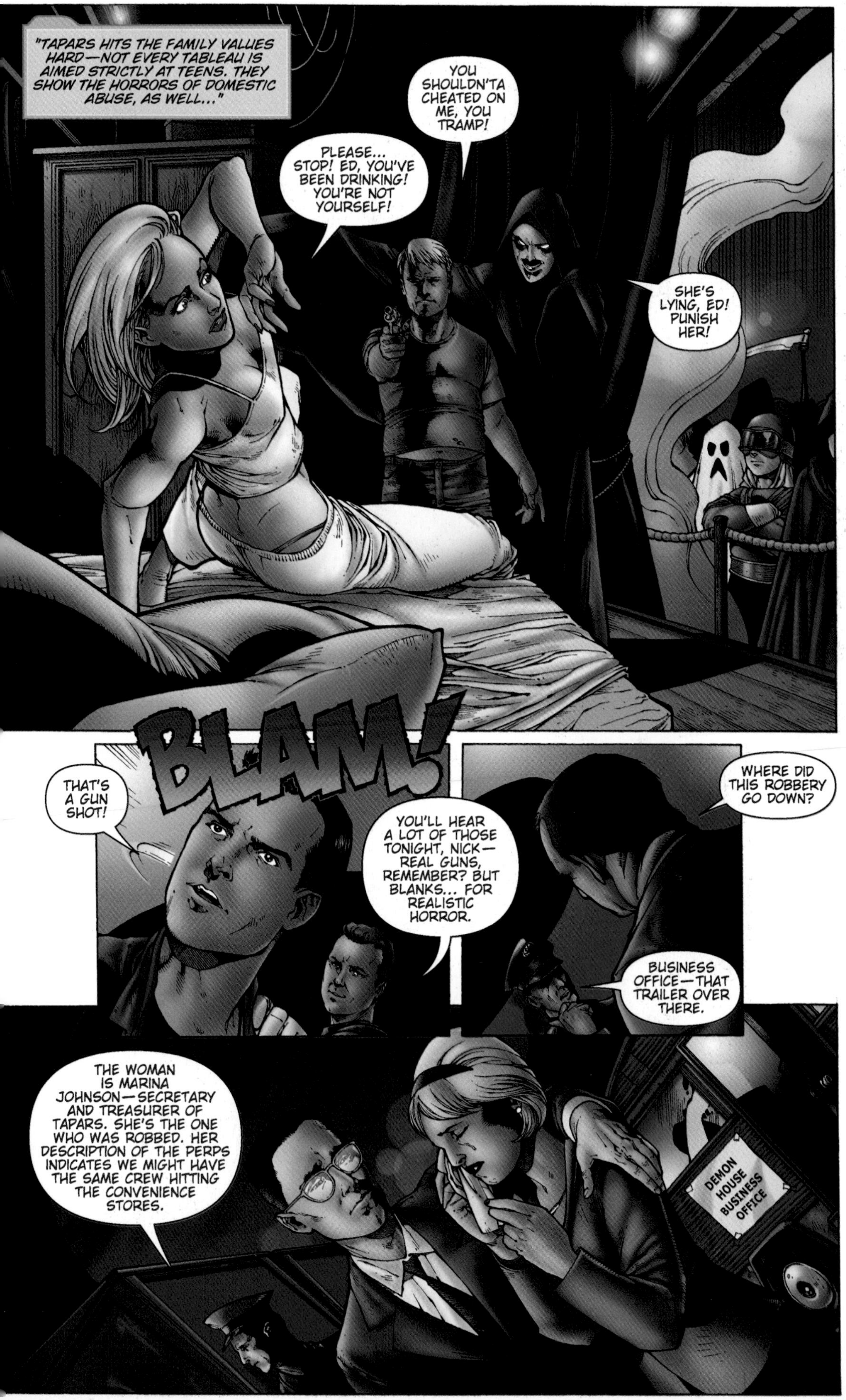
"TAPARS HITS THE FAMILY VALUES HARD—NOT EVERY TABLEAU IS AIMED STRICTLY AT TEENS. THEY SHOW THE HORRORS OF DOMESTIC ABUSE, AS WELL..."
YOU SHOULDN'TA CHEATED ON ME, YOU TRAMP!
PLEASE... STOP! ED, YOU'VE BEEN DRINKING! YOU'RE NOT YOURSELF!
SHE'S LYING, ED! PUNISH HER!
BLAM!
THAT'S A GUN SHOT!
YOU'LL HEAR A LOT OF THOSE TONIGHT, NICK—REAL GUNS, REMEMBER? BUT BLANKS... FOR REALISTIC HORROR.
WHERE DID THIS ROBBERY GO DOWN?
BUSINESS OFFICE—THAT TRAILER OVER THERE.
THE WOMAN IS MARINA JOHNSON—SECRETARY AND TREASURER OF TAPARS. SHE'S THE ONE WHO WAS ROBBED. HER DESCRIPTION OF THE PERPS INDICATES WE MIGHT HAVE THE SAME CREW HITTING THE CONVENIENCE STORES.
DEMON HOUSE BUSINESS OFFICE

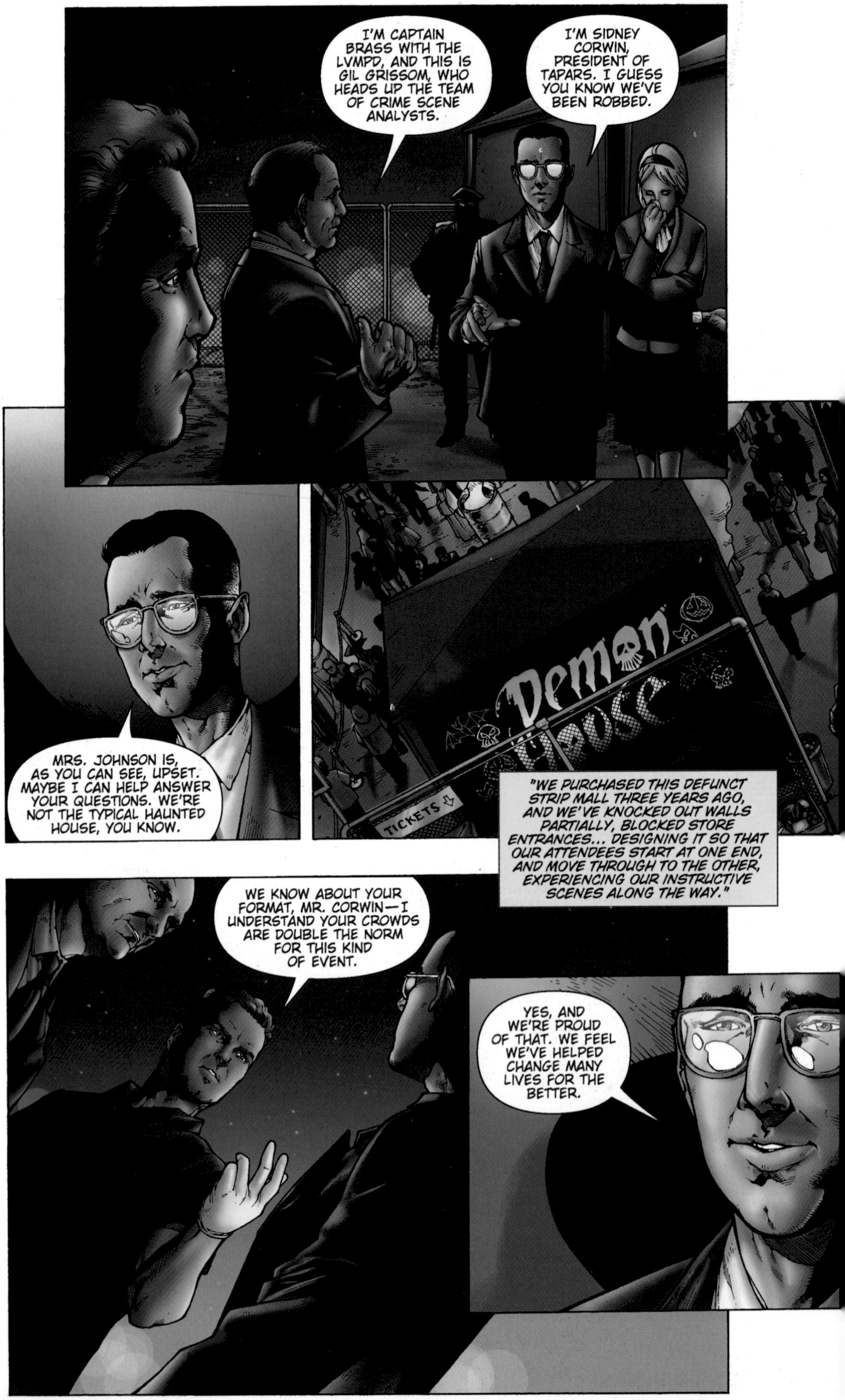
I'M CAPTAIN BRASS WITH THE LVMPD, AND THIS IS GIL GRISSOM, WHO HEADS UP THE TEAM OF CRIME SCENE ANALYSTS.
I'M SIDNEY CORWIN, PRESIDENT OF TAPARS. I GUESS YOU KNOW WE'VE BEEN ROBBED.
MRS. JOHNSON IS, AS YOU CAN SEE, UPSET. MAYBE I CAN HELP ANSWER YOUR QUESTIONS. WE'RE NOT THE TYPICAL HAUNTED HOUSE, YOU KNOW.
Demon House
TICKETS
"WE PURCHASED THIS DEFUNCT STRIP MALL THREE YEARS AGO, AND WE'VE KNOCKED OUT WALLS PARTIALLY, BLOCKED STORE ENTRANCES... DESIGNING IT SO THAT OUR ATTENDEES START AT ONE END, AND MOVE THROUGH TO THE OTHER, EXPERIENCING OUR INSTRUCTIVE SCENES ALONG THE WAY."
WE KNOW ABOUT YOUR FORMAT, MR. CORWIN—I UNDERSTAND YOUR CROWDS ARE DOUBLE THE NORM FOR THIS KIND OF EVENT.
YES, AND WE'RE PROUD OF THAT. WE FEEL WE'VE HELPED CHANGE MANY LIVES FOR THE BETTER.

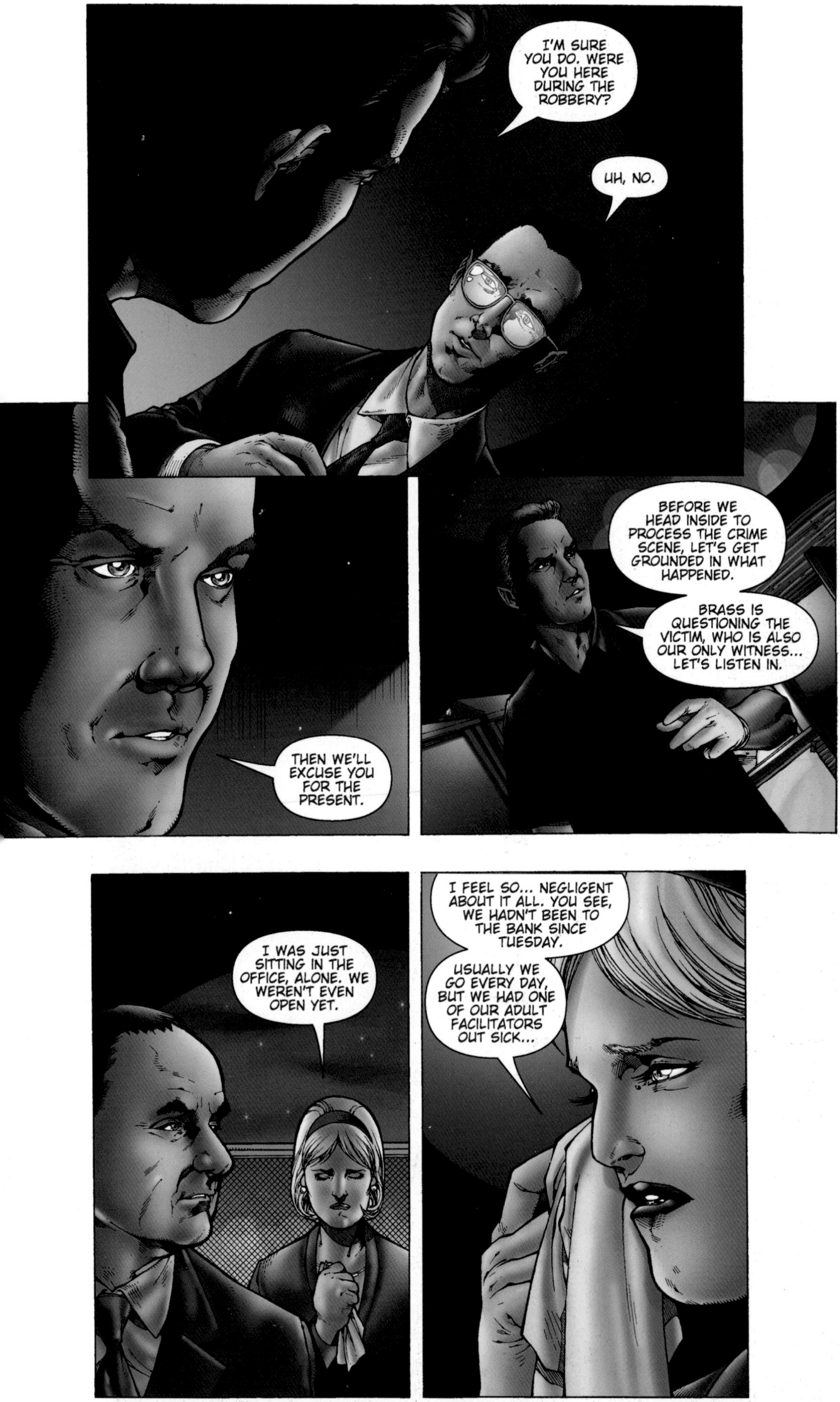
I'M SURE YOU DO. WERE YOU HERE DURING THE ROBBERY?
UH, NO.
THEN WE'LL EXCUSE YOU FOR THE PRESENT.
BEFORE WE HEAD INSIDE TO PROCESS THE CRIME SCENE, LET'S GET GROUNDED IN WHAT HAPPENED.
BRASS IS QUESTIONING THE VICTIM, WHO IS ALSO OUR ONLY WITNESS... LET'S LISTEN IN.
I WAS JUST SITTING IN THE OFFICE, ALONE. WE WEREN'T EVEN OPEN YET.
I FEEL SO... NEGLIGENT ABOUT IT ALL. YOU SEE, WE HADN'T BEEN TO THE BANK SINCE TUESDAY.
USUALLY WE GO EVERY DAY, BUT WE HAD ONE OF OUR ADULT FACILITATORS OUT SICK...

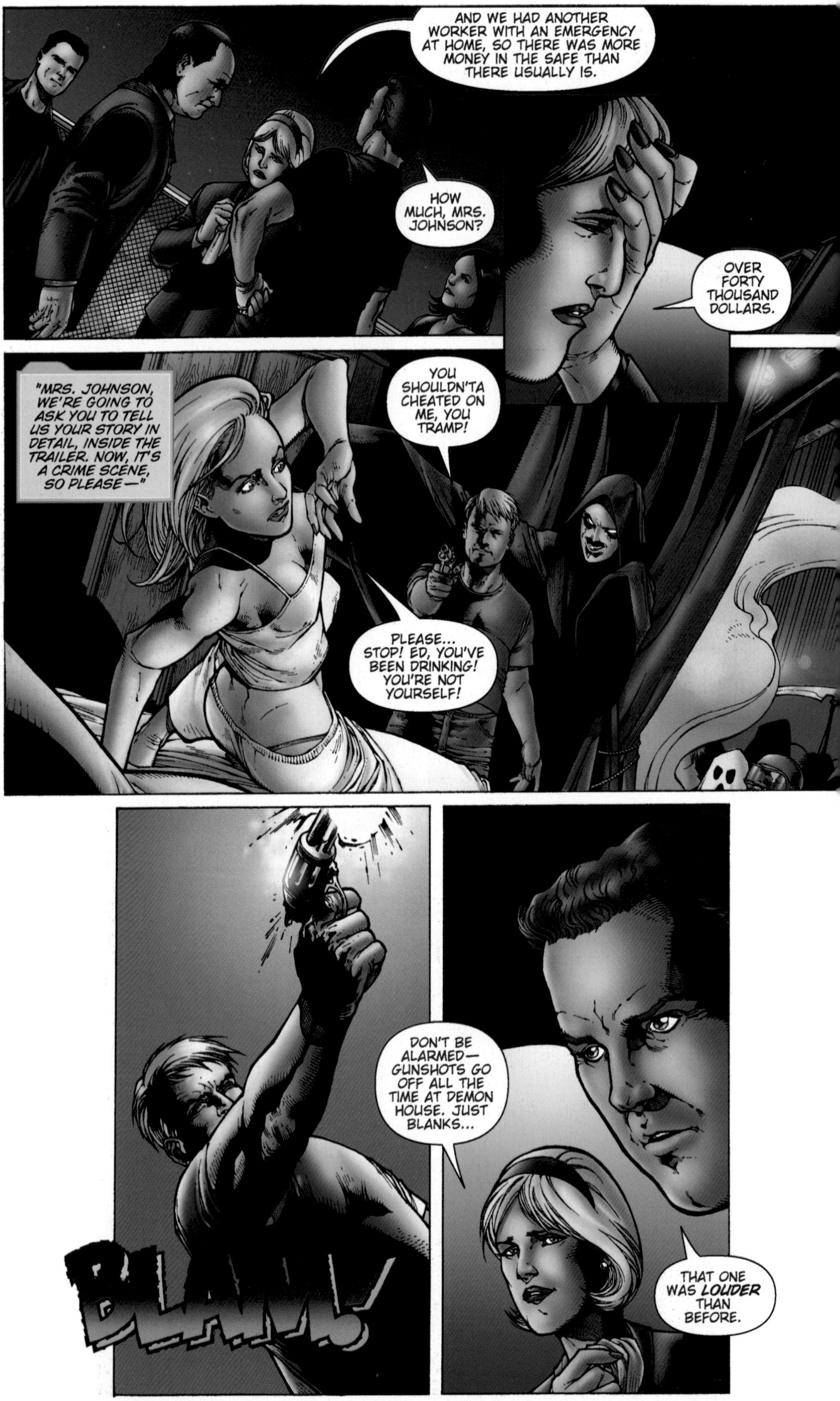
AND WE HAD ANOTHER WORKER WITH AN EMERGENCY AT HOME, SO THERE WAS MORE MONEY IN THE SAFE THAN THERE USUALLY IS.
HOW MUCH, MRS. JOHNSON?
OVER FORTY THOUSAND DOLLARS.
"MRS. JOHNSON, WE'RE GOING TO ASK YOU TO TELL US YOUR STORY IN DETAIL, INSIDE THE TRAILER. NOW, IT'S A CRIME SCENE, SO PLEASE—"
YOU SHOULDN'TA CHEATED ON ME, YOU TRAMP!
PLEASE... STOP! ED, YOU'VE BEEN DRINKING! YOU'RE NOT YOURSELF!
BLAM!
DON'T BE ALARMED— GUNSHOTS GO OFF ALL THE TIME AT DEMON HOUSE. JUST BLANKS...
THAT ONE WAS LOUDER THAN BEFORE.

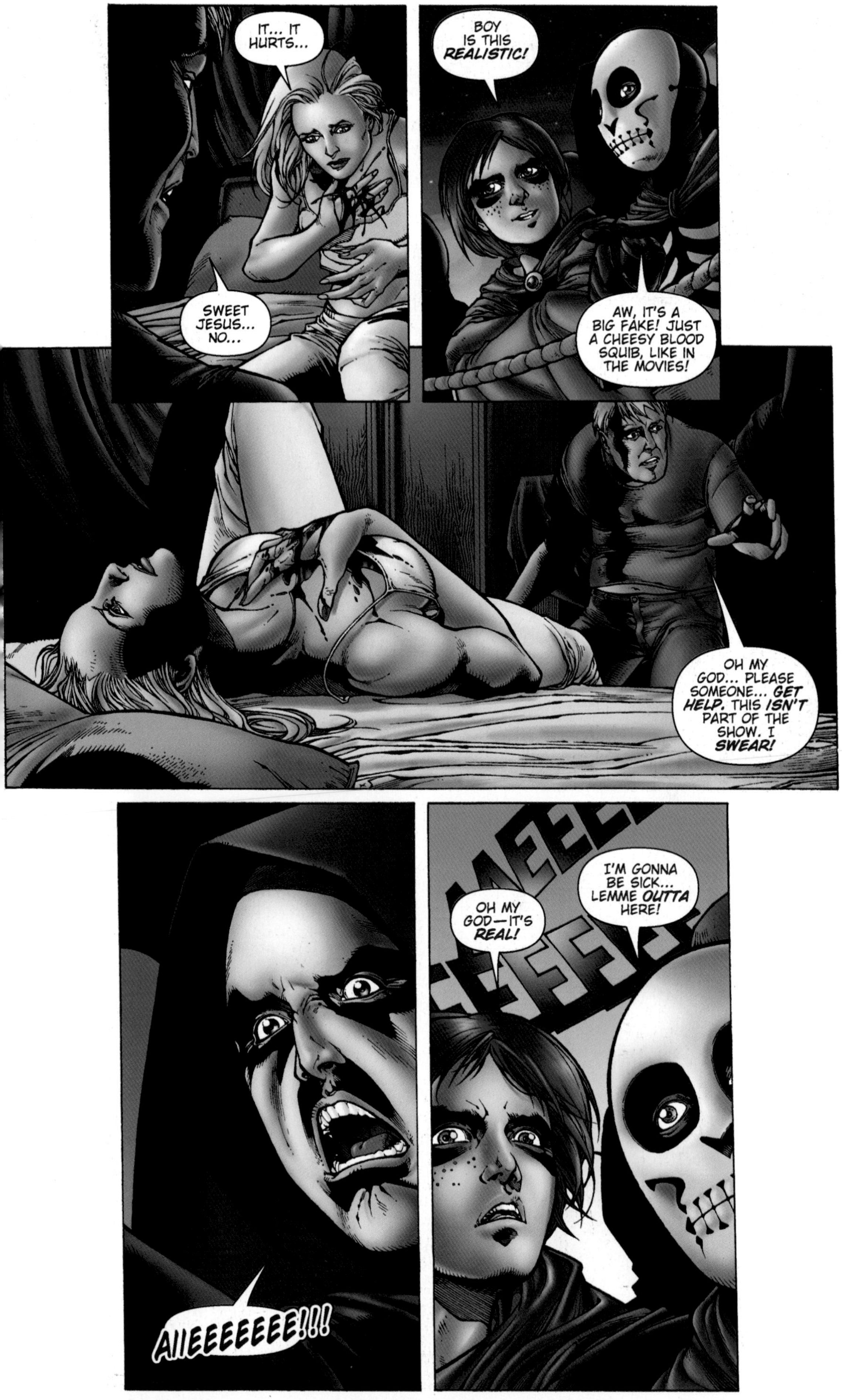
IT... IT HURTS...
SWEET JESUS... NO...
BOY IS THIS REALISTIC!
AW, IT'S A BIG FAKE! JUST A CHEESY BLOOD SQUIB, LIKE IN THE MOVIES!
OH MY GOD... PLEASE SOMEONE... GET HELP. THIS ISN'T PART OF THE SHOW. I SWEAR!
AIIEEEEEEE!!!
OH MY GOD—IT'S REAL!
I'M GONNA BE SICK... LEMME OUTTA HERE!

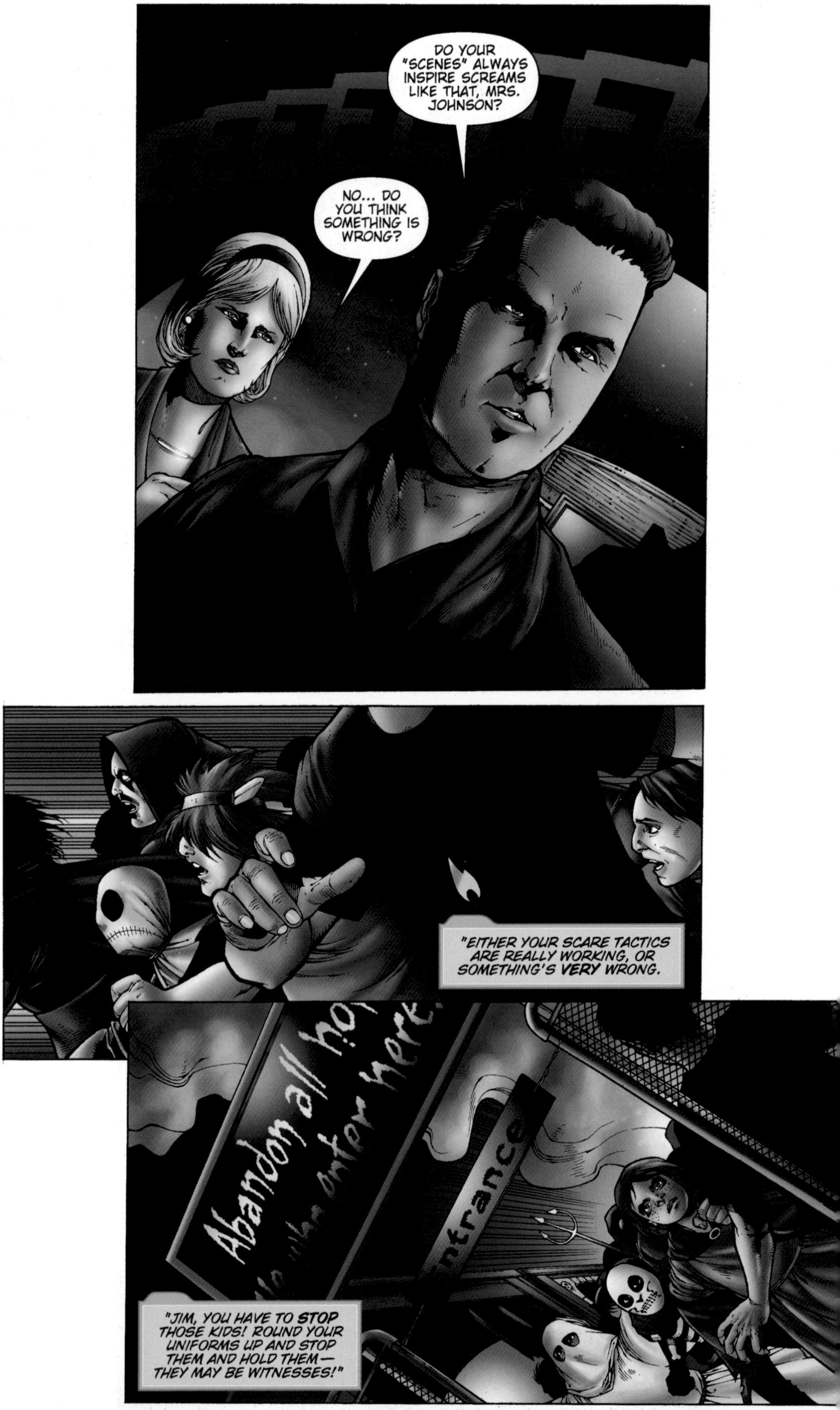

DO YOUR "SCENES" ALWAYS INSPIRE SCREAMS LIKE THAT, MRS. JOHNSON?
NO... DO YOU THINK SOMETHING IS WRONG?
"EITHER YOUR SCARE TACTICS ARE REALLY WORKING, OR SOMETHING'S **VERY** WRONG.
"JIM, YOU HAVE TO **STOP** THOSE KIDS! ROUND YOUR UNIFORMS UP AND STOP THEM AND HOLD THEM— THEY MAY BE WITNESSES!"

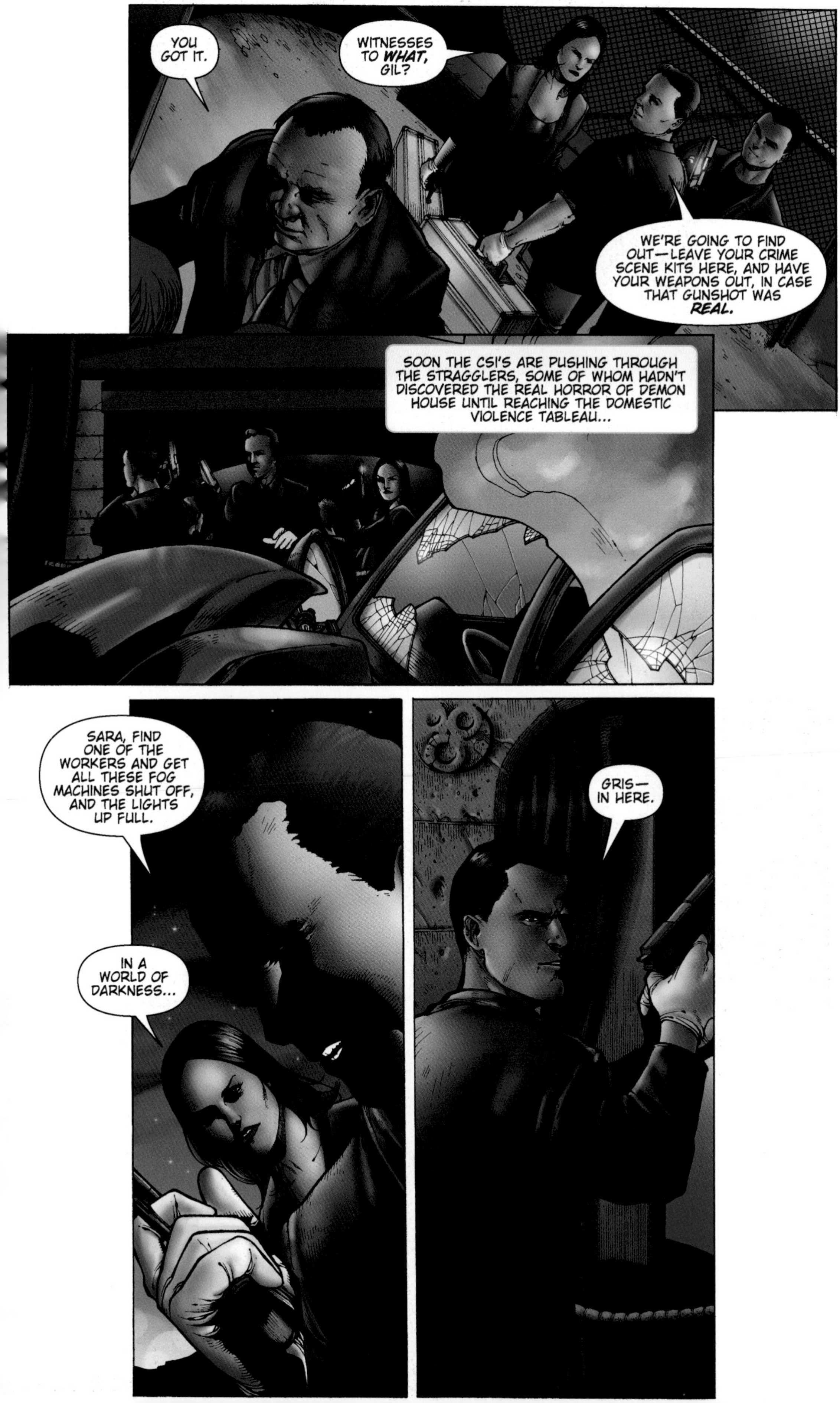
YOU GOT IT.
WITNESSES TO **WHAT,** GIL?
WE'RE GOING TO FIND OUT—LEAVE YOUR CRIME SCENE KITS HERE, AND HAVE YOUR WEAPONS OUT, IN CASE THAT GUNSHOT WAS **REAL.**
SOON THE CSI'S ARE PUSHING THROUGH THE STRAGGLERS, SOME OF WHOM HADN'T DISCOVERED THE REAL HORROR OF DEMON HOUSE UNTIL REACHING THE DOMESTIC VIOLENCE TABLEAU...
SARA, FIND ONE OF THE WORKERS AND GET ALL THESE FOG MACHINES SHUT OFF, AND THE LIGHTS UP FULL.
IN A WORLD OF DARKNESS...
GRIS— IN HERE.

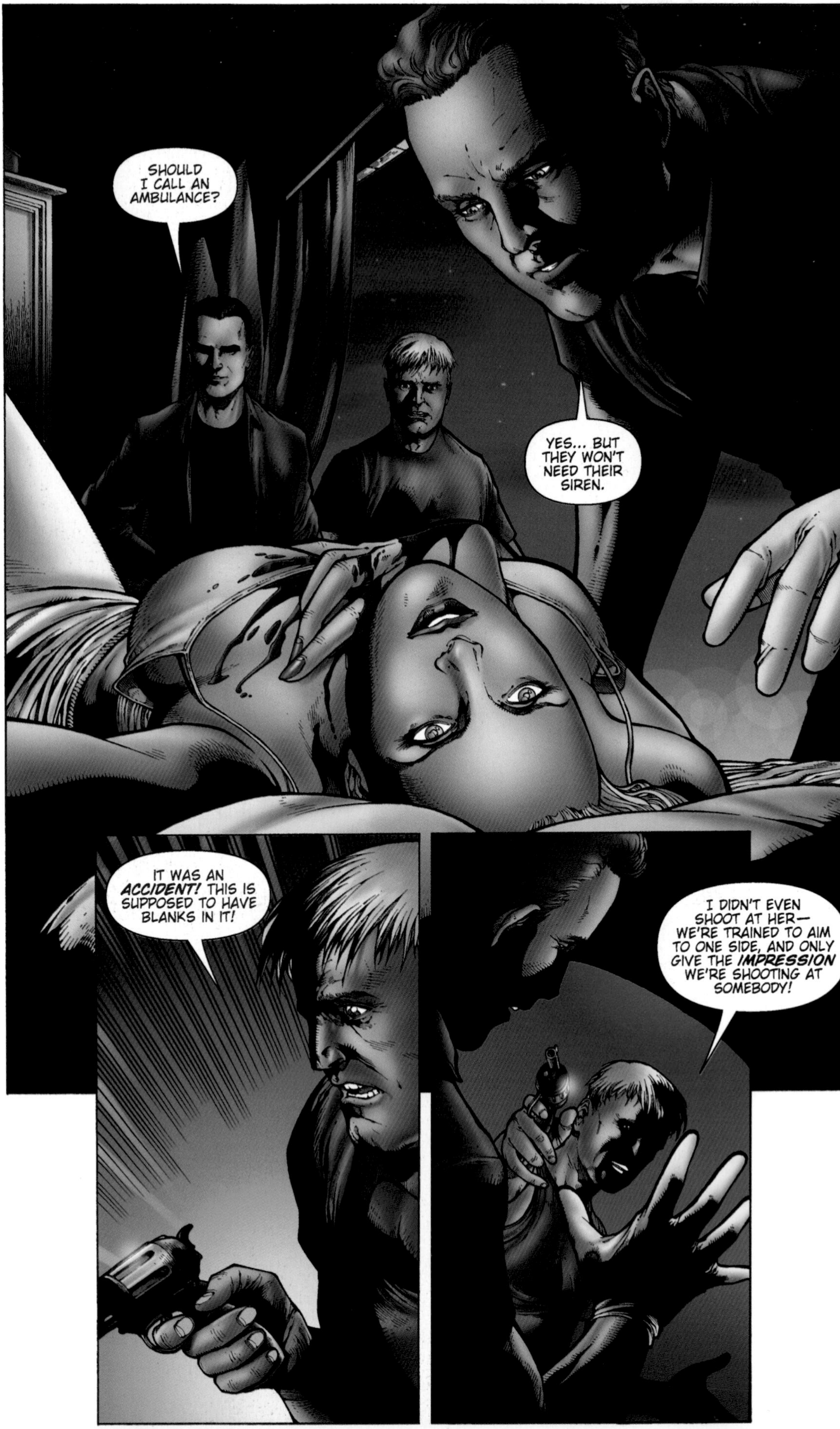

SHOULD I CALL AN AMBULANCE?
YES... BUT THEY WON'T NEED THEIR SIREN.
IT WAS AN *ACCIDENT!* THIS IS SUPPOSED TO HAVE BLANKS IN IT!
I DIDN'T EVEN SHOOT AT HER— WE'RE TRAINED TO AIM TO ONE SIDE, AND ONLY GIVE THE *IMPRESSION* WE'RE SHOOTING AT SOMEBODY!

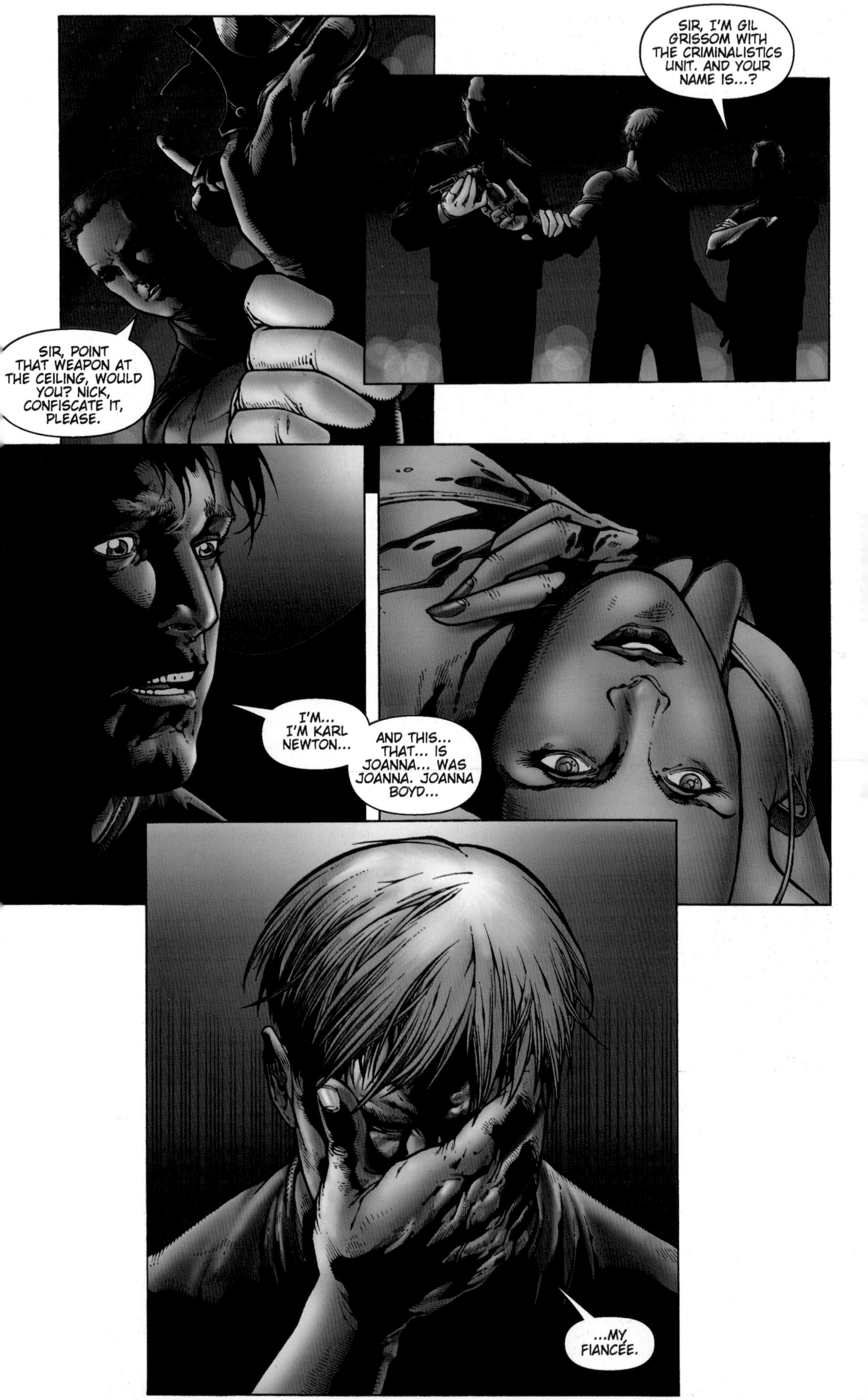
SIR, POINT THAT WEAPON AT THE CEILING, WOULD YOU? NICK, CONFISCATE IT, PLEASE.
SIR, I'M GIL GRISSOM WITH THE CRIMINALISTICS UNIT. AND YOUR NAME IS...?
I'M... I'M KARL NEWTON...
AND THIS... THAT... IS JOANNA... WAS JOANNA. JOANNA BOYD...
...MY FIANCÉE.

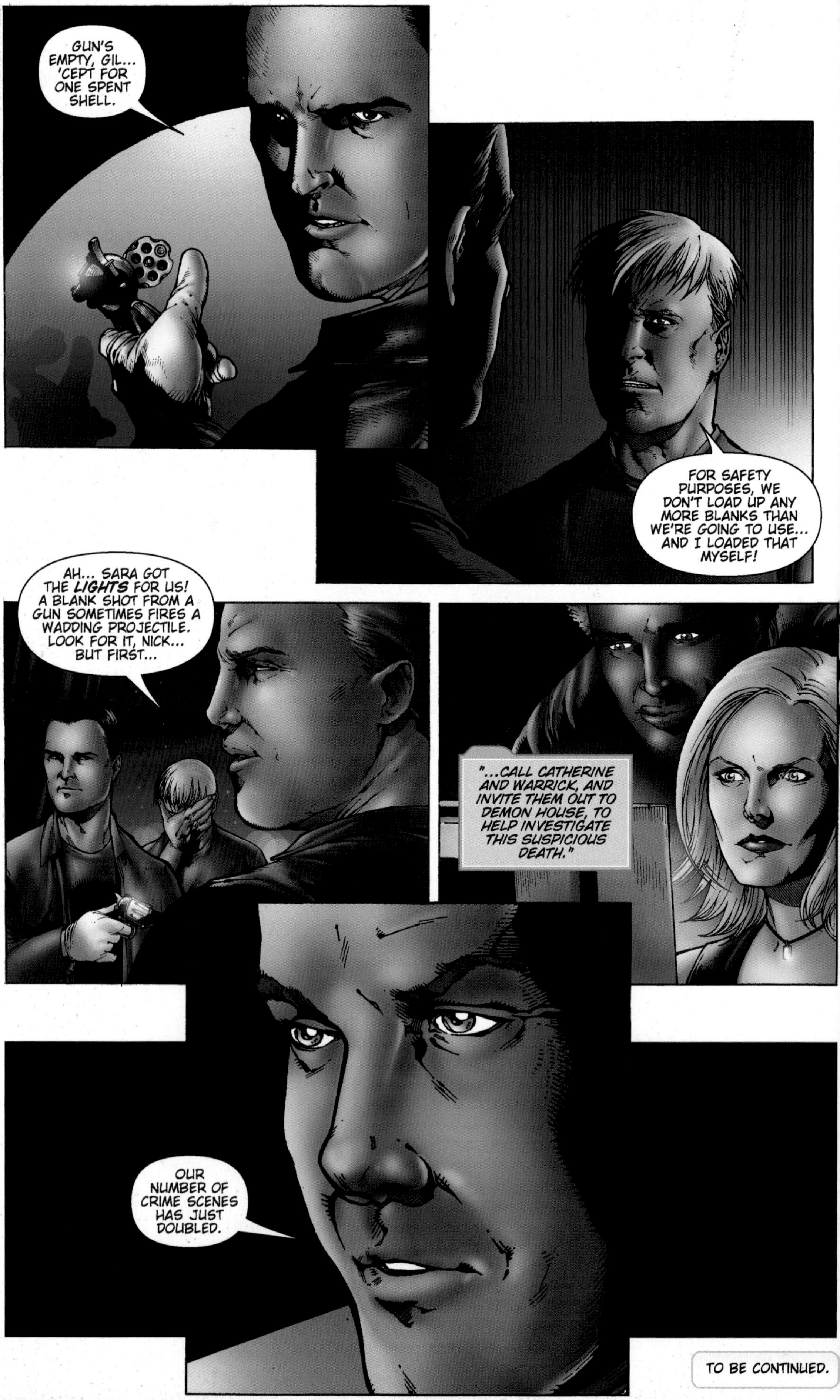
GUN'S EMPTY, GIL... 'CEPT FOR ONE SPENT SHELL.
FOR SAFETY PURPOSES, WE DON'T LOAD UP ANY MORE BLANKS THAN WE'RE GOING TO USE... AND I LOADED THAT MYSELF!
AH... SARA GOT THE *LIGHTS* FOR US! A BLANK SHOT FROM A GUN SOMETIMES FIRES A WADDING PROJECTILE. LOOK FOR IT, NICK... BUT FIRST...
"...CALL CATHERINE AND WARRICK, AND INVITE THEM OUT TO DEMON HOUSE, TO HELP INVESTIGATE THIS SUSPICIOUS DEATH."
OUR NUMBER OF CRIME SCENES HAS JUST DOUBLED.
TO BE CONTINUED.

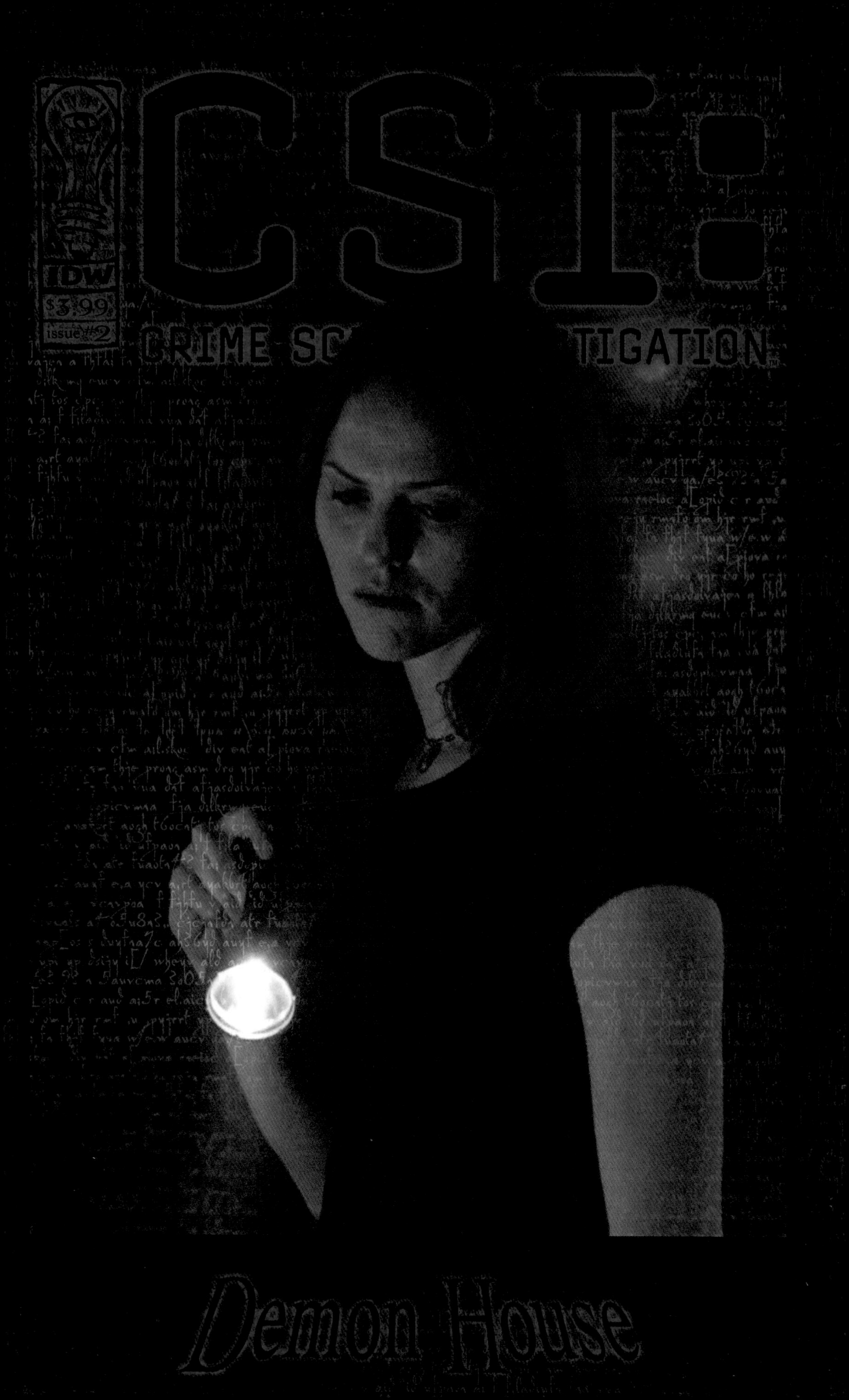

IDW
$3.99
issue #2
CSI:
CRIME SC TIGATION
Demon House

chapter two

Magic Town

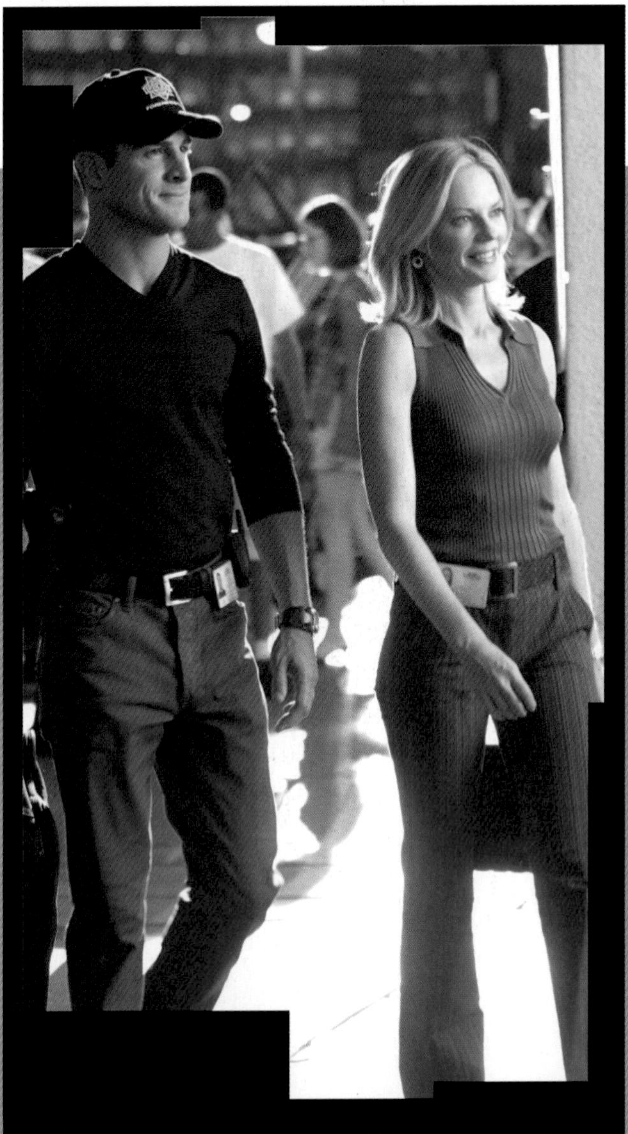

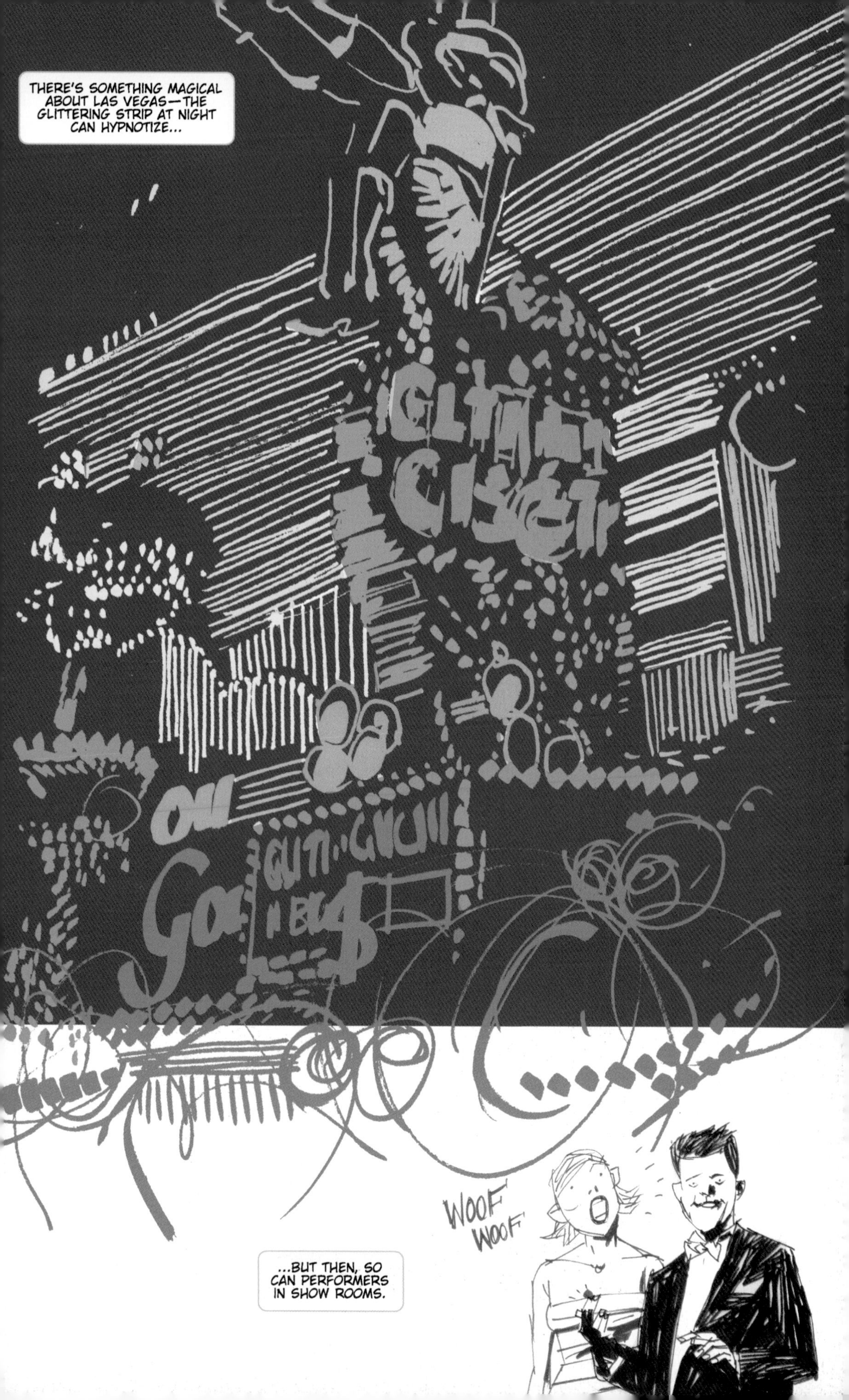
THERE'S SOMETHING MAGICAL ABOUT LAS VEGAS—THE GLITTERING STRIP AT NIGHT CAN HYPNOTIZE...
...BUT THEN, SO CAN PERFORMERS IN SHOW ROOMS.
WOOF WOOF

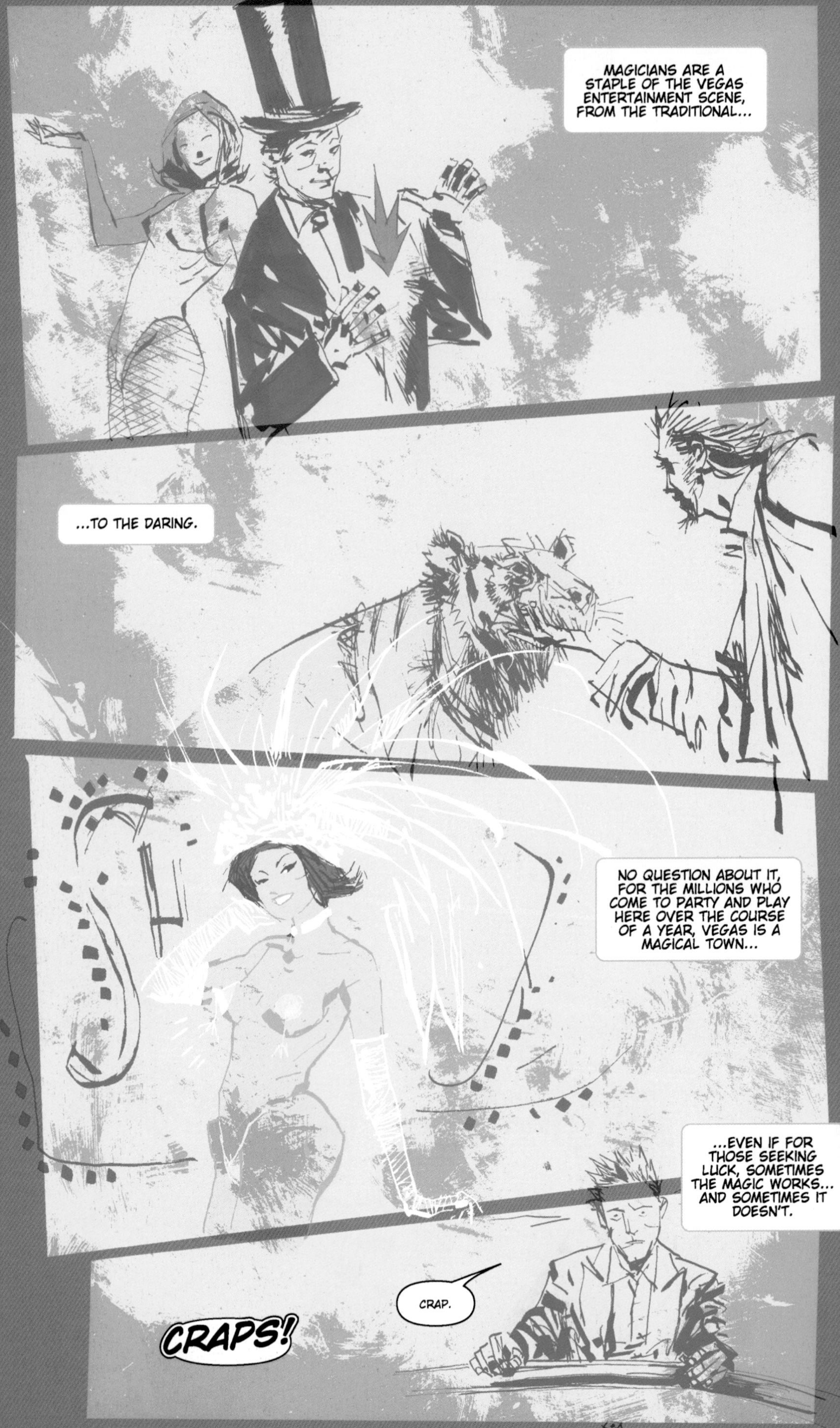
MAGICIANS ARE A STAPLE OF THE VEGAS ENTERTAINMENT SCENE, FROM THE TRADITIONAL...
...TO THE DARING.
NO QUESTION ABOUT IT, FOR THE MILLIONS WHO COME TO PARTY AND PLAY HERE OVER THE COURSE OF A YEAR, VEGAS IS A MAGICAL TOWN...
...EVEN IF FOR THOSE SEEKING LUCK, SOMETIMES THE MAGIC WORKS... AND SOMETIMES IT DOESN'T.
CRAPS!
CRAP.

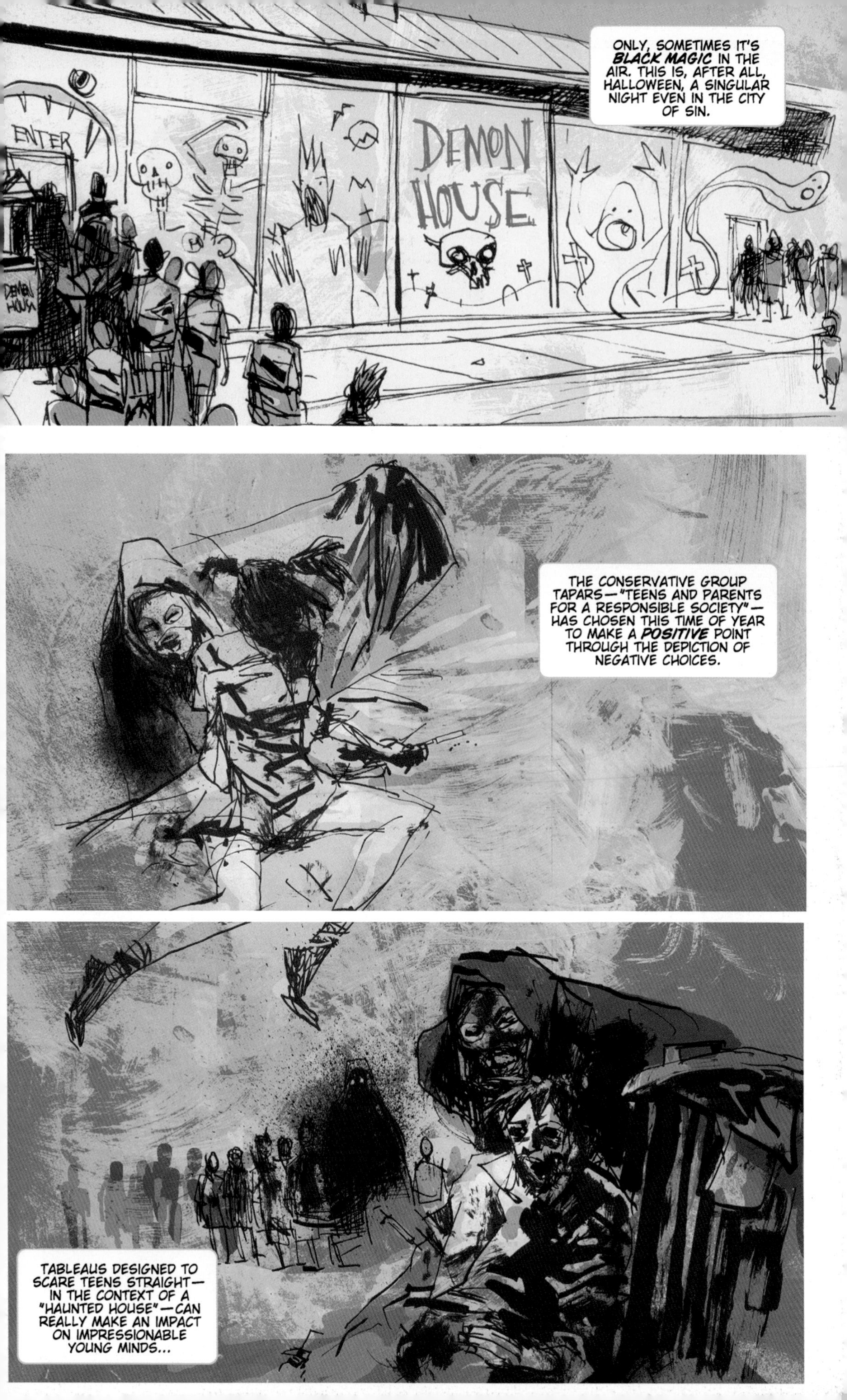
ONLY, SOMETIMES IT'S ***BLACK MAGIC*** IN THE AIR. THIS IS, AFTER ALL, HALLOWEEN, A SINGULAR NIGHT EVEN IN THE CITY OF SIN.
ENTER
DEMON HOUSE
THE CONSERVATIVE GROUP TAPARS—"TEENS AND PARENTS FOR A RESPONSIBLE SOCIETY"—HAS CHOSEN THIS TIME OF YEAR TO MAKE A ***POSITIVE*** POINT THROUGH THE DEPICTION OF NEGATIVE CHOICES.
TABLEAUS DESIGNED TO SCARE TEENS STRAIGHT—IN THE CONTEXT OF A "HAUNTED HOUSE"—CAN REALLY MAKE AN IMPACT ON IMPRESSIONABLE YOUNG MINDS...

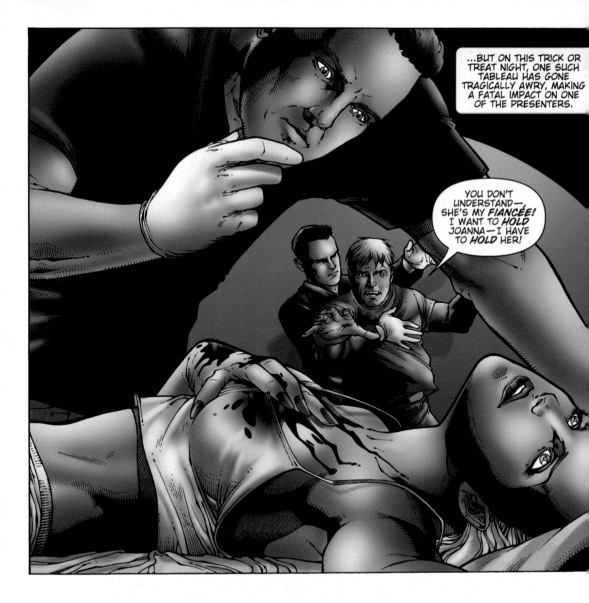

...BUT ON THIS TRICK OR TREAT NIGHT, ONE SUCH TABLEAU HAS GONE TRAGICALLY AWRY, MAKING A FATAL IMPACT ON ONE OF THE PRESENTERS.

YOU DON'T UNDERSTAND— SHE'S MY *FIANCÉE!* I WANT TO *HOLD* JOANNA—I HAVE TO *HOLD* HER!

SIR—YOUR FIANCÉE IS DEAD. YOU WON'T BE DOING HER, OR YOURSELF, ANY GOOD BY TAINTING THIS CRIME SCENE.

CRIME? I *DID* THIS... I DON'T *DENY* IT... BUT IT WAS AN *ACCIDENT!* YOU CAN'T THINK—

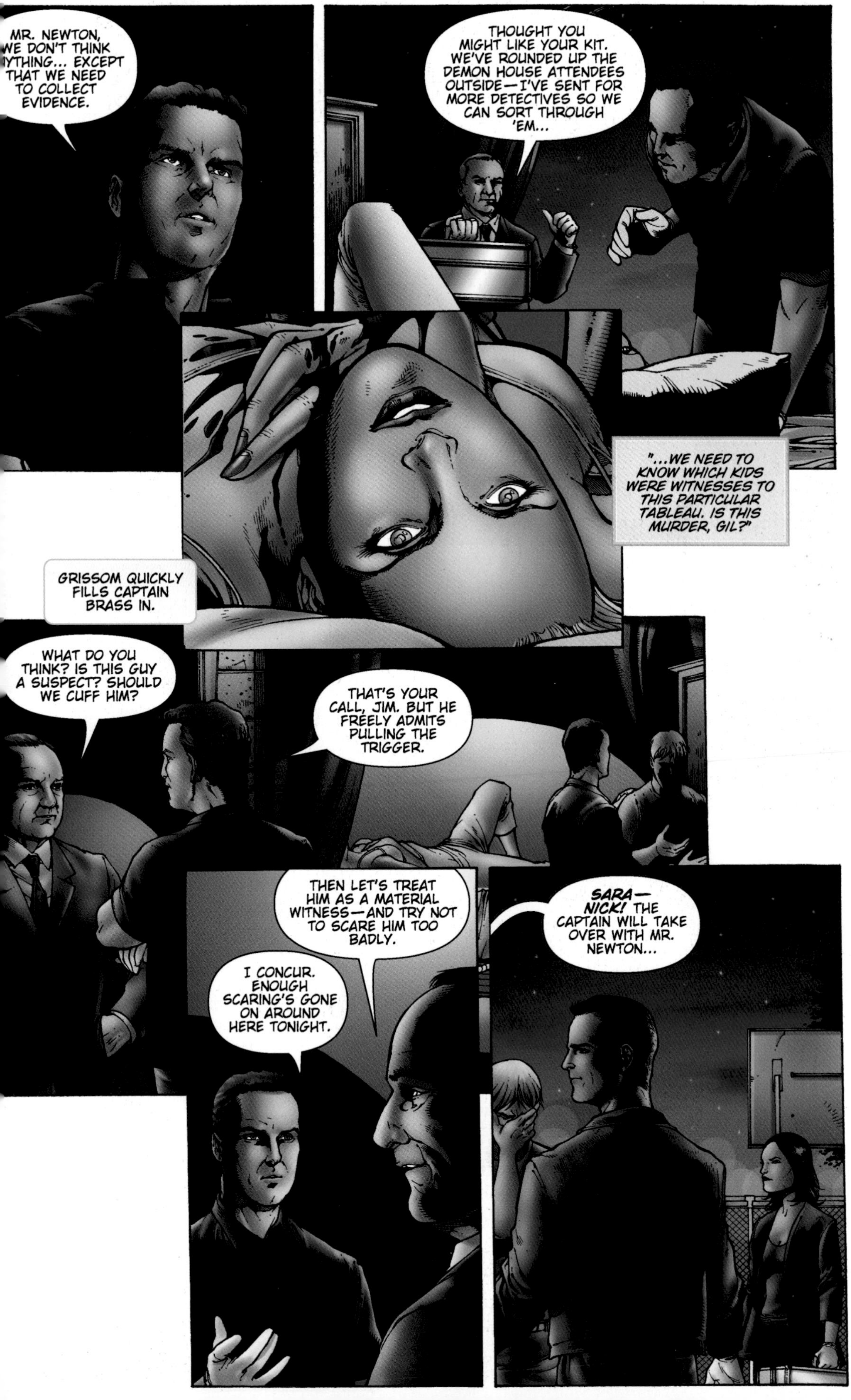
MR. NEWTON, WE DON'T THINK ANYTHING... EXCEPT THAT WE NEED TO COLLECT EVIDENCE.
THOUGHT YOU MIGHT LIKE YOUR KIT. WE'VE ROUNDED UP THE DEMON HOUSE ATTENDEES OUTSIDE—I'VE SENT FOR MORE DETECTIVES SO WE CAN SORT THROUGH 'EM...
"...WE NEED TO KNOW WHICH KIDS WERE WITNESSES TO THIS PARTICULAR TABLEAU. IS THIS MURDER, GIL?"
GRISSOM QUICKLY FILLS CAPTAIN BRASS IN.
WHAT DO YOU THINK? IS THIS GUY A SUSPECT? SHOULD WE CUFF HIM?
THAT'S YOUR CALL, JIM. BUT HE FREELY ADMITS PULLING THE TRIGGER.
THEN LET'S TREAT HIM AS A MATERIAL WITNESS—AND TRY NOT TO SCARE HIM TOO BADLY.
I CONCUR. ENOUGH SCARING'S GONE ON AROUND HERE TONIGHT.
SARA—NICK! THE CAPTAIN WILL TAKE OVER WITH MR. NEWTON...

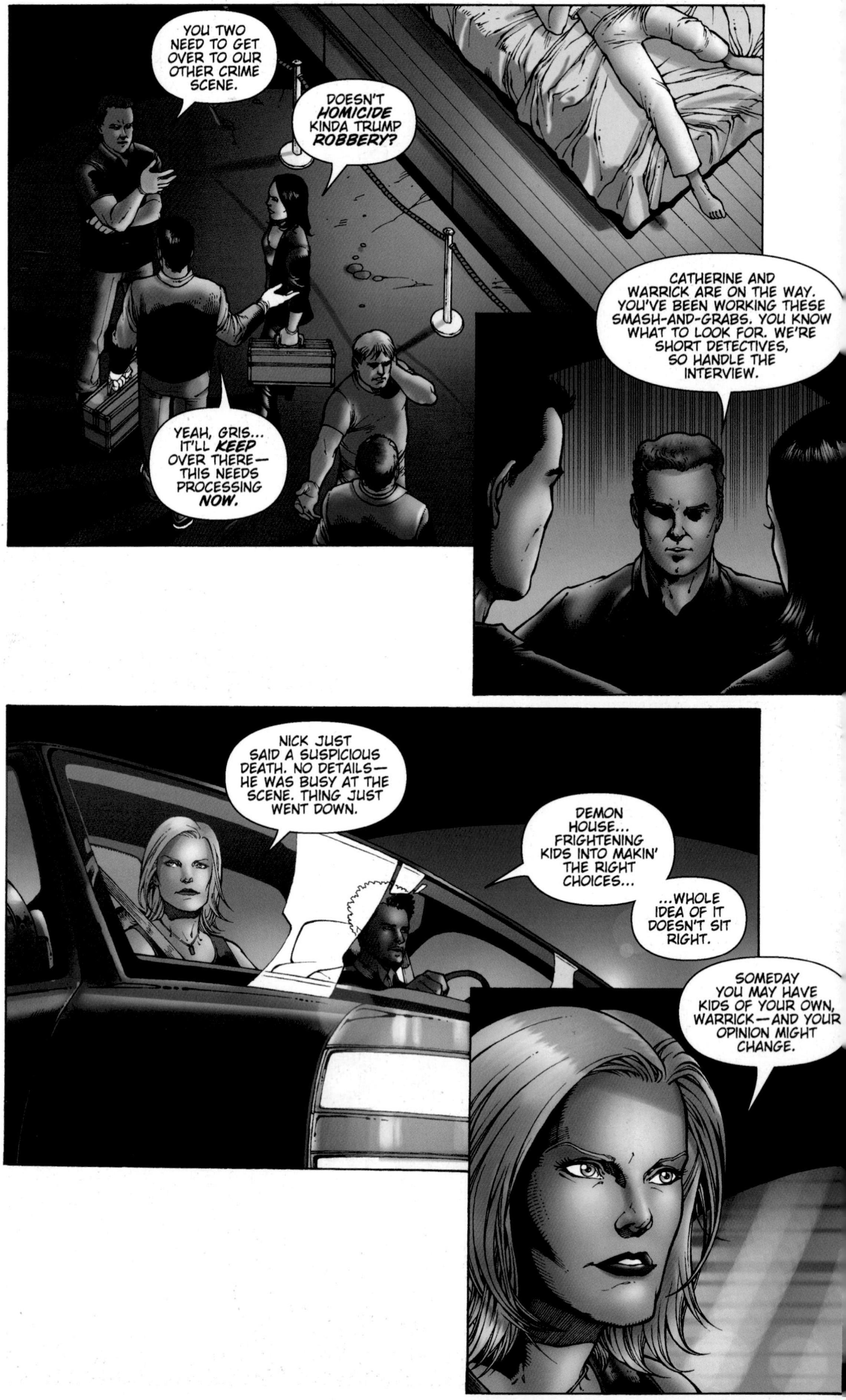
YOU TWO NEED TO GET OVER TO OUR OTHER CRIME SCENE.
DOESN'T HOMICIDE KINDA TRUMP ROBBERY?
YEAH, GRIS... IT'LL KEEP OVER THERE— THIS NEEDS PROCESSING NOW.
CATHERINE AND WARRICK ARE ON THE WAY. YOU'VE BEEN WORKING THESE SMASH-AND-GRABS. YOU KNOW WHAT TO LOOK FOR. WE'RE SHORT DETECTIVES, SO HANDLE THE INTERVIEW.
NICK JUST SAID A SUSPICIOUS DEATH. NO DETAILS— HE WAS BUSY AT THE SCENE. THING JUST WENT DOWN.
DEMON HOUSE... FRIGHTENING KIDS INTO MAKIN' THE RIGHT CHOICES...
...WHOLE IDEA OF IT DOESN'T SIT RIGHT.
SOMEDAY YOU MAY HAVE KIDS OF YOUR OWN, WARRICK—AND YOUR OPINION MIGHT CHANGE.

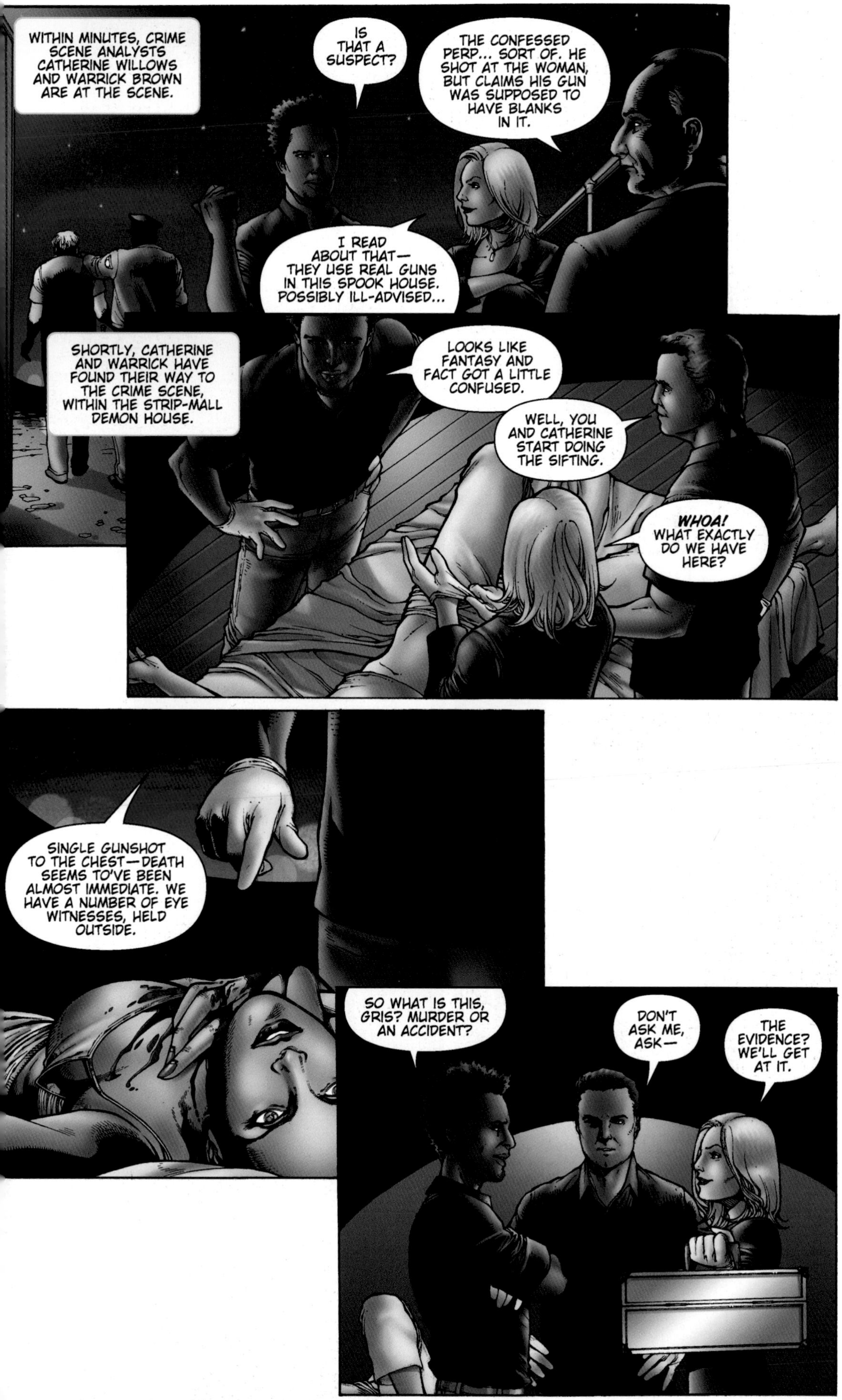
WITHIN MINUTES, CRIME SCENE ANALYSTS CATHERINE WILLOWS AND WARRICK BROWN ARE AT THE SCENE.
IS THAT A SUSPECT?
THE CONFESSED PERP... SORT OF. HE SHOT AT THE WOMAN, BUT CLAIMS HIS GUN WAS SUPPOSED TO HAVE BLANKS IN IT.
I READ ABOUT THAT—THEY USE REAL GUNS IN THIS SPOOK HOUSE. POSSIBLY ILL-ADVISED...
SHORTLY, CATHERINE AND WARRICK HAVE FOUND THEIR WAY TO THE CRIME SCENE, WITHIN THE STRIP-MALL DEMON HOUSE.
LOOKS LIKE FANTASY AND FACT GOT A LITTLE CONFUSED.
WELL, YOU AND CATHERINE START DOING THE SIFTING.
WHOA! WHAT EXACTLY DO WE HAVE HERE?
SINGLE GUNSHOT TO THE CHEST—DEATH SEEMS TO'VE BEEN ALMOST IMMEDIATE. WE HAVE A NUMBER OF EYE WITNESSES, HELD OUTSIDE.
SO WHAT IS THIS, GRIS? MURDER OR AN ACCIDENT?
DON'T ASK ME, ASK—
THE EVIDENCE? WE'LL GET AT IT.

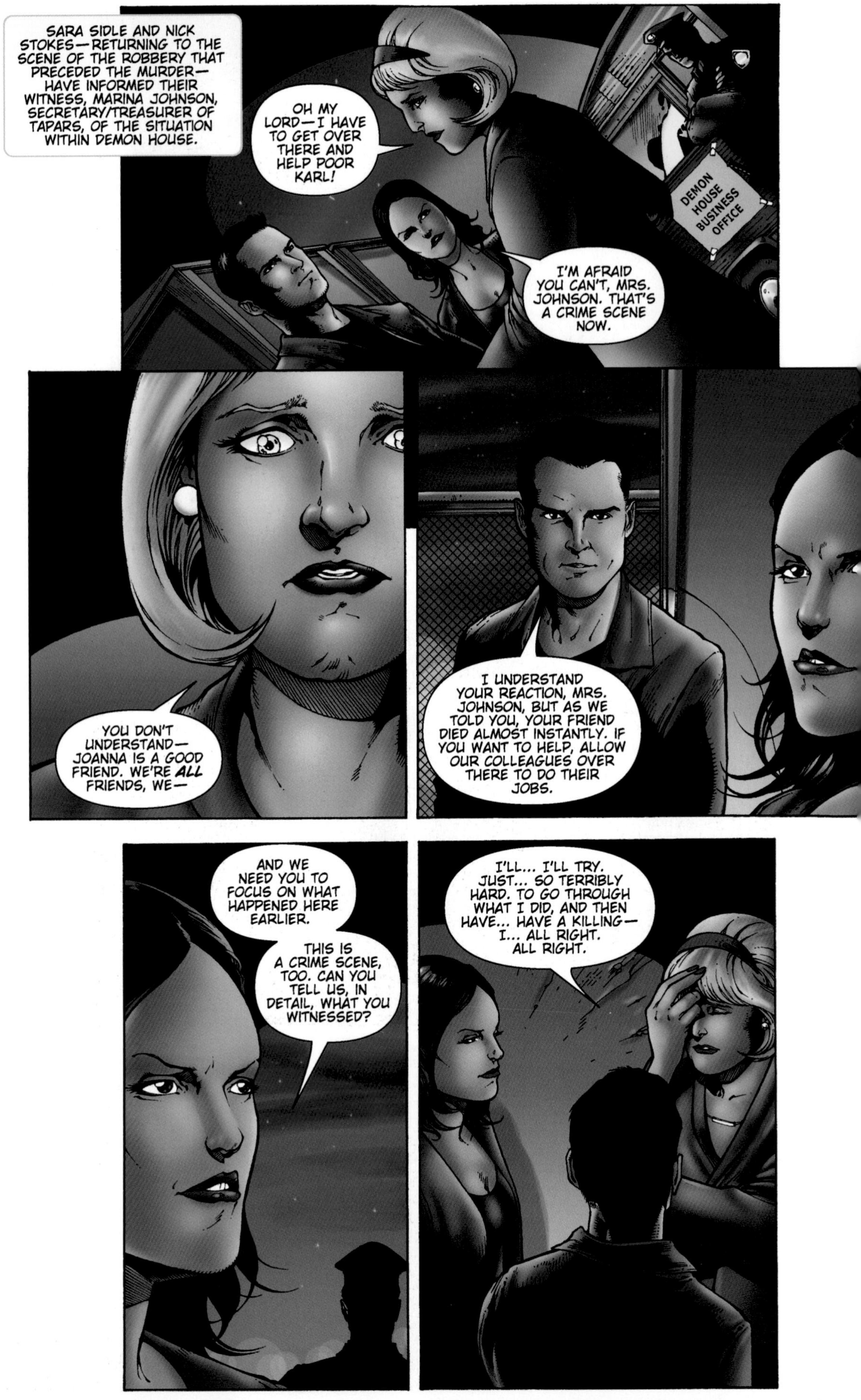
SARA SIDLE AND NICK STOKES—RETURNING TO THE SCENE OF THE ROBBERY THAT PRECEDED THE MURDER—HAVE INFORMED THEIR WITNESS, MARINA JOHNSON, SECRETARY/TREASURER OF TAPARS, OF THE SITUATION WITHIN DEMON HOUSE.
OH MY LORD—I HAVE TO GET OVER THERE AND HELP POOR KARL!
DEMON HOUSE BUSINESS OFFICE
I'M AFRAID YOU CAN'T, MRS. JOHNSON. THAT'S A CRIME SCENE NOW.
YOU DON'T UNDERSTAND—JOANNA IS A GOOD FRIEND. WE'RE *ALL* FRIENDS, WE—
I UNDERSTAND YOUR REACTION, MRS. JOHNSON, BUT AS WE TOLD YOU, YOUR FRIEND DIED ALMOST INSTANTLY. IF YOU WANT TO HELP, ALLOW OUR COLLEAGUES OVER THERE TO DO THEIR JOBS.
AND WE NEED YOU TO FOCUS ON WHAT HAPPENED HERE EARLIER.
THIS IS A CRIME SCENE, TOO. CAN YOU TELL US, IN DETAIL, WHAT YOU WITNESSED?
I'LL... I'LL TRY. JUST... SO TERRIBLY HARD. TO GO THROUGH WHAT I DID, AND THEN HAVE... HAVE A KILLING—I... ALL RIGHT. ALL RIGHT.

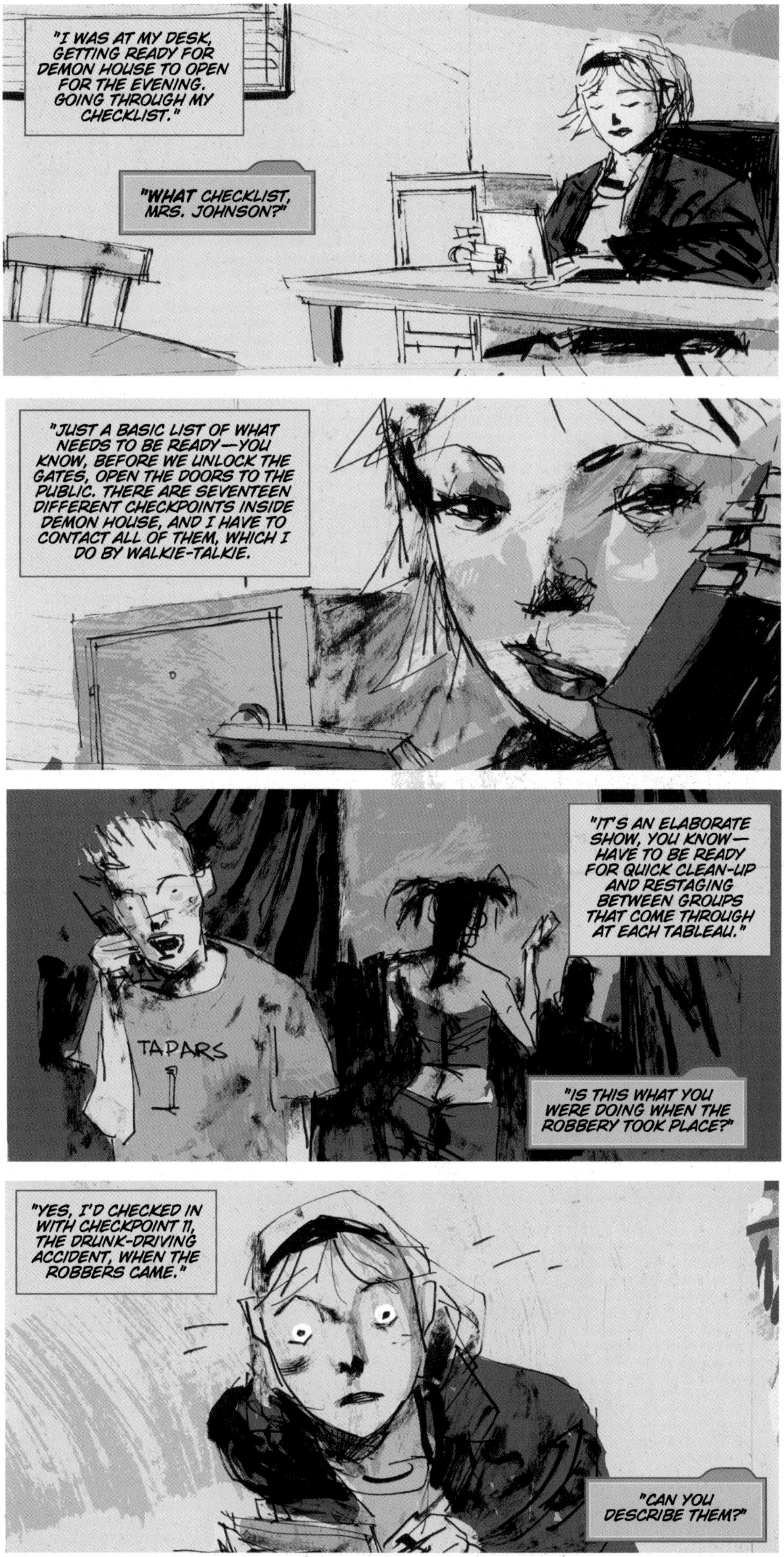
"I WAS AT MY DESK, GETTING READY FOR DEMON HOUSE TO OPEN FOR THE EVENING. GOING THROUGH MY CHECKLIST."
"WHAT CHECKLIST, MRS. JOHNSON?"
"JUST A BASIC LIST OF WHAT NEEDS TO BE READY—YOU KNOW, BEFORE WE UNLOCK THE GATES, OPEN THE DOORS TO THE PUBLIC. THERE ARE SEVENTEEN DIFFERENT CHECKPOINTS INSIDE DEMON HOUSE, AND I HAVE TO CONTACT ALL OF THEM, WHICH I DO BY WALKIE-TALKIE.
"IT'S AN ELABORATE SHOW, YOU KNOW—HAVE TO BE READY FOR QUICK CLEAN-UP AND RESTAGING BETWEEN GROUPS THAT COME THROUGH AT EACH TABLEAU."
TAPARS
"IS THIS WHAT YOU WERE DOING WHEN THE ROBBERY TOOK PLACE?"
"YES, I'D CHECKED IN WITH CHECKPOINT 11, THE DRUNK-DRIVING ACCIDENT, WHEN THE ROBBERS CAME."
"CAN YOU DESCRIBE THEM?"

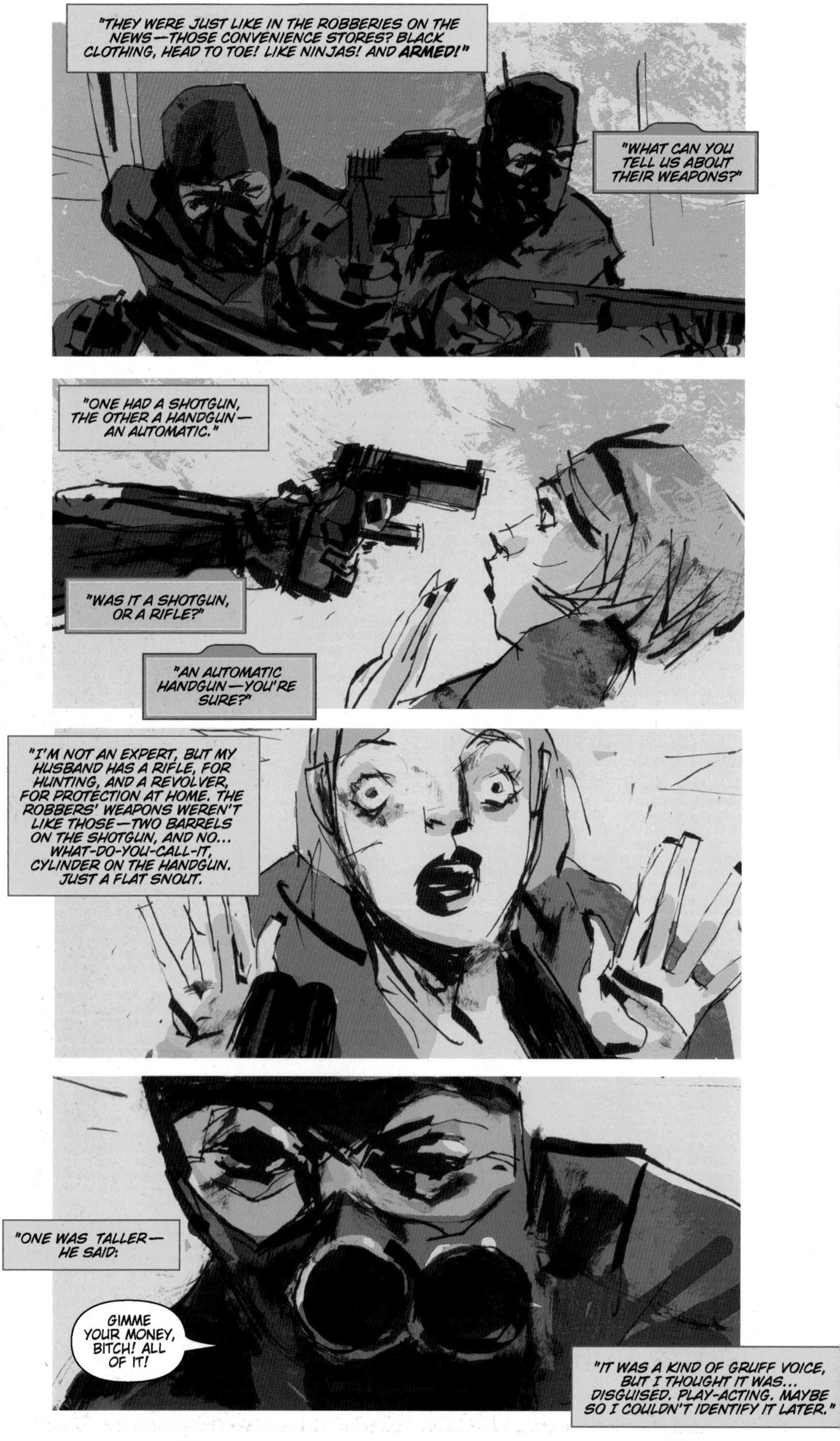
"THEY WERE JUST LIKE IN THE ROBBERIES ON THE NEWS—THOSE CONVENIENCE STORES? BLACK CLOTHING, HEAD TO TOE! LIKE NINJAS! AND ARMED!"
"WHAT CAN YOU TELL US ABOUT THEIR WEAPONS?"
"ONE HAD A SHOTGUN, THE OTHER A HANDGUN—AN AUTOMATIC."
"WAS IT A SHOTGUN, OR A RIFLE?"
"AN AUTOMATIC HANDGUN—YOU'RE SURE?"
"I'M NOT AN EXPERT, BUT MY HUSBAND HAS A RIFLE, FOR HUNTING, AND A REVOLVER, FOR PROTECTION AT HOME. THE ROBBERS' WEAPONS WEREN'T LIKE THOSE—TWO BARRELS ON THE SHOTGUN, AND NO... WHAT-DO-YOU-CALL-IT, CYLINDER ON THE HANDGUN. JUST A FLAT SNOUT.
"ONE WAS TALLER—HE SAID:
GIMME YOUR MONEY, BITCH! ALL OF IT!
"IT WAS A KIND OF GRUFF VOICE, BUT I THOUGHT IT WAS... DISGUISED. PLAY-ACTING. MAYBE SO I COULDN'T IDENTIFY IT LATER."

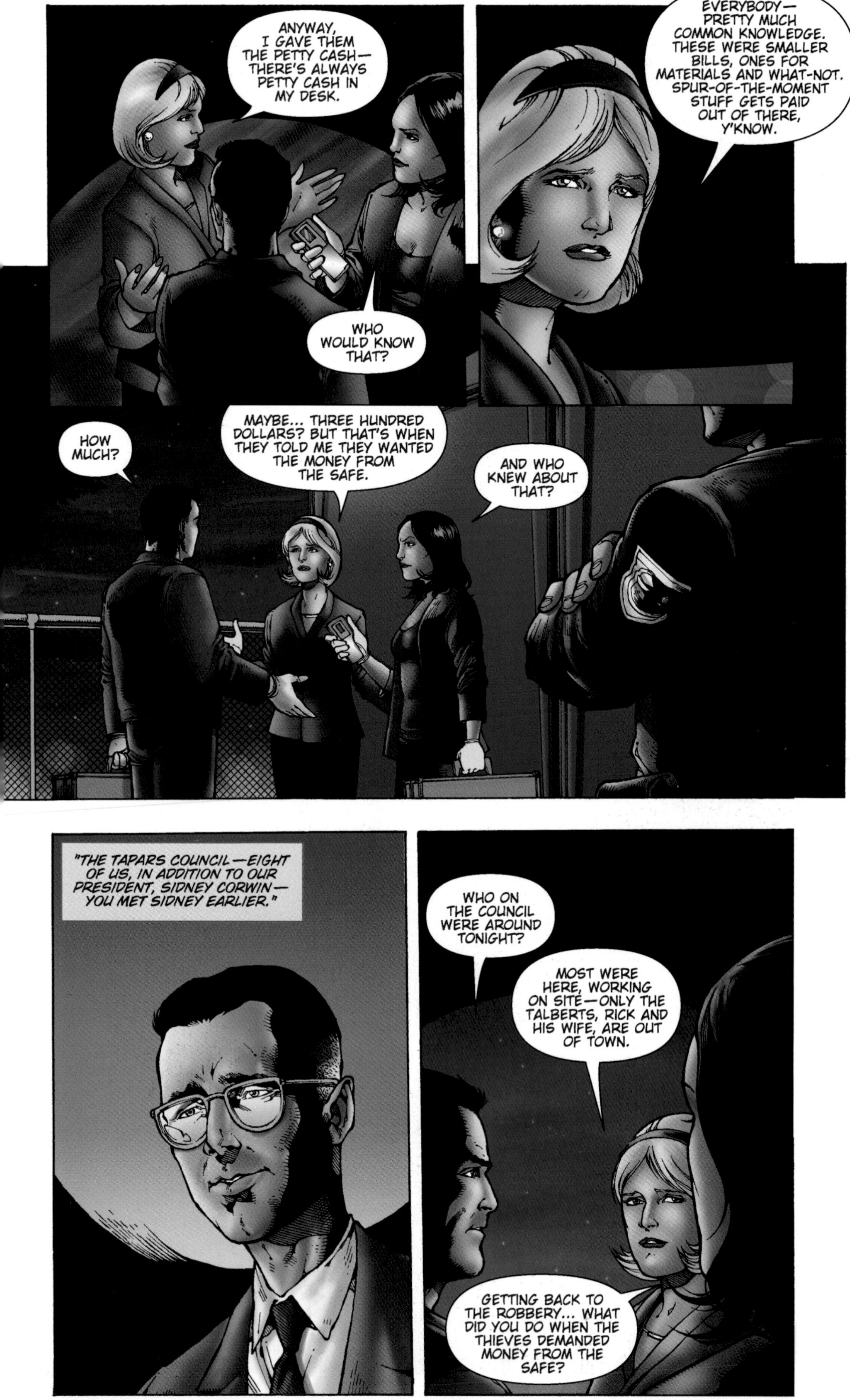

ANYWAY, I GAVE THEM THE PETTY CASH— THERE'S ALWAYS PETTY CASH IN MY DESK.
WHO WOULD KNOW THAT?
EVERYBODY— PRETTY MUCH COMMON KNOWLEDGE. THESE WERE SMALLER BILLS, ONES FOR MATERIALS AND WHAT-NOT. SPUR-OF-THE-MOMENT STUFF GETS PAID OUT OF THERE, Y'KNOW.
HOW MUCH?
MAYBE... THREE HUNDRED DOLLARS? BUT THAT'S WHEN THEY TOLD ME THEY WANTED THE MONEY FROM THE SAFE.
AND WHO KNEW ABOUT THAT?
"THE TAPARS COUNCIL—EIGHT OF US, IN ADDITION TO OUR PRESIDENT, SIDNEY CORWIN— YOU MET SIDNEY EARLIER."
WHO ON THE COUNCIL WERE AROUND TONIGHT?
MOST WERE HERE, WORKING ON SITE—ONLY THE TALBERTS, RICK AND HIS WIFE, ARE OUT OF TOWN.
GETTING BACK TO THE ROBBERY... WHAT DID YOU DO WHEN THE THIEVES DEMANDED MONEY FROM THE SAFE?

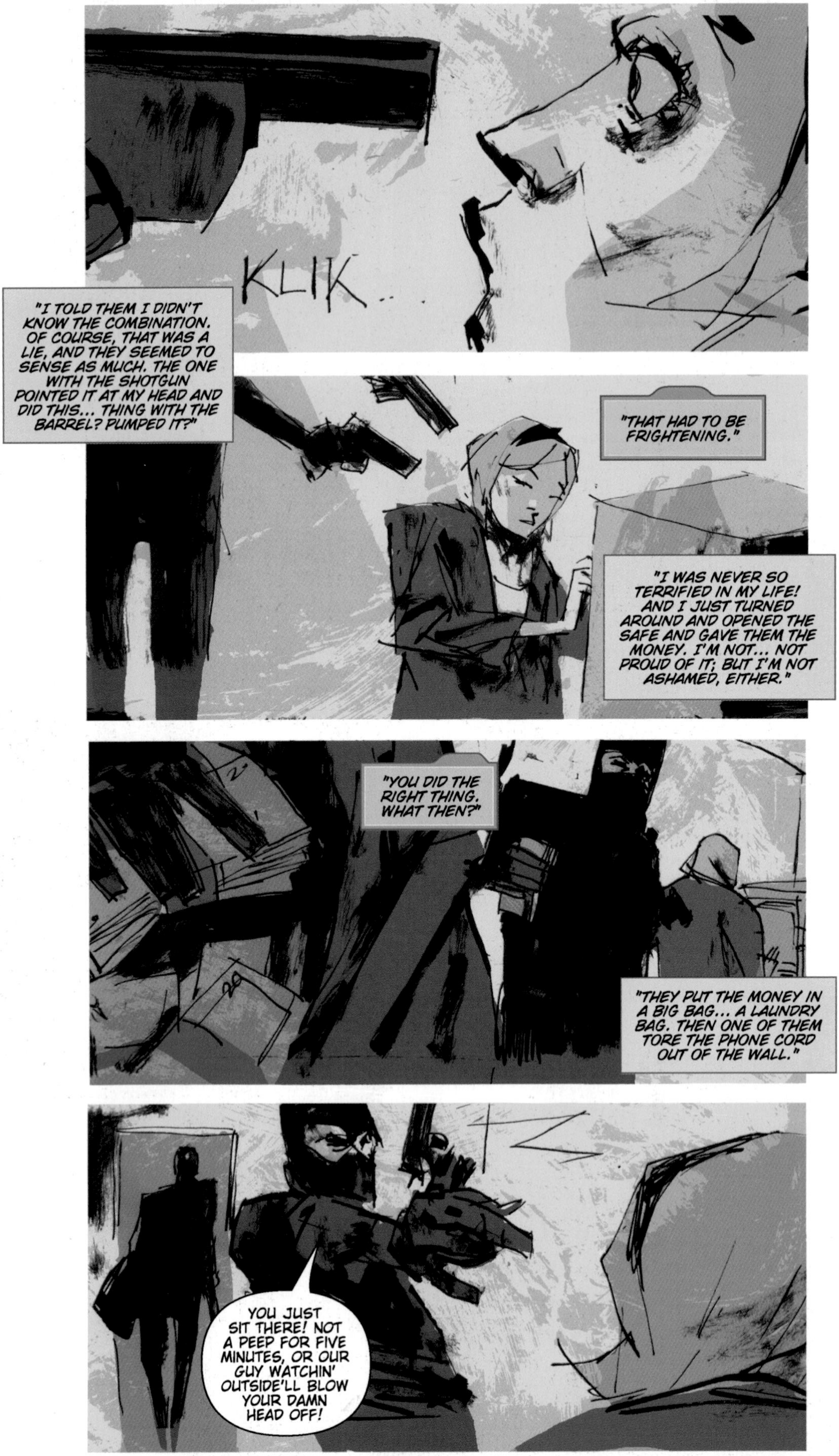
KLIK...
"I TOLD THEM I DIDN'T KNOW THE COMBINATION. OF COURSE, THAT WAS A LIE, AND THEY SEEMED TO SENSE AS MUCH. THE ONE WITH THE SHOTGUN POINTED IT AT MY HEAD AND DID THIS... THING WITH THE BARREL? PUMPED IT?"
"THAT HAD TO BE FRIGHTENING."
"I WAS NEVER SO TERRIFIED IN MY LIFE! AND I JUST TURNED AROUND AND OPENED THE SAFE AND GAVE THEM THE MONEY. I'M NOT... NOT PROUD OF IT; BUT I'M NOT ASHAMED, EITHER."
"YOU DID THE RIGHT THING. WHAT THEN?"
"THEY PUT THE MONEY IN A BIG BAG... A LAUNDRY BAG. THEN ONE OF THEM TORE THE PHONE CORD OUT OF THE WALL."
YOU JUST SIT THERE! NOT A PEEP FOR FIVE MINUTES, OR OUR GUY WATCHIN' OUTSIDE'LL BLOW YOUR DAMN HEAD OFF!

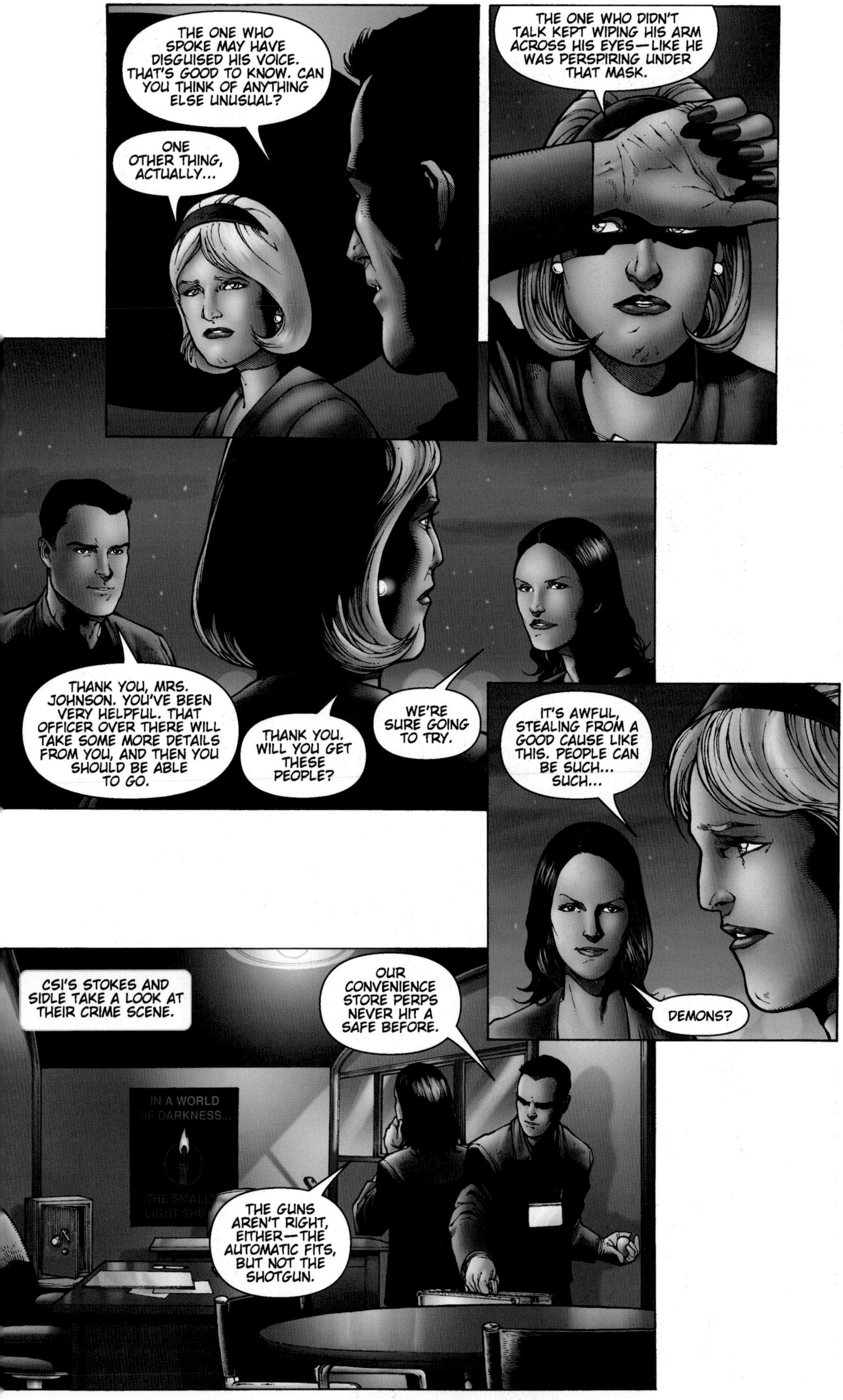
THE ONE WHO SPOKE MAY HAVE DISGUISED HIS VOICE. THAT'S GOOD TO KNOW. CAN YOU THINK OF ANYTHING ELSE UNUSUAL?
ONE OTHER THING, ACTUALLY...
THE ONE WHO DIDN'T TALK KEPT WIPING HIS ARM ACROSS HIS EYES—LIKE HE WAS PERSPIRING UNDER THAT MASK.
THANK YOU, MRS. JOHNSON. YOU'VE BEEN VERY HELPFUL. THAT OFFICER OVER THERE WILL TAKE SOME MORE DETAILS FROM YOU, AND THEN YOU SHOULD BE ABLE TO GO.
THANK YOU. WILL YOU GET THESE PEOPLE?
WE'RE SURE GOING TO TRY.
IT'S AWFUL, STEALING FROM A GOOD CAUSE LIKE THIS. PEOPLE CAN BE SUCH... SUCH...
DEMONS?
CSI'S STOKES AND SIDLE TAKE A LOOK AT THEIR CRIME SCENE.
OUR CONVENIENCE STORE PERPS NEVER HIT A SAFE BEFORE.
IN A WORLD OF DARKNESS...
THE GUNS AREN'T RIGHT, EITHER—THE AUTOMATIC FITS, BUT NOT THE SHOTGUN.

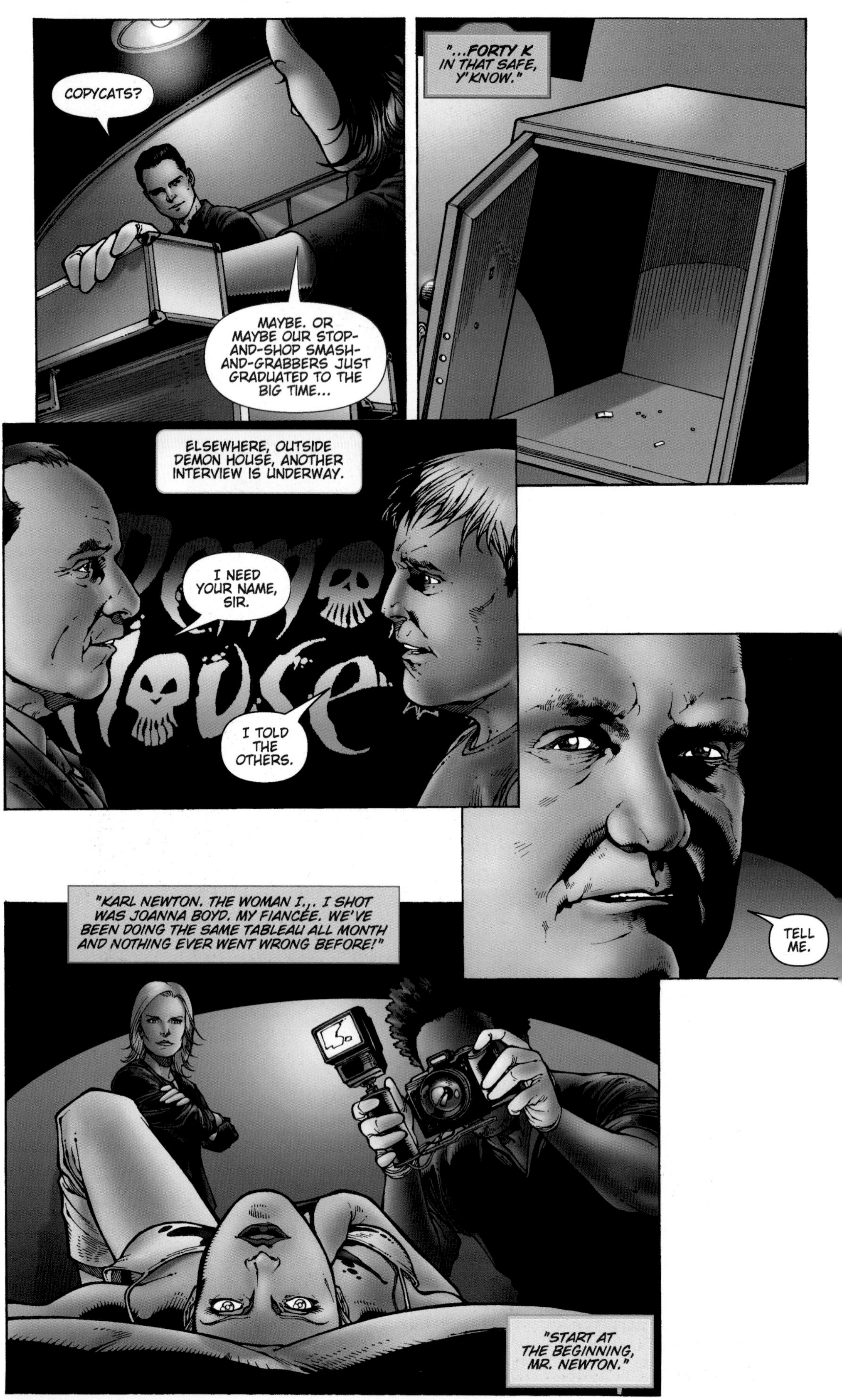
COPYCATS?
MAYBE. OR MAYBE OUR STOP-AND-SHOP SMASH-AND-GRABBERS JUST GRADUATED TO THE BIG TIME...
"...FORTY K IN THAT SAFE, Y'KNOW."
ELSEWHERE, OUTSIDE DEMON HOUSE, ANOTHER INTERVIEW IS UNDERWAY.
I NEED YOUR NAME, SIR.
I TOLD THE OTHERS.
TELL ME.
"KARL NEWTON. THE WOMAN I... I SHOT WAS JOANNA BOYD. MY FIANCÉE. WE'VE BEEN DOING THE SAME TABLEAU ALL MONTH AND NOTHING EVER WENT WRONG BEFORE!"
"START AT THE BEGINNING, MR. NEWTON."

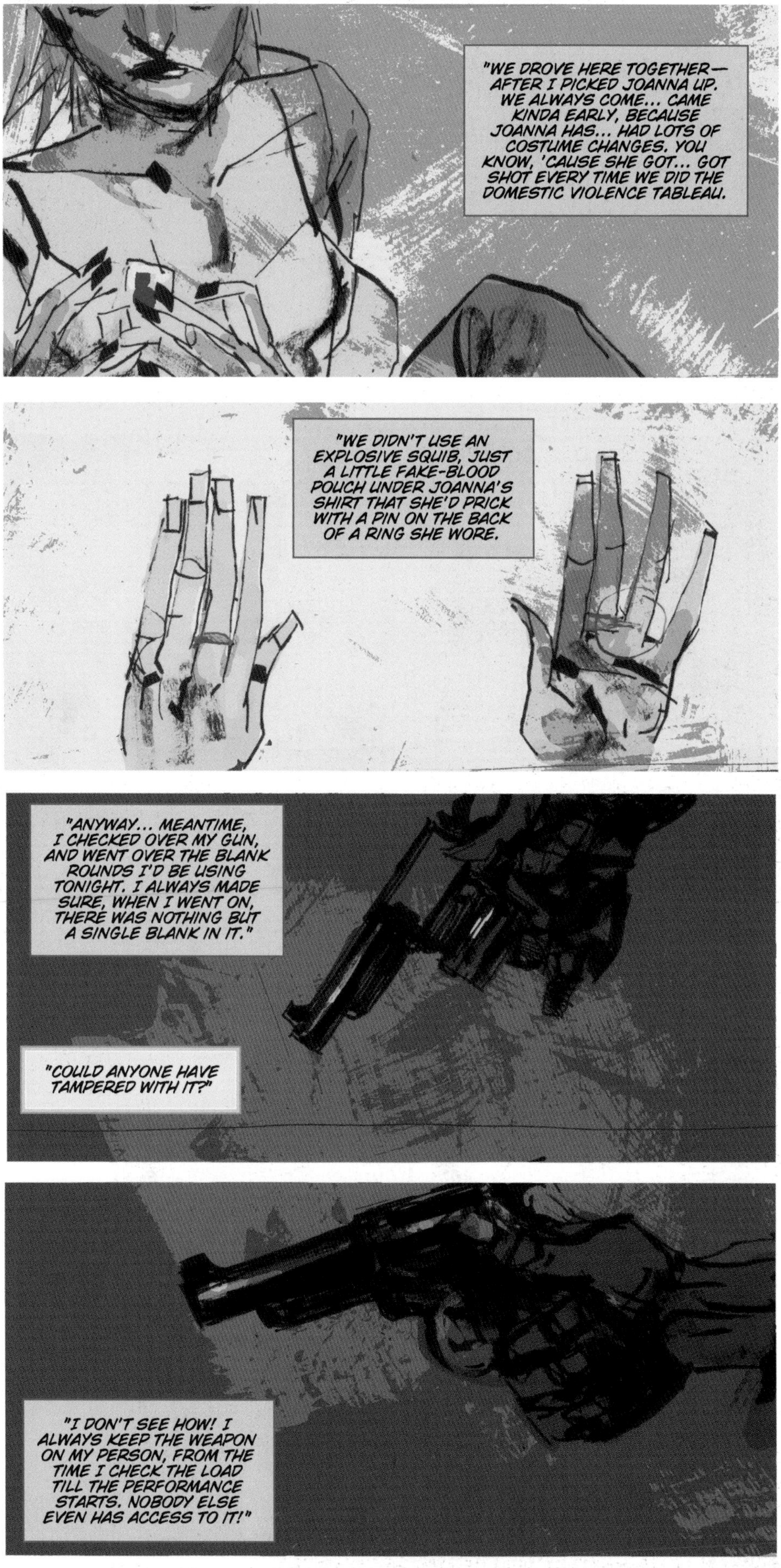
"WE DROVE HERE TOGETHER— AFTER I PICKED JOANNA UP. WE ALWAYS COME... CAME KINDA EARLY, BECAUSE JOANNA HAS... HAD LOTS OF COSTUME CHANGES. YOU KNOW, 'CAUSE SHE GOT... GOT SHOT EVERY TIME WE DID THE DOMESTIC VIOLENCE TABLEAU.
"WE DIDN'T USE AN EXPLOSIVE SQUIB, JUST A LITTLE FAKE-BLOOD POUCH UNDER JOANNA'S SHIRT THAT SHE'D PRICK WITH A PIN ON THE BACK OF A RING SHE WORE.
"ANYWAY... MEANTIME, I CHECKED OVER MY GUN, AND WENT OVER THE BLANK ROUNDS I'D BE USING TONIGHT. I ALWAYS MADE SURE, WHEN I WENT ON, THERE WAS NOTHING BUT A SINGLE BLANK IN IT."
"COULD ANYONE HAVE TAMPERED WITH IT?"
"I DON'T SEE HOW! I ALWAYS KEEP THE WEAPON ON MY PERSON, FROM THE TIME I CHECK THE LOAD TILL THE PERFORMANCE STARTS. NOBODY ELSE EVEN HAS ACCESS TO IT!"

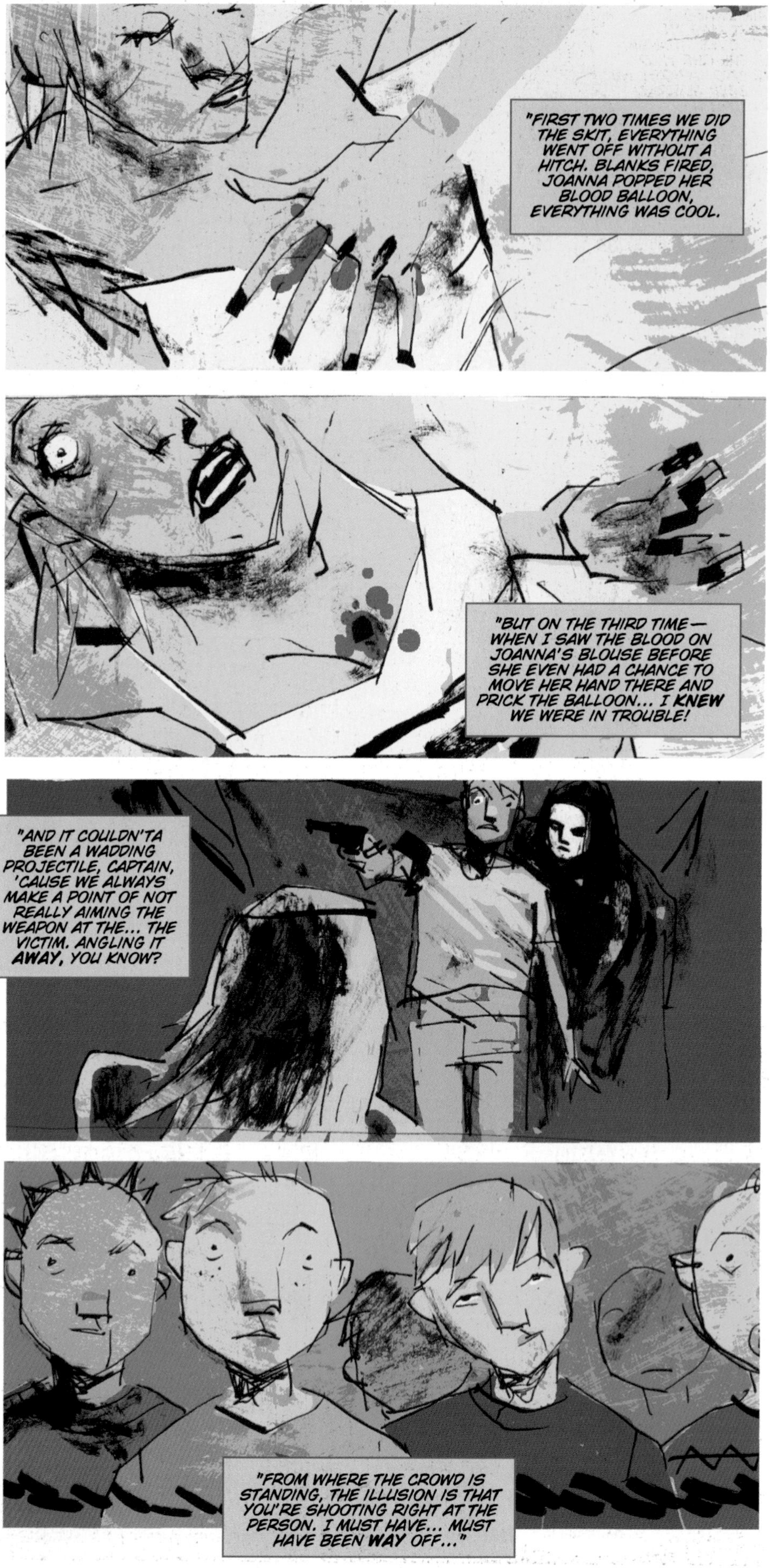
"FIRST TWO TIMES WE DID THE SKIT, EVERYTHING WENT OFF WITHOUT A HITCH. BLANKS FIRED, JOANNA POPPED HER BLOOD BALLOON, EVERYTHING WAS COOL.
"BUT ON THE THIRD TIME— WHEN I SAW THE BLOOD ON JOANNA'S BLOUSE BEFORE SHE EVEN HAD A CHANCE TO MOVE HER HAND THERE AND PRICK THE BALLOON... I KNEW WE WERE IN TROUBLE!
"AND IT COULDN'TA BEEN A WADDING PROJECTILE, CAPTAIN, 'CAUSE WE ALWAYS MAKE A POINT OF NOT REALLY AIMING THE WEAPON AT THE... THE VICTIM. ANGLING IT AWAY, YOU KNOW?
"FROM WHERE THE CROWD IS STANDING, THE ILLUSION IS THAT YOU'RE SHOOTING RIGHT AT THE PERSON. I MUST HAVE... MUST HAVE BEEN WAY OFF..."

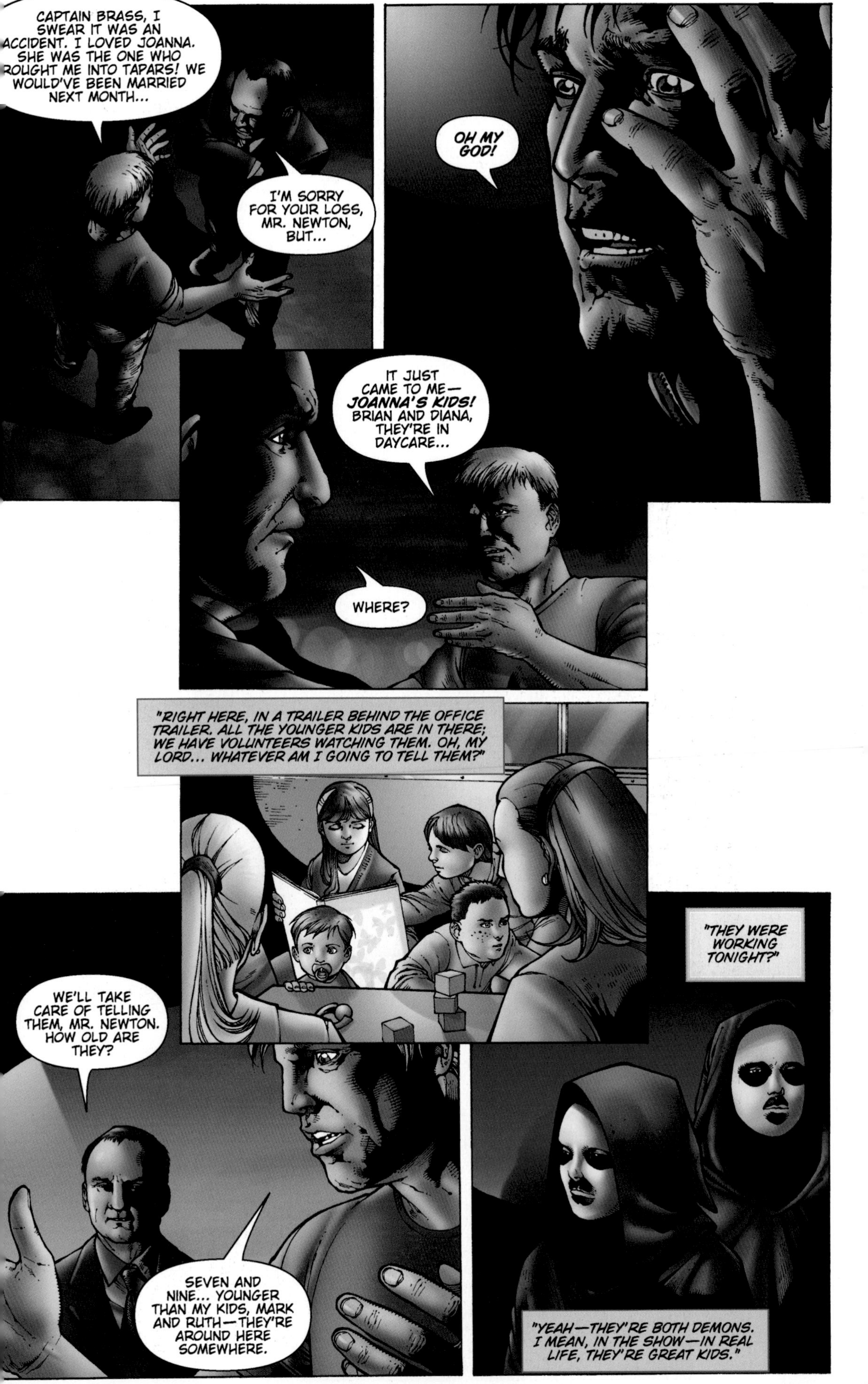
CAPTAIN BRASS, I SWEAR IT WAS AN ACCIDENT. I LOVED JOANNA. SHE WAS THE ONE WHO BROUGHT ME INTO TAPARS! WE WOULD'VE BEEN MARRIED NEXT MONTH...
I'M SORRY FOR YOUR LOSS, MR. NEWTON, BUT...
OH MY GOD!
IT JUST CAME TO ME— JOANNA'S KIDS! BRIAN AND DIANA, THEY'RE IN DAYCARE...
WHERE?
"RIGHT HERE, IN A TRAILER BEHIND THE OFFICE TRAILER. ALL THE YOUNGER KIDS ARE IN THERE; WE HAVE VOLUNTEERS WATCHING THEM. OH, MY LORD... WHATEVER AM I GOING TO TELL THEM?"
WE'LL TAKE CARE OF TELLING THEM, MR. NEWTON. HOW OLD ARE THEY?
SEVEN AND NINE... YOUNGER THAN MY KIDS, MARK AND RUTH—THEY'RE AROUND HERE SOMEWHERE.
"THEY WERE WORKING TONIGHT?"
"YEAH—THEY'RE BOTH DEMONS. I MEAN, IN THE SHOW—IN REAL LIFE, THEY'RE GREAT KIDS."

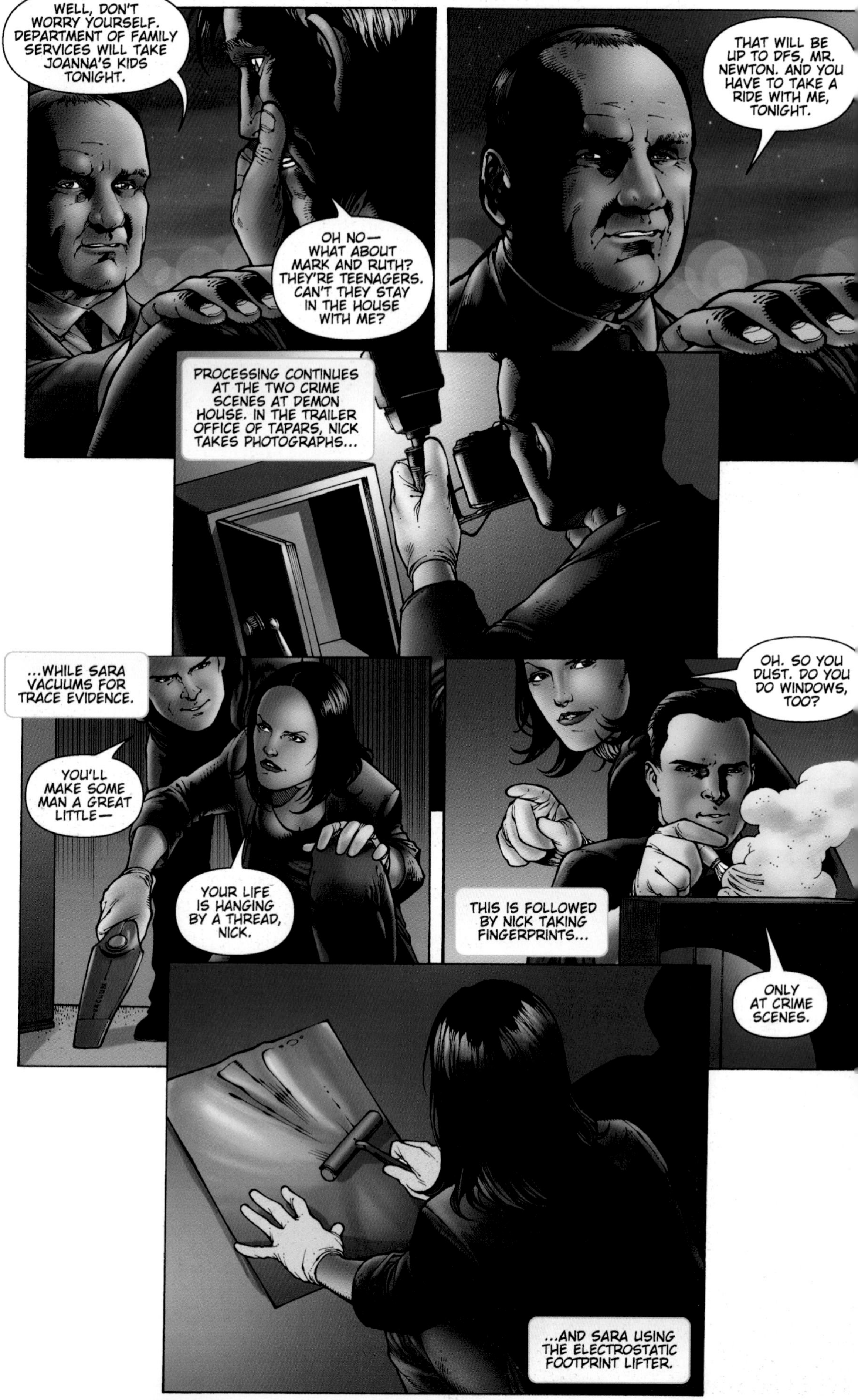

WELL, DON'T WORRY YOURSELF. DEPARTMENT OF FAMILY SERVICES WILL TAKE JOANNA'S KIDS TONIGHT.
OH NO— WHAT ABOUT MARK AND RUTH? THEY'RE TEENAGERS. CAN'T THEY STAY IN THE HOUSE WITH ME?
THAT WILL BE UP TO DFS, MR. NEWTON. AND YOU HAVE TO TAKE A RIDE WITH ME, TONIGHT.
PROCESSING CONTINUES AT THE TWO CRIME SCENES AT DEMON HOUSE. IN THE TRAILER OFFICE OF TAPARS, NICK TAKES PHOTOGRAPHS...
...WHILE SARA VACUUMS FOR TRACE EVIDENCE.
YOU'LL MAKE SOME MAN A GREAT LITTLE—
YOUR LIFE IS HANGING BY A THREAD, NICK.
OH. SO YOU DUST. DO YOU DO WINDOWS, TOO?
THIS IS FOLLOWED BY NICK TAKING FINGERPRINTS...
ONLY AT CRIME SCENES.
...AND SARA USING THE ELECTROSTATIC FOOTPRINT LIFTER.

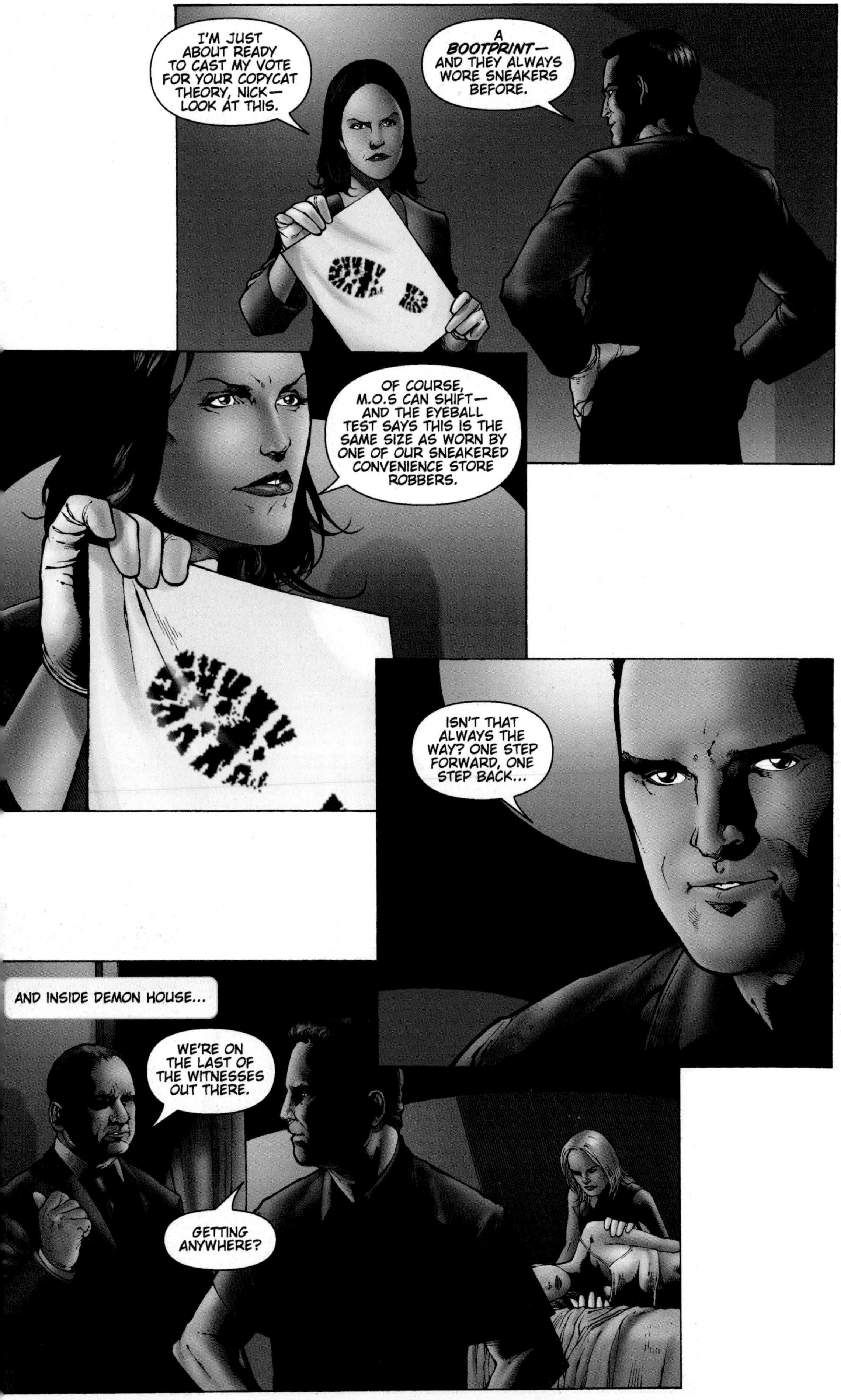
I'M JUST ABOUT READY TO CAST MY VOTE FOR YOUR COPYCAT THEORY, NICK— LOOK AT THIS.
A BOOTPRINT— AND THEY ALWAYS WORE SNEAKERS BEFORE.
OF COURSE, M.O.S CAN SHIFT— AND THE EYEBALL TEST SAYS THIS IS THE SAME SIZE AS WORN BY ONE OF OUR SNEAKERED CONVENIENCE STORE ROBBERS.
ISN'T THAT ALWAYS THE WAY? ONE STEP FORWARD, ONE STEP BACK...
AND INSIDE DEMON HOUSE...
WE'RE ON THE LAST OF THE WITNESSES OUT THERE.
GETTING ANYWHERE?

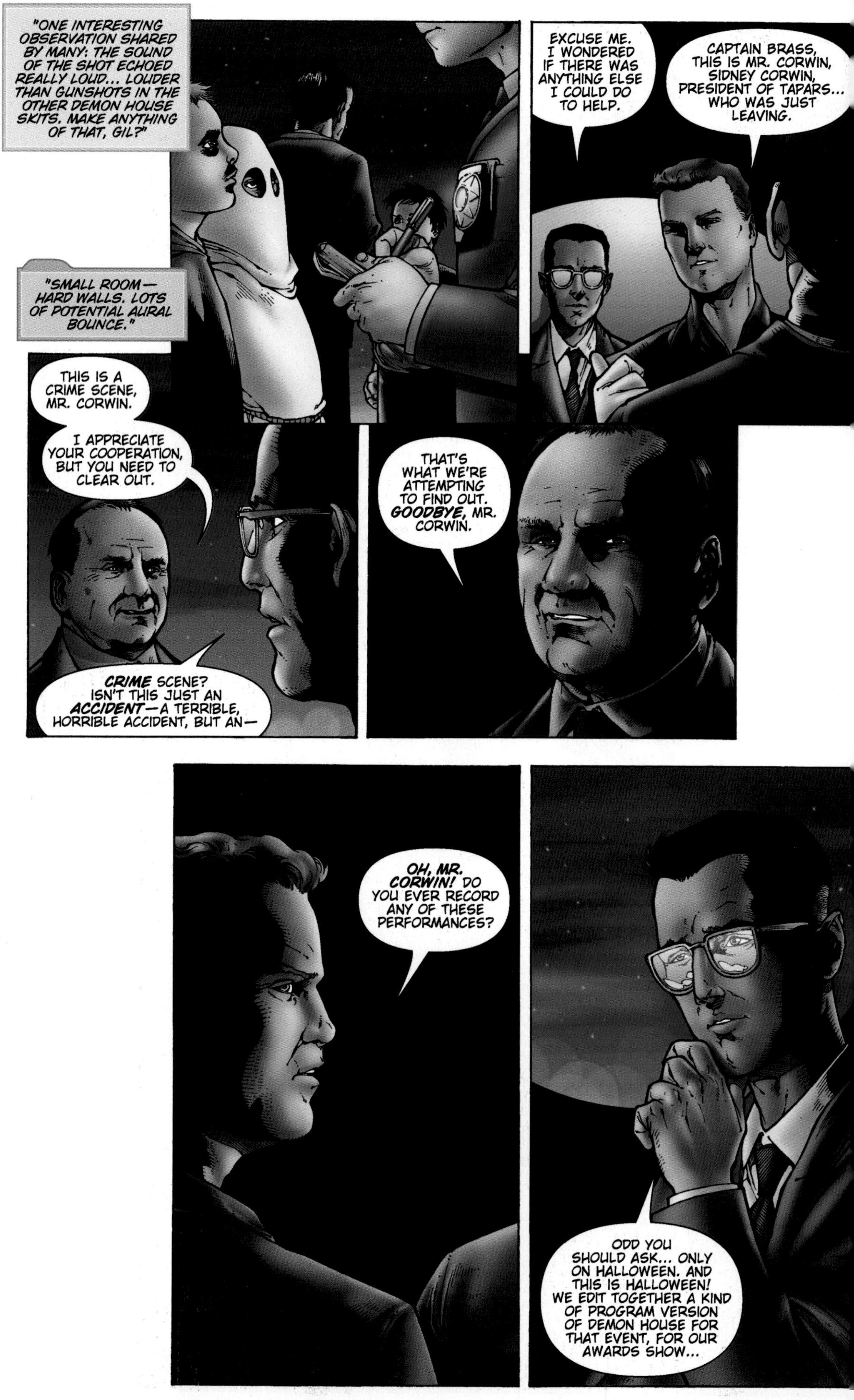
"ONE INTERESTING OBSERVATION SHARED BY MANY: THE SOUND OF THE SHOT ECHOED REALLY LOUD... LOUDER THAN GUNSHOTS IN THE OTHER DEMON HOUSE SKITS. MAKE ANYTHING OF THAT, GIL?"
"SMALL ROOM— HARD WALLS. LOTS OF POTENTIAL AURAL BOUNCE."
EXCUSE ME. I WONDERED IF THERE WAS ANYTHING ELSE I COULD DO TO HELP.
CAPTAIN BRASS, THIS IS MR. CORWIN, SIDNEY CORWIN, PRESIDENT OF TAPARS... WHO WAS JUST LEAVING.
THIS IS A CRIME SCENE, MR. CORWIN.
I APPRECIATE YOUR COOPERATION, BUT YOU NEED TO CLEAR OUT.
CRIME SCENE? ISN'T THIS JUST AN ACCIDENT—A TERRIBLE, HORRIBLE ACCIDENT, BUT AN—
THAT'S WHAT WE'RE ATTEMPTING TO FIND OUT. GOODBYE, MR. CORWIN.
OH, MR. CORWIN! DO YOU EVER RECORD ANY OF THESE PERFORMANCES?
ODD YOU SHOULD ASK... ONLY ON HALLOWEEN. AND THIS IS HALLOWEEN! WE EDIT TOGETHER A KIND OF PROGRAM VERSION OF DEMON HOUSE FOR THAT EVENT, FOR OUR AWARDS SHOW...

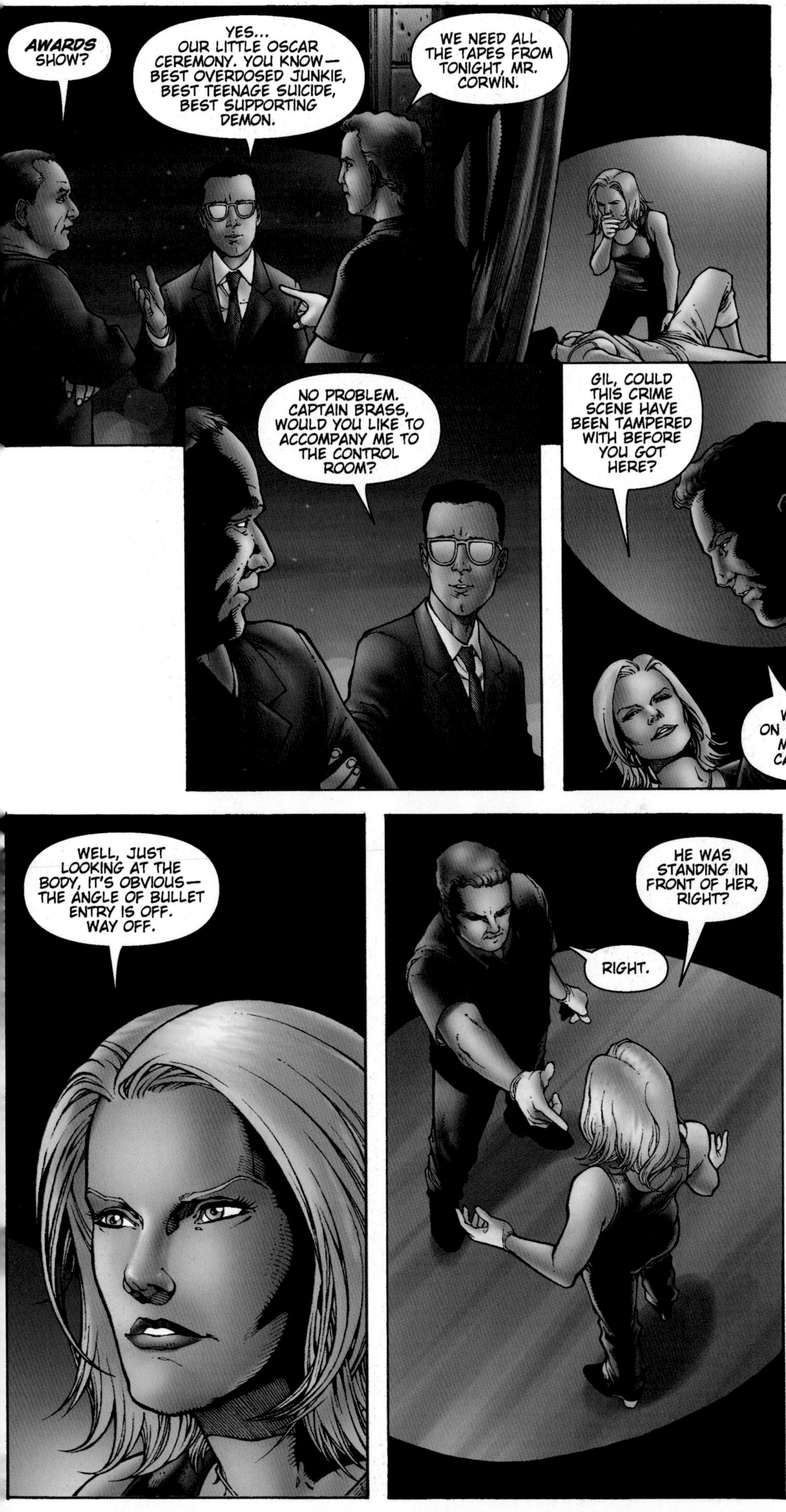
AWARDS SHOW?
YES... OUR LITTLE OSCAR CEREMONY. YOU KNOW— BEST OVERDOSED JUNKIE, BEST TEENAGE SUICIDE, BEST SUPPORTING DEMON.
WE NEED ALL THE TAPES FROM TONIGHT, MR. CORWIN.
NO PROBLEM. CAPTAIN BRASS, WOULD YOU LIKE TO ACCOMPANY ME TO THE CONTROL ROOM?
GIL, COULD THIS CRIME SCENE HAVE BEEN TAMPERED WITH BEFORE YOU GOT HERE?
WE WERE ON SITE WITHIN MOMENTS, CATHERINE.
WELL, JUST LOOKING AT THE BODY, IT'S OBVIOUS— THE ANGLE OF BULLET ENTRY IS OFF. WAY OFF.
HE WAS STANDING IN FRONT OF HER, RIGHT?
RIGHT.

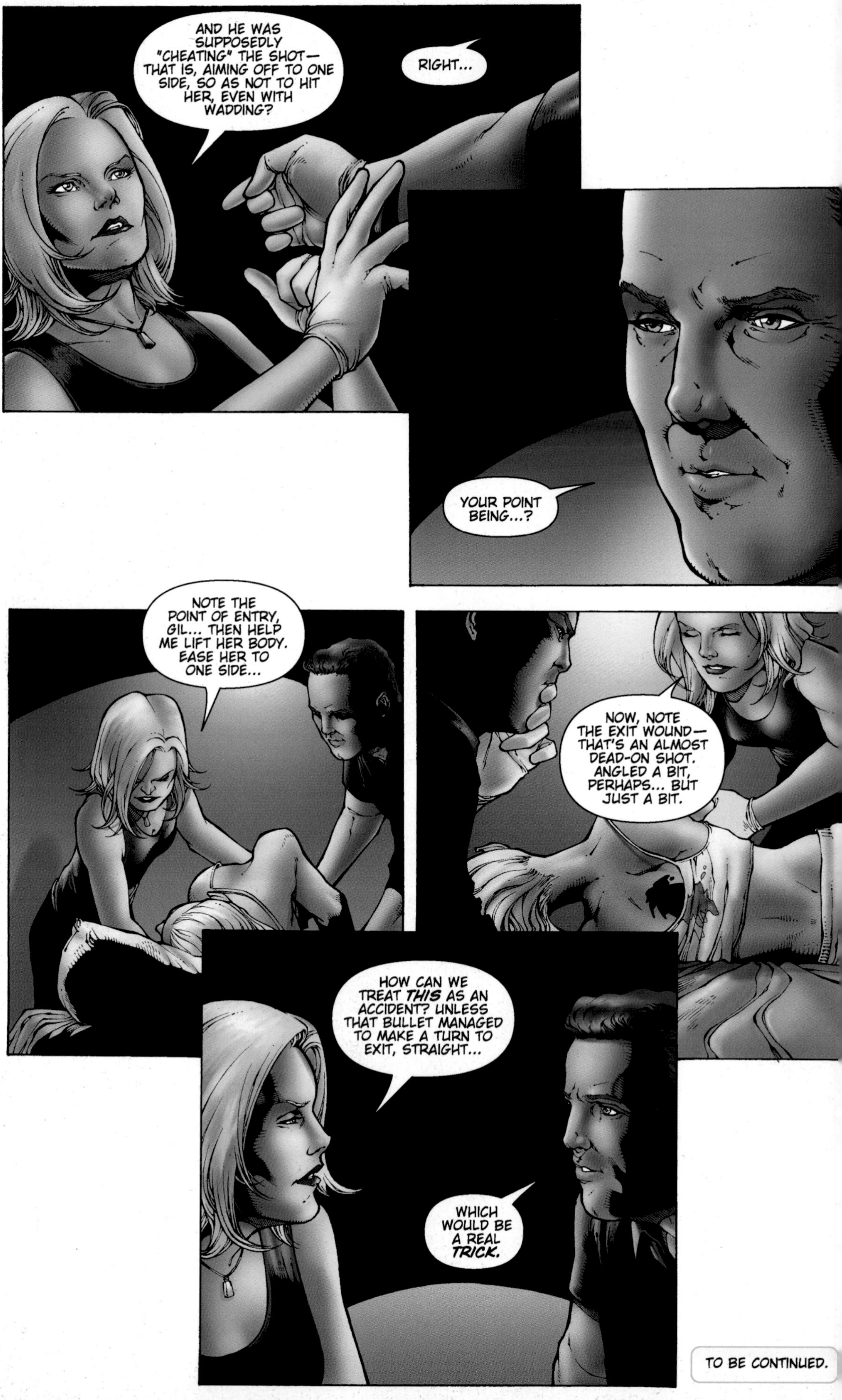
AND HE WAS SUPPOSEDLY "CHEATING" THE SHOT— THAT IS, AIMING OFF TO ONE SIDE, SO AS NOT TO HIT HER, EVEN WITH WADDING?
RIGHT...
YOUR POINT BEING...?
NOTE THE POINT OF ENTRY, GIL... THEN HELP ME LIFT HER BODY. EASE HER TO ONE SIDE...
NOW, NOTE THE EXIT WOUND— THAT'S AN ALMOST DEAD-ON SHOT. ANGLED A BIT, PERHAPS... BUT JUST A BIT.
HOW CAN WE TREAT THIS AS AN ACCIDENT? UNLESS THAT BULLET MANAGED TO MAKE A TURN TO EXIT, STRAIGHT...
WHICH WOULD BE A REAL TRICK.
TO BE CONTINUED.

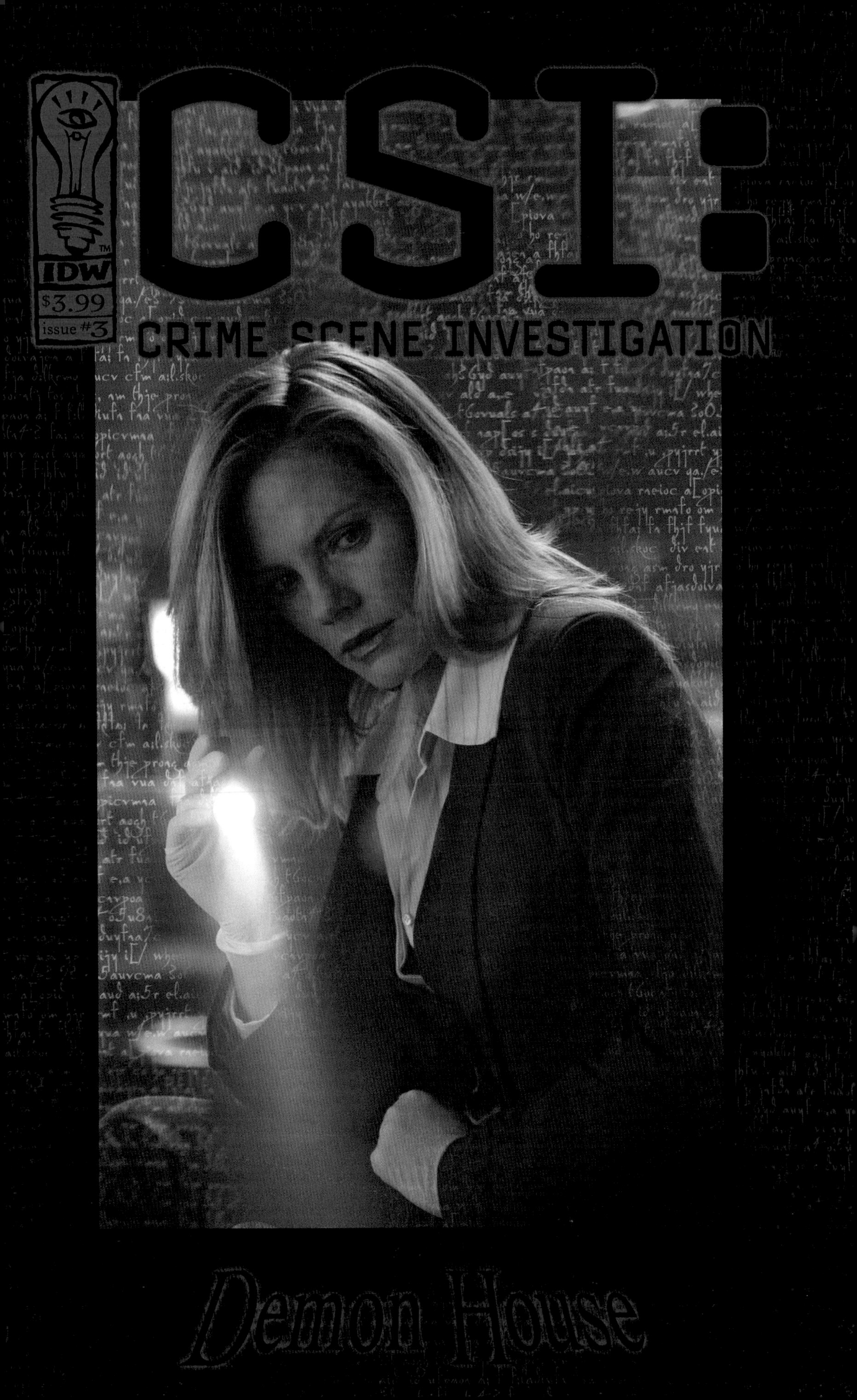
IDW
$3.99
issue #3
CSI:
CRIME SCENE INVESTIGATION
Demon House

chapter three

Curtains For Joanna

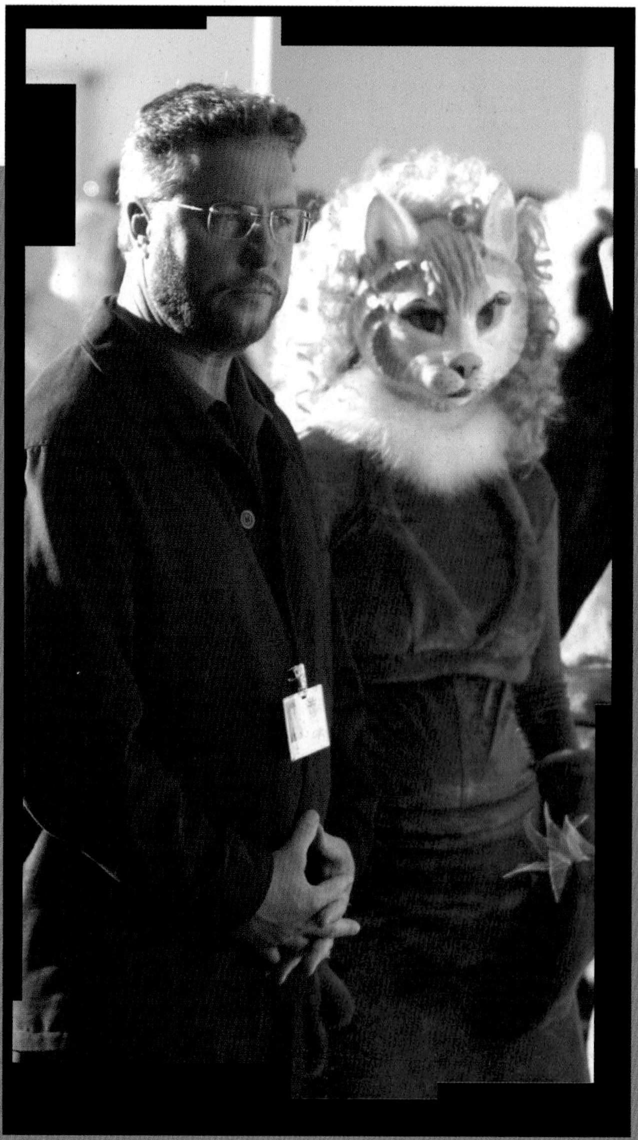

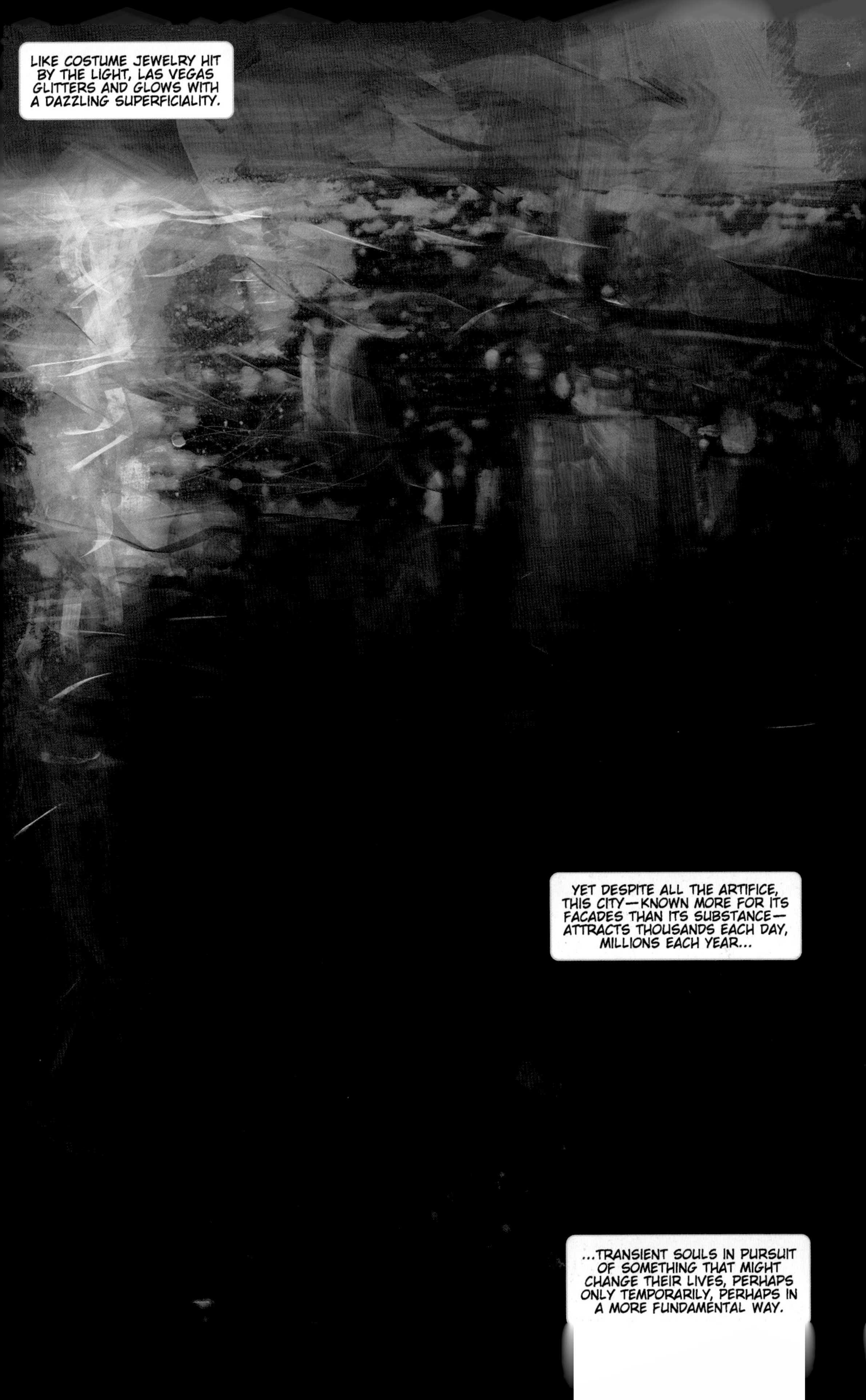
LIKE COSTUME JEWELRY HIT BY THE LIGHT, LAS VEGAS GLITTERS AND GLOWS WITH A DAZZLING SUPERFICIALITY.
YET DESPITE ALL THE ARTIFICE, THIS CITY—KNOWN MORE FOR ITS FACADES THAN ITS SUBSTANCE—ATTRACTS THOUSANDS EACH DAY, MILLIONS EACH YEAR...
...TRANSIENT SOULS IN PURSUIT OF SOMETHING THAT MIGHT CHANGE THEIR LIVES, PERHAPS ONLY TEMPORARILY, PERHAPS IN A MORE FUNDAMENTAL WAY.

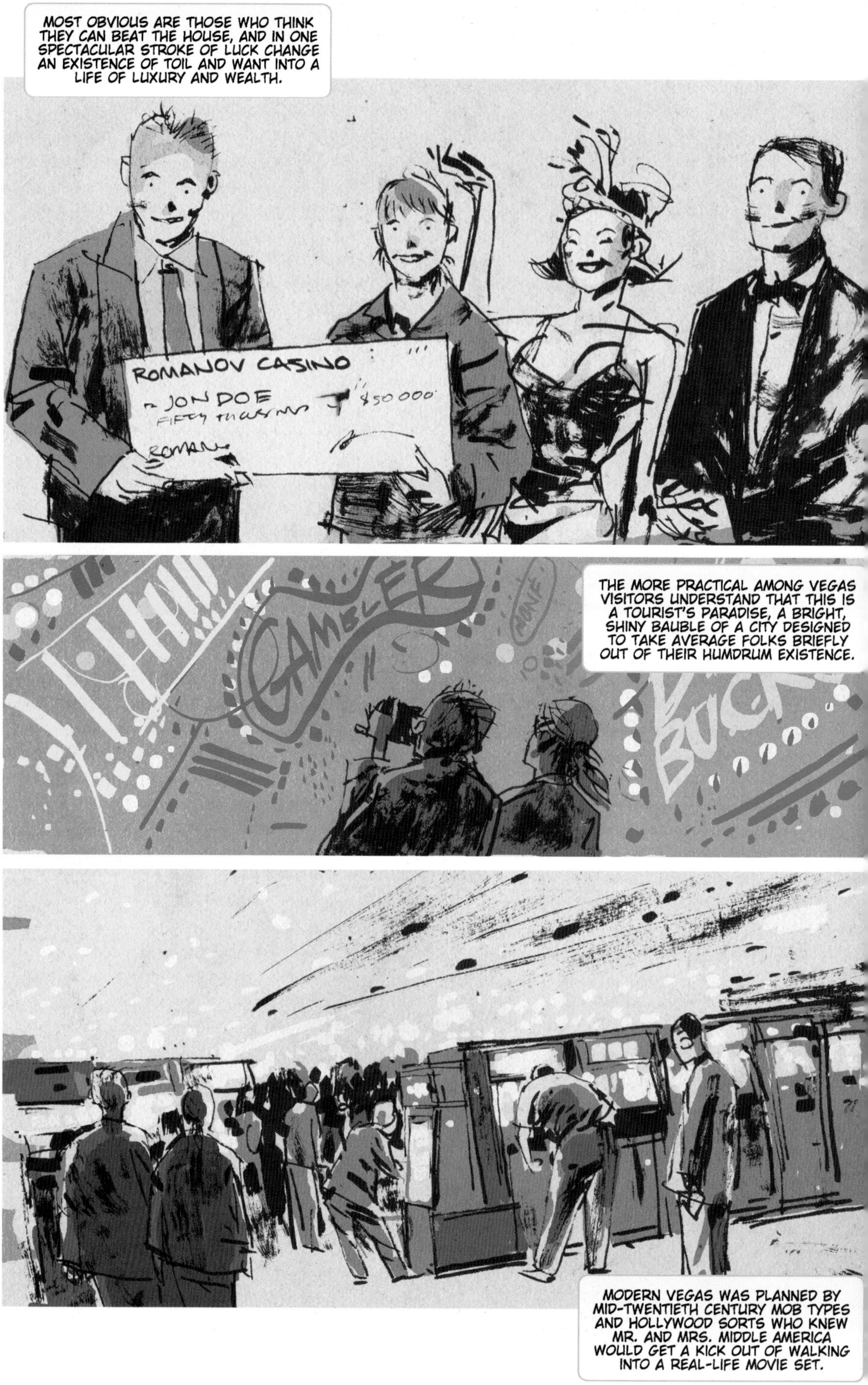
MOST OBVIOUS ARE THOSE WHO THINK THEY CAN BEAT THE HOUSE, AND IN ONE SPECTACULAR STROKE OF LUCK CHANGE AN EXISTENCE OF TOIL AND WANT INTO A LIFE OF LUXURY AND WEALTH.
ROMANOV CASINO
JON DOE
$50 000
GAMBLER
THE MORE PRACTICAL AMONG VEGAS VISITORS UNDERSTAND THAT THIS IS A TOURIST'S PARADISE, A BRIGHT, SHINY BAUBLE OF A CITY DESIGNED TO TAKE AVERAGE FOLKS BRIEFLY OUT OF THEIR HUMDRUM EXISTENCE.
MODERN VEGAS WAS PLANNED BY MID-TWENTIETH CENTURY MOB TYPES AND HOLLYWOOD SORTS WHO KNEW MR. AND MRS. MIDDLE AMERICA WOULD GET A KICK OUT OF WALKING INTO A REAL-LIFE MOVIE SET.

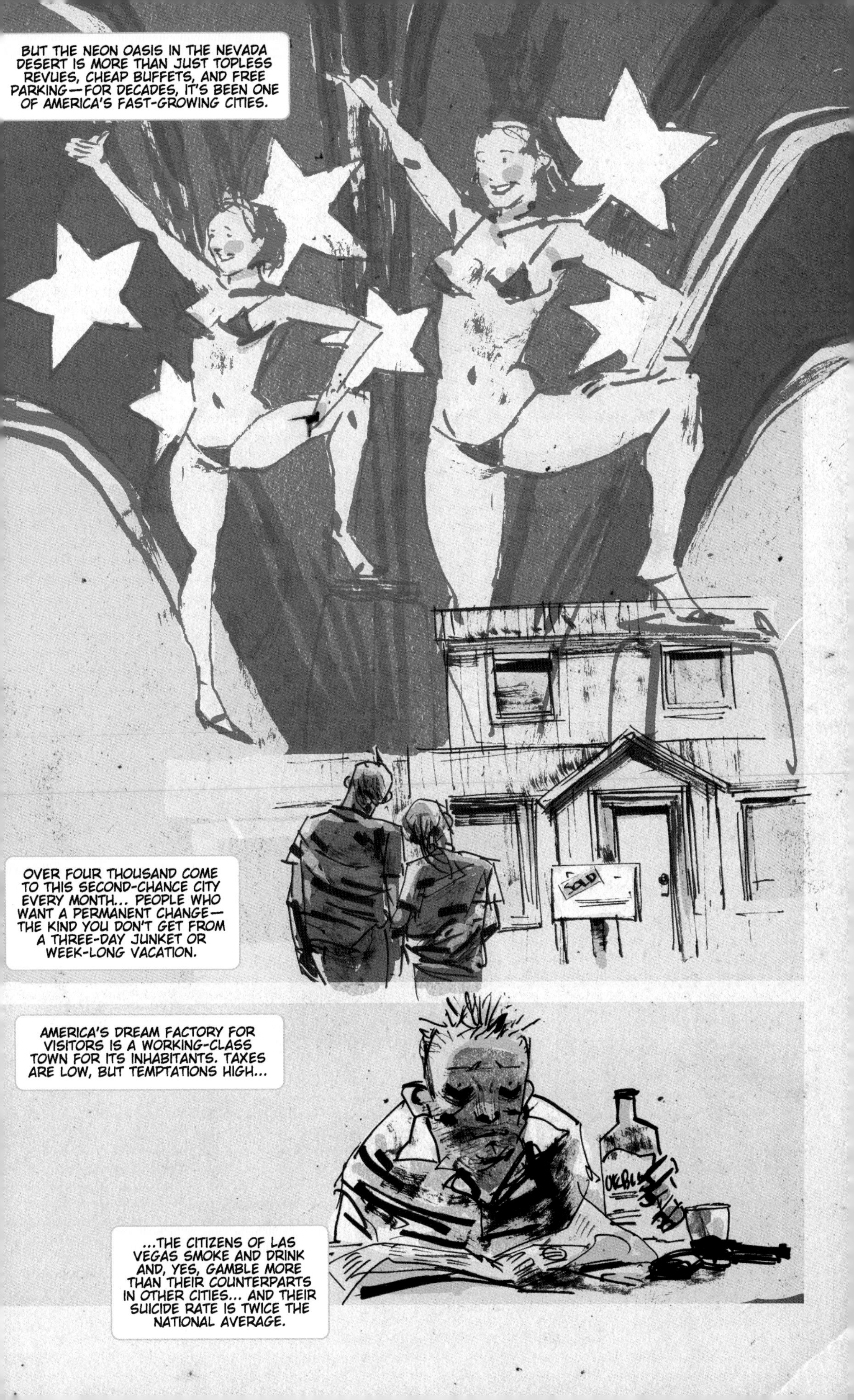
BUT THE NEON OASIS IN THE NEVADA DESERT IS MORE THAN JUST TOPLESS REVUES, CHEAP BUFFETS, AND FREE PARKING—FOR DECADES, IT'S BEEN ONE OF AMERICA'S FAST-GROWING CITIES.
OVER FOUR THOUSAND COME TO THIS SECOND-CHANCE CITY EVERY MONTH... PEOPLE WHO WANT A PERMANENT CHANGE—THE KIND YOU DON'T GET FROM A THREE-DAY JUNKET OR WEEK-LONG VACATION.
SOLD
AMERICA'S DREAM FACTORY FOR VISITORS IS A WORKING-CLASS TOWN FOR ITS INHABITANTS. TAXES ARE LOW, BUT TEMPTATIONS HIGH...
...THE CITIZENS OF LAS VEGAS SMOKE AND DRINK AND, YES, GAMBLE MORE THAN THEIR COUNTERPARTS IN OTHER CITIES... AND THEIR SUICIDE RATE IS TWICE THE NATIONAL AVERAGE.

AND JUST AS A POP STAR MAY MAKE A BAD JUDGMENT IN A QUICKIE MARRIAGE IN ONE OF THE MANY WEDDING CHAPELS IN TOWN...

...SO MIGHT OTHERS SEEK THE MORE TRADITIONAL VALUES OF FAITH THAT CAN SIGNAL A PROFOUND CHANGE IN LIFESTYLE.

NO SURPRISE, THEN, THAT THE CONSERVATIVE VALUES OF THOSE BEHIND THE CAUTIONARY TABLEAUS IN THE "HAUNTED HOUSE" STAGED BY THE TAPARS* KIDS, WERE EXPRESSED WITH A CERTAIN SPLASHY VEGAS-STYLE PANACHE.

*ACRONYM FOR "TEENS AND PARENTS FOR A RESPONSIBLE SOCIETY"—ED.

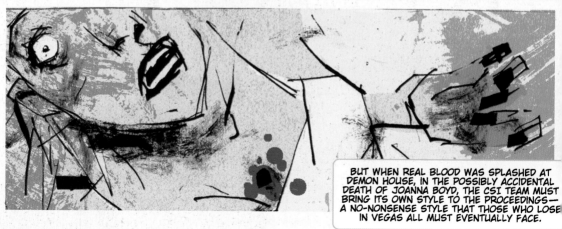

BUT WHEN REAL BLOOD WAS SPLASHED AT DEMON HOUSE, IN THE POSSIBLY ACCIDENTAL DEATH OF JOANNA BOYD, THE CSI TEAM MUST BRING ITS OWN STYLE TO THE PROCEEDINGS— A NO-NONSENSE STYLE THAT THOSE WHO LOSE IN VEGAS ALL MUST EVENTUALLY FACE.

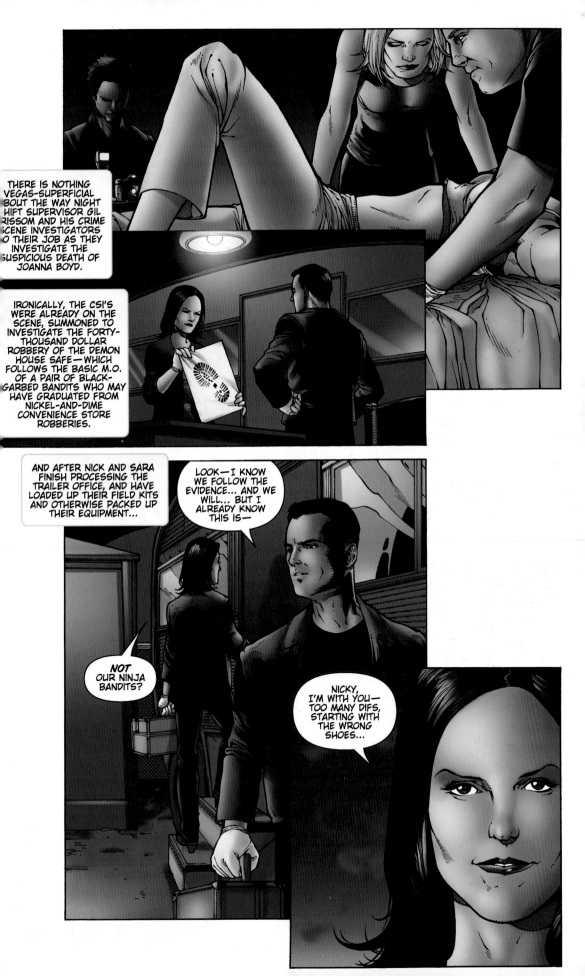

THERE IS NOTHING VEGAS-SUPERFICIAL ABOUT THE WAY NIGHT SHIFT SUPERVISOR GIL GRISSOM AND HIS CRIME SCENE INVESTIGATORS DO THEIR JOB AS THEY INVESTIGATE THE SUSPICIOUS DEATH OF JOANNA BOYD.

IRONICALLY, THE CSI'S WERE ALREADY ON THE SCENE, SUMMONED TO INVESTIGATE THE FORTY-THOUSAND DOLLAR ROBBERY OF THE DEMON HOUSE SAFE—WHICH FOLLOWS THE BASIC M.O. OF A PAIR OF BLACK-GARBED BANDITS WHO MAY HAVE GRADUATED FROM NICKEL-AND-DIME CONVENIENCE STORE ROBBERIES.

AND AFTER NICK AND SARA FINISH PROCESSING THE TRAILER OFFICE, AND HAVE LOADED UP THEIR FIELD KITS AND OTHERWISE PACKED UP THEIR EQUIPMENT...

LOOK—I KNOW WE FOLLOW THE EVIDENCE... AND WE WILL... BUT I ALREADY KNOW THIS IS—

NOT OUR NINJA BANDITS?

NICKY, I'M WITH YOU— TOO MANY DIFS, STARTING WITH THE WRONG SHOES...

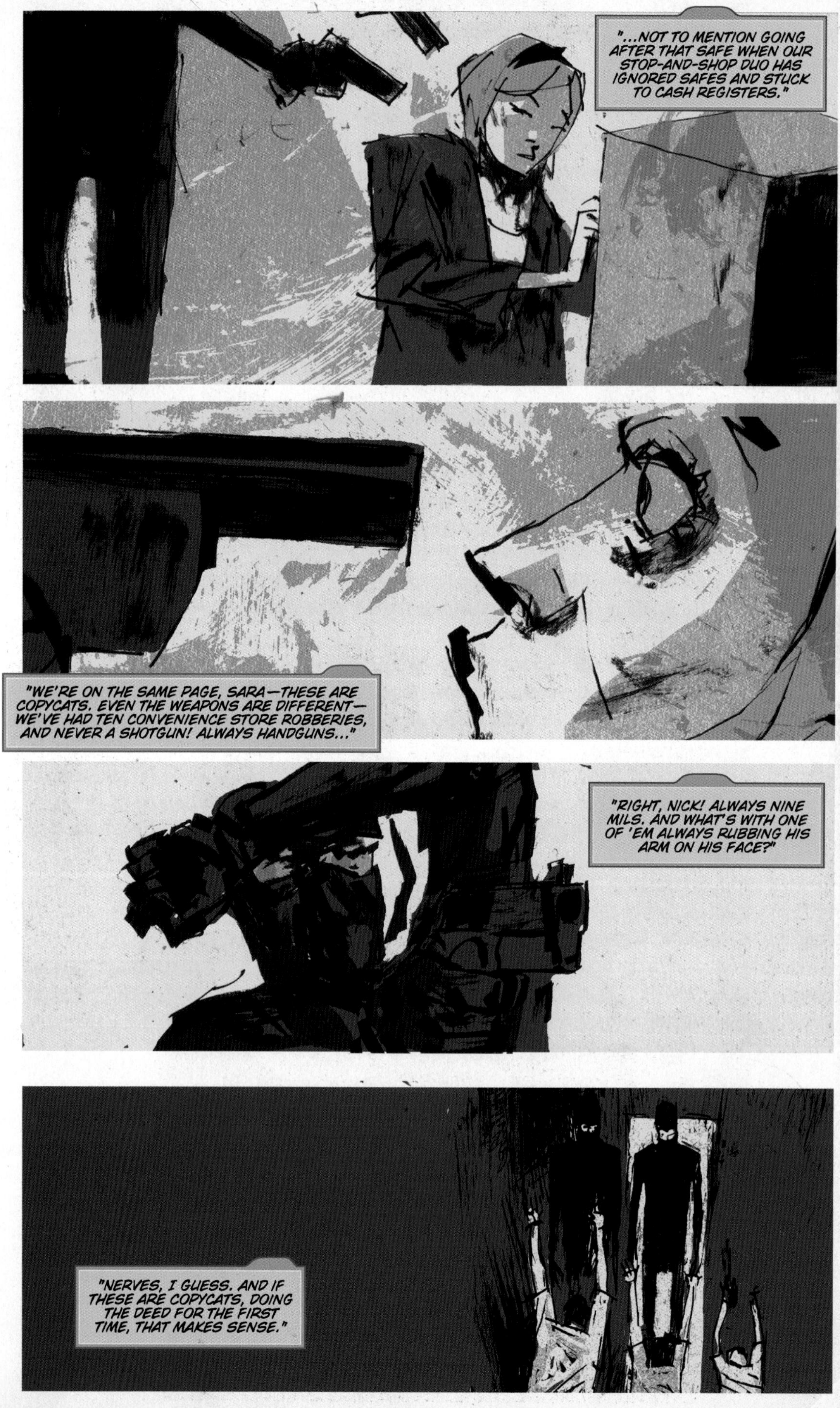

"...NOT TO MENTION GOING AFTER THAT SAFE WHEN OUR STOP-AND-SHOP DUO HAS IGNORED SAFES AND STUCK TO CASH REGISTERS."
"WE'RE ON THE SAME PAGE, SARA—THESE ARE COPYCATS. EVEN THE WEAPONS ARE DIFFERENT—WE'VE HAD TEN CONVENIENCE STORE ROBBERIES, AND NEVER A SHOTGUN! ALWAYS HANDGUNS..."
"RIGHT, NICK! ALWAYS NINE MILS. AND WHAT'S WITH ONE OF 'EM ALWAYS RUBBING HIS ARM ON HIS FACE?"
"NERVES, I GUESS. AND IF THESE ARE COPYCATS, DOING THE DEED FOR THE FIRST TIME, THAT MAKES SENSE."

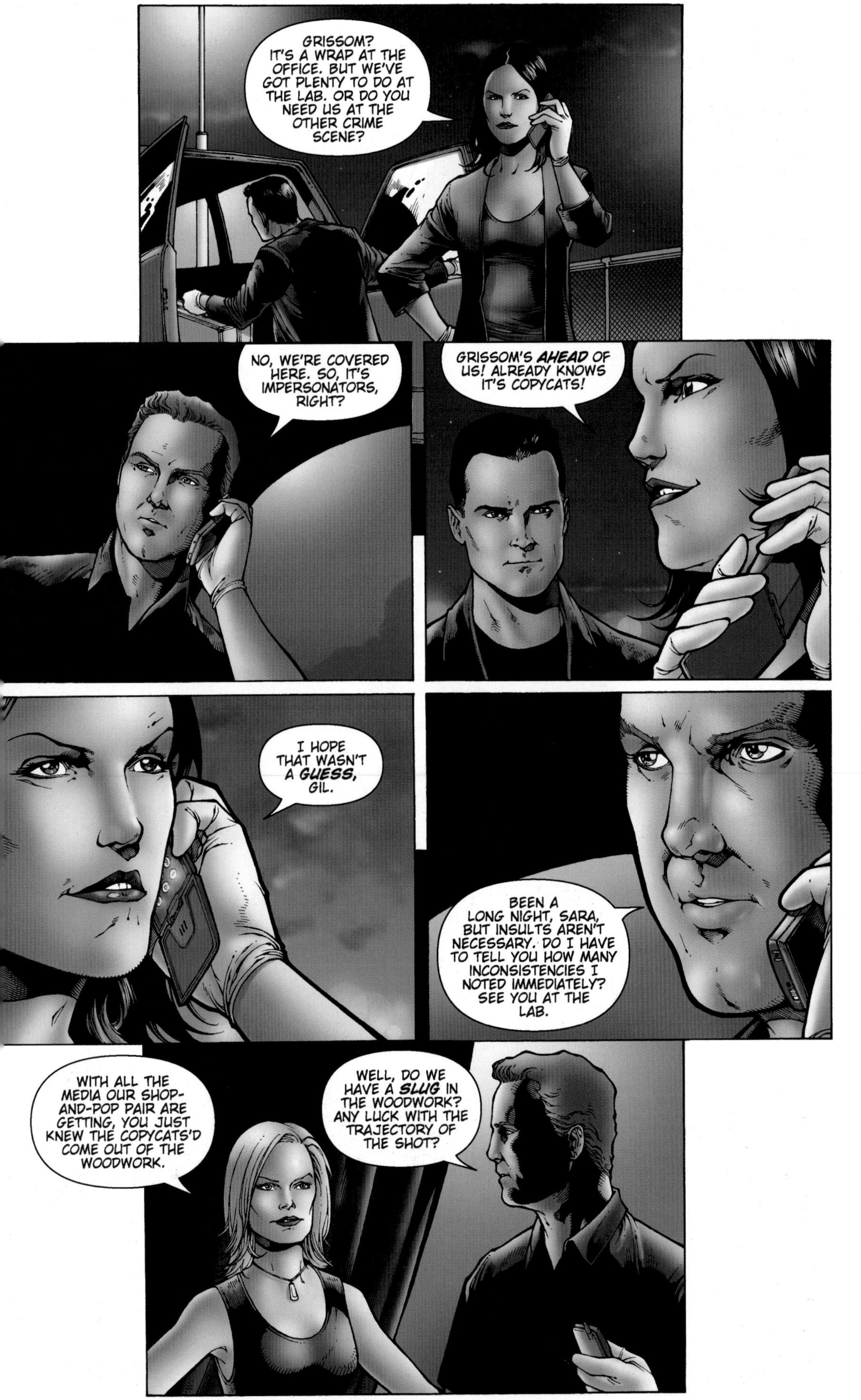
GRISSOM? IT'S A WRAP AT THE OFFICE. BUT WE'VE GOT PLENTY TO DO AT THE LAB. OR DO YOU NEED US AT THE OTHER CRIME SCENE?
NO, WE'RE COVERED HERE. SO, IT'S IMPERSONATORS, RIGHT?
GRISSOM'S AHEAD OF US! ALREADY KNOWS IT'S COPYCATS!
I HOPE THAT WASN'T A GUESS, GIL.
BEEN A LONG NIGHT, SARA, BUT INSULTS AREN'T NECESSARY. DO I HAVE TO TELL YOU HOW MANY INCONSISTENCIES I NOTED IMMEDIATELY? SEE YOU AT THE LAB.
WITH ALL THE MEDIA OUR SHOP-AND-POP PAIR ARE GETTING, YOU JUST KNEW THE COPYCATS'D COME OUT OF THE WOODWORK.
WELL, DO WE HAVE A SLUG IN THE WOODWORK? ANY LUCK WITH THE TRAJECTORY OF THE SHOT?

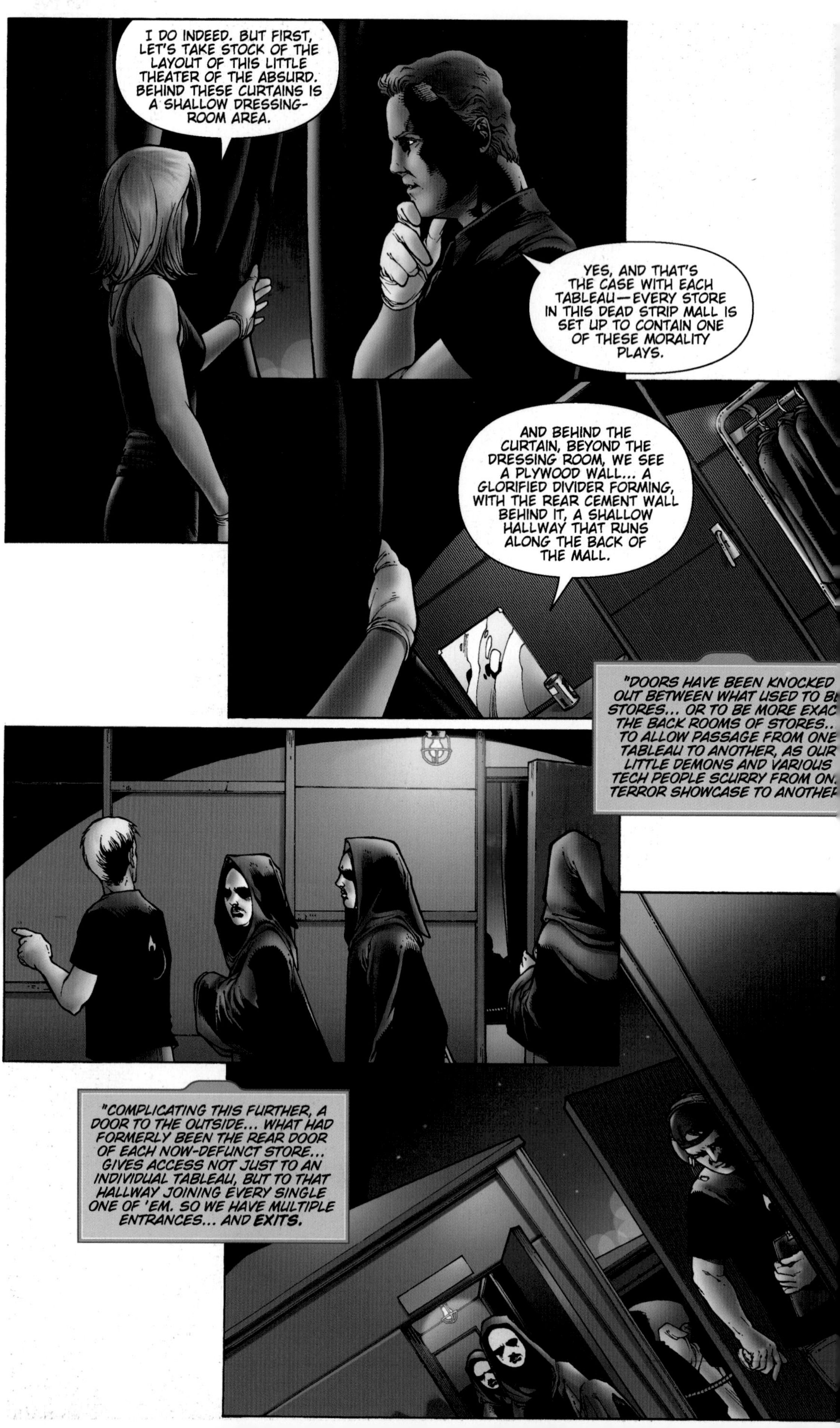
I DO INDEED. BUT FIRST, LET'S TAKE STOCK OF THE LAYOUT OF THIS LITTLE THEATER OF THE ABSURD. BEHIND THESE CURTAINS IS A SHALLOW DRESSING-ROOM AREA.
YES, AND THAT'S THE CASE WITH EACH TABLEAU—EVERY STORE IN THIS DEAD STRIP MALL IS SET UP TO CONTAIN ONE OF THESE MORALITY PLAYS.
AND BEHIND THE CURTAIN, BEYOND THE DRESSING ROOM, WE SEE A PLYWOOD WALL... A GLORIFIED DIVIDER FORMING, WITH THE REAR CEMENT WALL BEHIND IT, A SHALLOW HALLWAY THAT RUNS ALONG THE BACK OF THE MALL.
"DOORS HAVE BEEN KNOCKED OUT BETWEEN WHAT USED TO B STORES... OR TO BE MORE EXAC THE BACK ROOMS OF STORES... TO ALLOW PASSAGE FROM ONE TABLEAU TO ANOTHER, AS OUR LITTLE DEMONS AND VARIOUS TECH PEOPLE SCURRY FROM ON TERROR SHOWCASE TO ANOTHE
"COMPLICATING THIS FURTHER, A DOOR TO THE OUTSIDE... WHAT HAD FORMERLY BEEN THE REAR DOOR OF EACH NOW-DEFUNCT STORE... GIVES ACCESS NOT JUST TO AN INDIVIDUAL TABLEAU, BUT TO THAT HALLWAY JOINING EVERY SINGLE ONE OF 'EM. SO WE HAVE MULTIPLE ENTRANCES... AND EXITS.

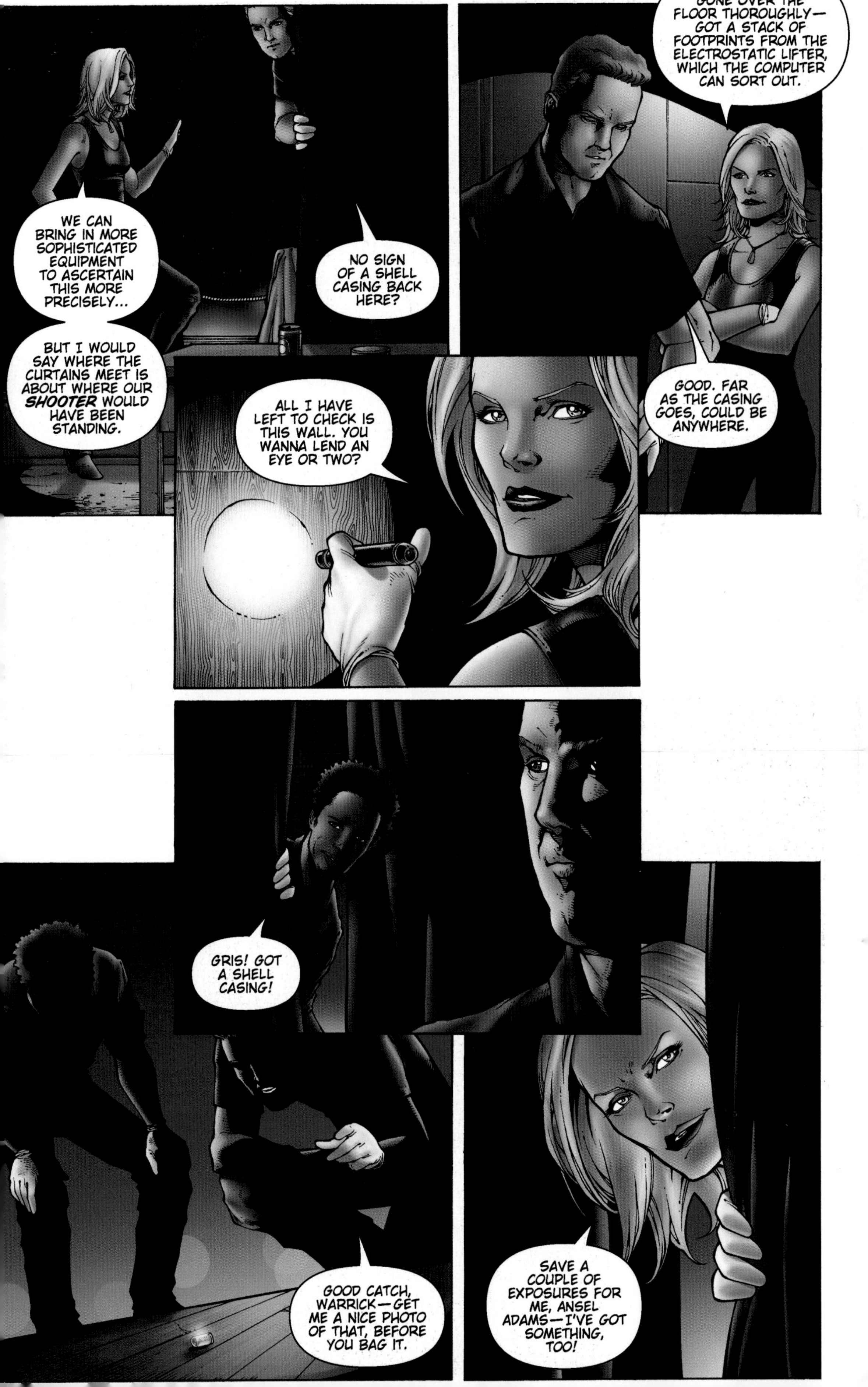
WE CAN BRING IN MORE SOPHISTICATED EQUIPMENT TO ASCERTAIN THIS MORE PRECISELY...
BUT I WOULD SAY WHERE THE CURTAINS MEET IS ABOUT WHERE OUR *SHOOTER* WOULD HAVE BEEN STANDING.
NO SIGN OF A SHELL CASING BACK HERE?
NO, AND I'VE GONE OVER THE FLOOR THOROUGHLY— GOT A STACK OF FOOTPRINTS FROM THE ELECTROSTATIC LIFTER, WHICH THE COMPUTER CAN SORT OUT.
GOOD. FAR AS THE CASING GOES, COULD BE ANYWHERE.
ALL I HAVE LEFT TO CHECK IS THIS WALL. YOU WANNA LEND AN EYE OR TWO?
GRIS! GOT A SHELL CASING!
GOOD CATCH, WARRICK—GET ME A NICE PHOTO OF THAT, BEFORE YOU BAG IT.
SAVE A COUPLE OF EXPOSURES FOR ME, ANSEL ADAMS—I'VE GOT SOMETHING, TOO!

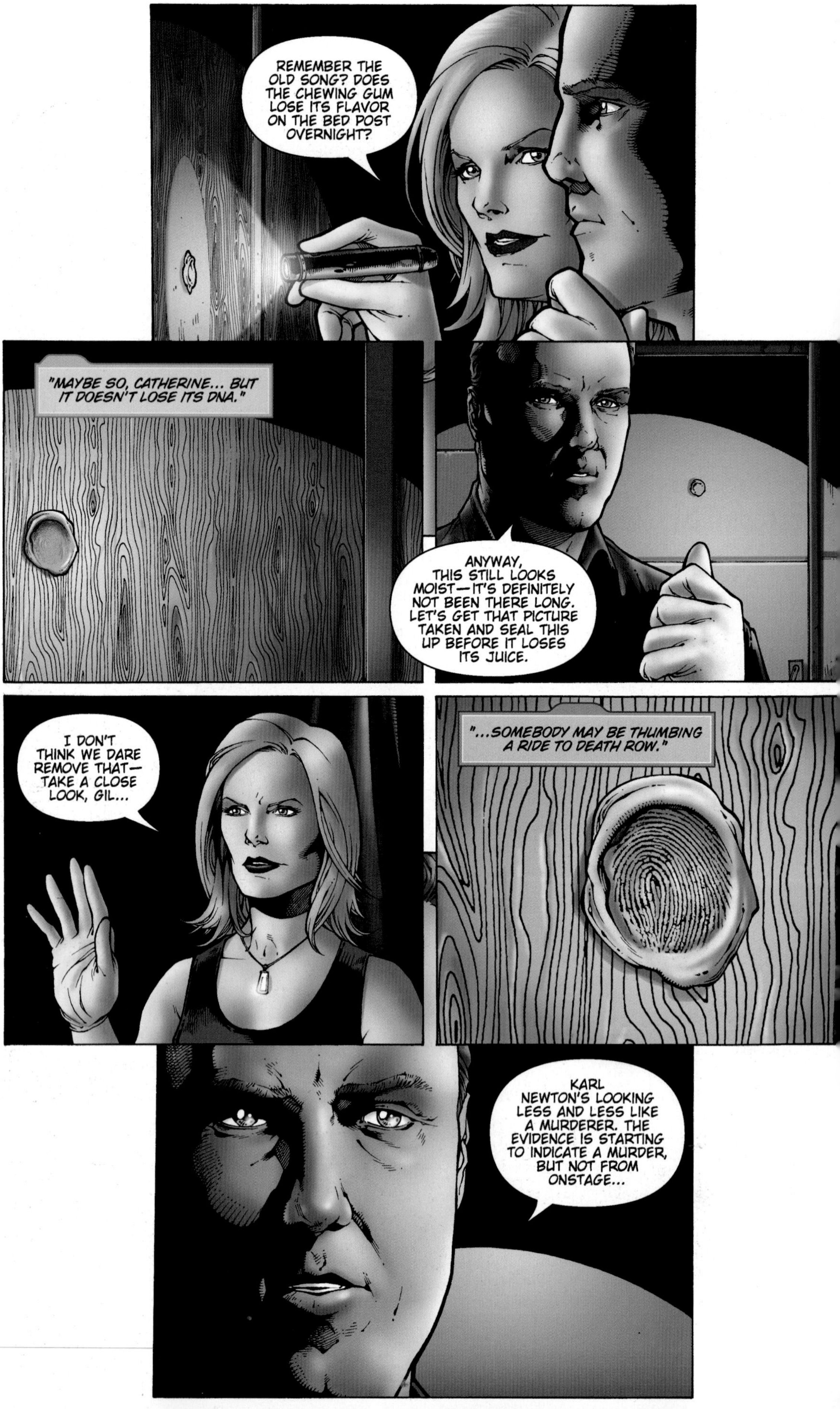
REMEMBER THE OLD SONG? DOES THE CHEWING GUM LOSE ITS FLAVOR ON THE BED POST OVERNIGHT?
"MAYBE SO, CATHERINE... BUT IT DOESN'T LOSE ITS DNA."
ANYWAY, THIS STILL LOOKS MOIST—IT'S DEFINITELY NOT BEEN THERE LONG. LET'S GET THAT PICTURE TAKEN AND SEAL THIS UP BEFORE IT LOSES ITS JUICE.
I DON'T THINK WE DARE REMOVE THAT—TAKE A CLOSE LOOK, GIL...
"...SOMEBODY MAY BE THUMBING A RIDE TO DEATH ROW."
KARL NEWTON'S LOOKING LESS AND LESS LIKE A MURDERER. THE EVIDENCE IS STARTING TO INDICATE A MURDER, BUT NOT FROM ONSTAGE...

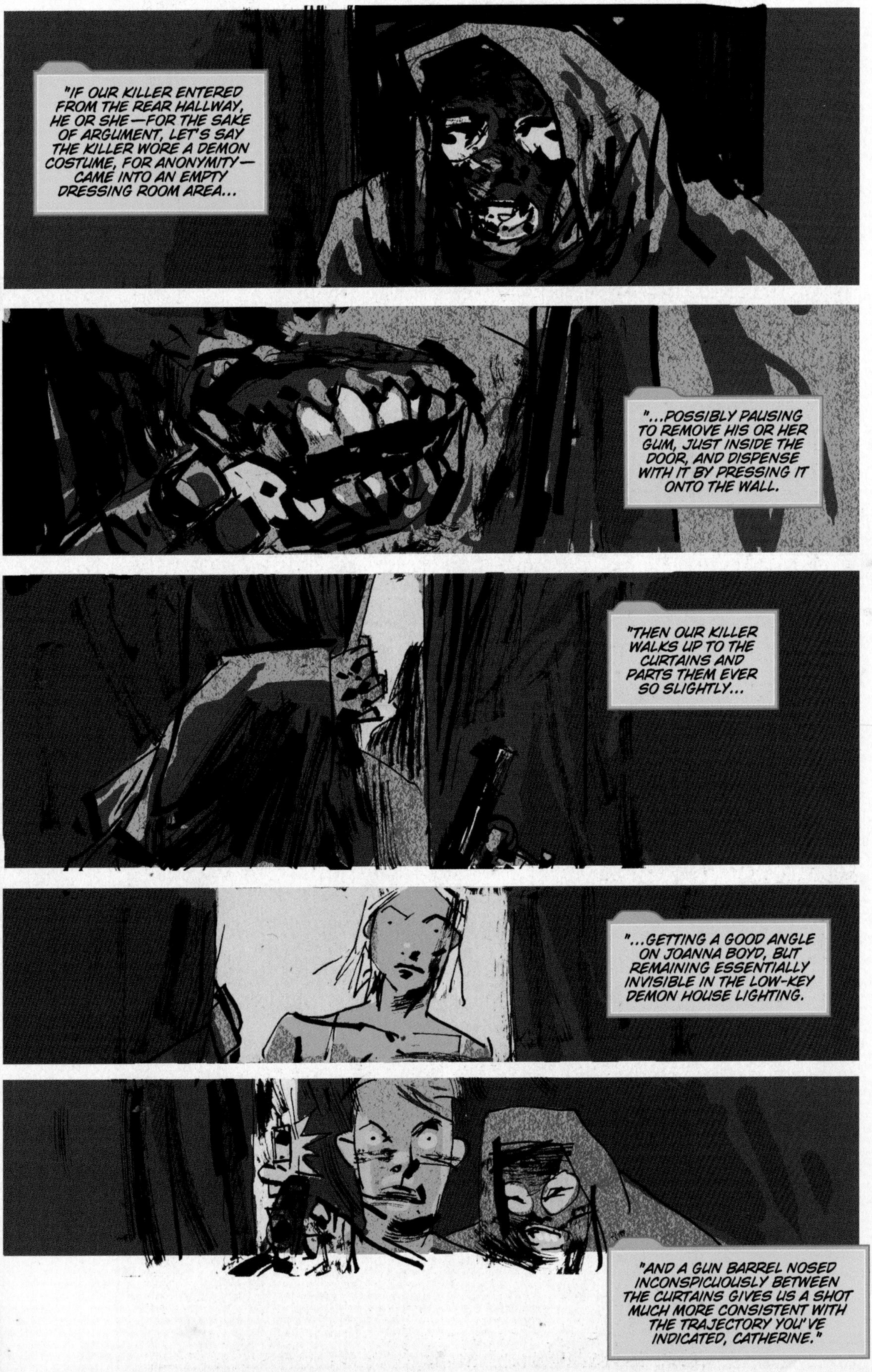
"IF OUR KILLER ENTERED FROM THE REAR HALLWAY, HE OR SHE—FOR THE SAKE OF ARGUMENT, LET'S SAY THE KILLER WORE A DEMON COSTUME, FOR ANONYMITY—CAME INTO AN EMPTY DRESSING ROOM AREA...
"...POSSIBLY PAUSING TO REMOVE HIS OR HER GUM, JUST INSIDE THE DOOR, AND DISPENSE WITH IT BY PRESSING IT ONTO THE WALL.
"THEN OUR KILLER WALKS UP TO THE CURTAINS AND PARTS THEM EVER SO SLIGHTLY...
"...GETTING A GOOD ANGLE ON JOANNA BOYD, BUT REMAINING ESSENTIALLY INVISIBLE IN THE LOW-KEY DEMON HOUSE LIGHTING.
"AND A GUN BARREL NOSED INCONSPICUOUSLY BETWEEN THE CURTAINS GIVES US A SHOT MUCH MORE CONSISTENT WITH THE TRAJECTORY YOU'VE INDICATED, CATHERINE."

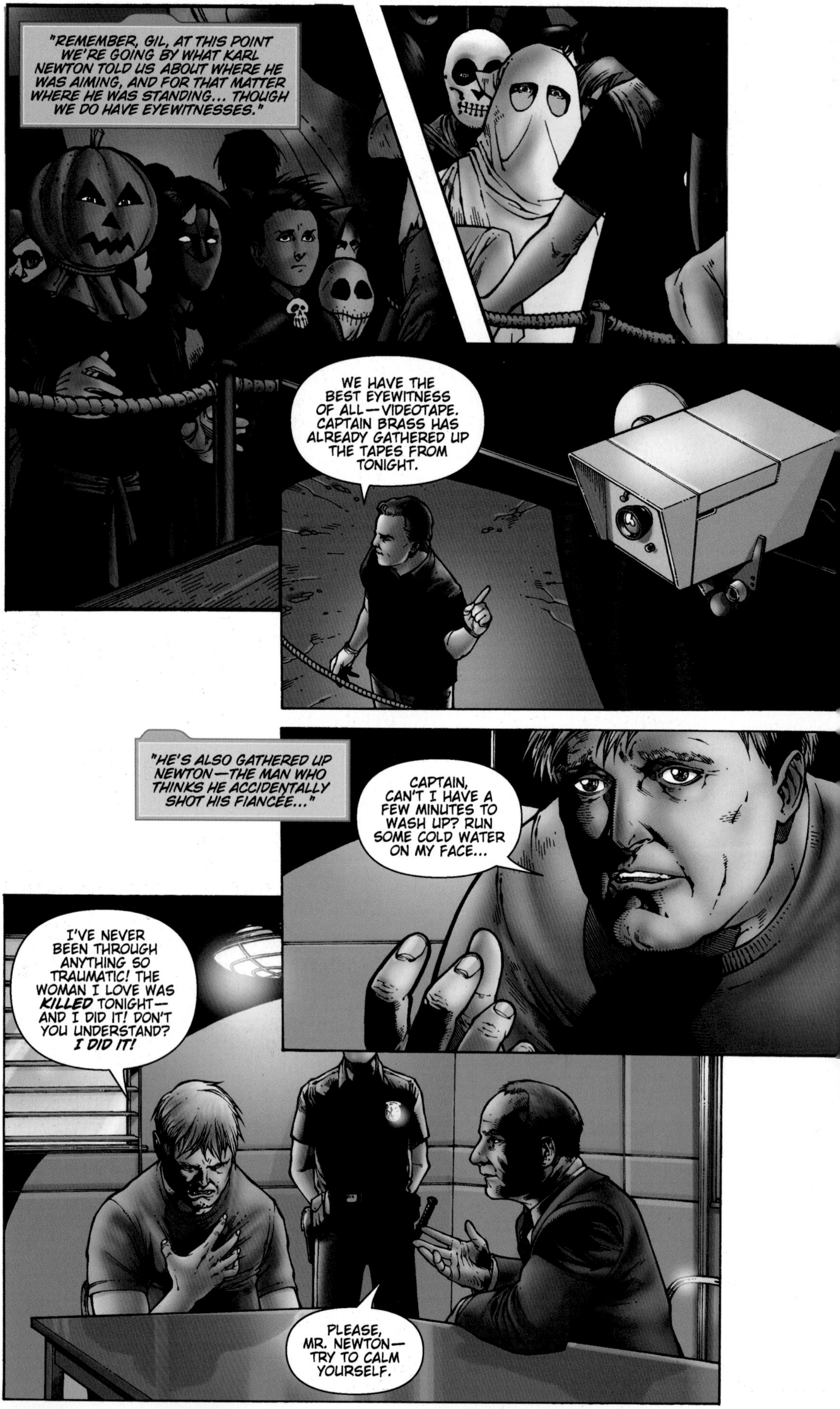
"REMEMBER, GIL, AT THIS POINT WE'RE GOING BY WHAT KARL NEWTON TOLD US ABOUT WHERE HE WAS AIMING, AND FOR THAT MATTER WHERE HE WAS STANDING... THOUGH WE DO HAVE EYEWITNESSES."
WE HAVE THE BEST EYEWITNESS OF ALL—VIDEOTAPE. CAPTAIN BRASS HAS ALREADY GATHERED UP THE TAPES FROM TONIGHT.
"HE'S ALSO GATHERED UP NEWTON—THE MAN WHO THINKS HE ACCIDENTALLY SHOT HIS FIANCÉE..."
CAPTAIN, CAN'T I HAVE A FEW MINUTES TO WASH UP? RUN SOME COLD WATER ON MY FACE...
I'VE NEVER BEEN THROUGH ANYTHING SO TRAUMATIC! THE WOMAN I LOVE WAS KILLED TONIGHT—AND I DID IT! DON'T YOU UNDERSTAND? I DID IT!
PLEASE, MR. NEWTON—TRY TO CALM YOURSELF.

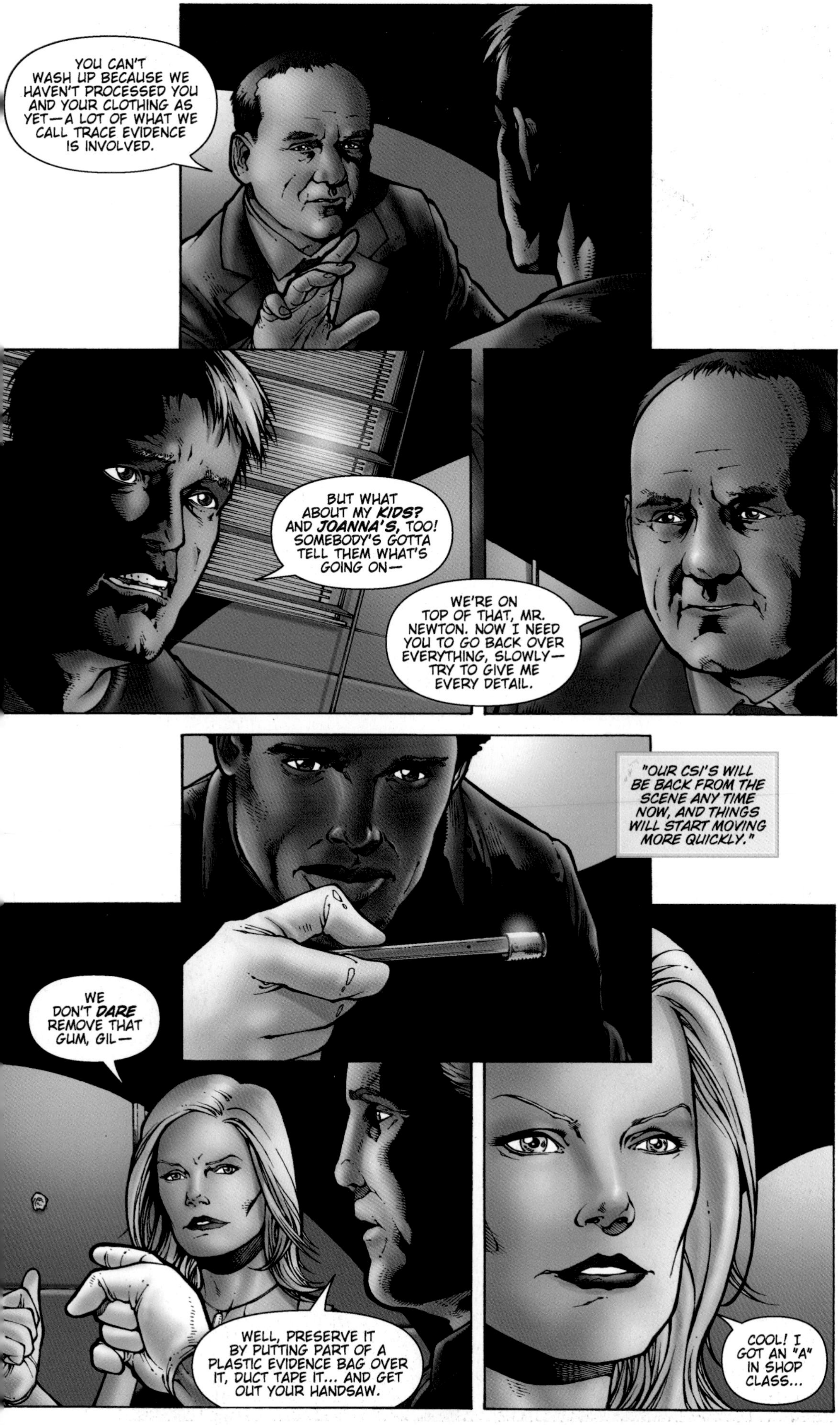

YOU CAN'T WASH UP BECAUSE WE HAVEN'T PROCESSED YOU AND YOUR CLOTHING AS YET—A LOT OF WHAT WE CALL TRACE EVIDENCE IS INVOLVED.
BUT WHAT ABOUT MY KIDS? AND JOANNA'S, TOO! SOMEBODY'S GOTTA TELL THEM WHAT'S GOING ON—
WE'RE ON TOP OF THAT, MR. NEWTON. NOW I NEED YOU TO GO BACK OVER EVERYTHING, SLOWLY—TRY TO GIVE ME EVERY DETAIL.
"OUR CSI'S WILL BE BACK FROM THE SCENE ANY TIME NOW, AND THINGS WILL START MOVING MORE QUICKLY."
WE DON'T DARE REMOVE THAT GUM, GIL—
WELL, PRESERVE IT BY PUTTING PART OF A PLASTIC EVIDENCE BAG OVER IT, DUCT TAPE IT... AND GET OUT YOUR HANDSAW.
COOL! I GOT AN "A" IN SHOP CLASS...

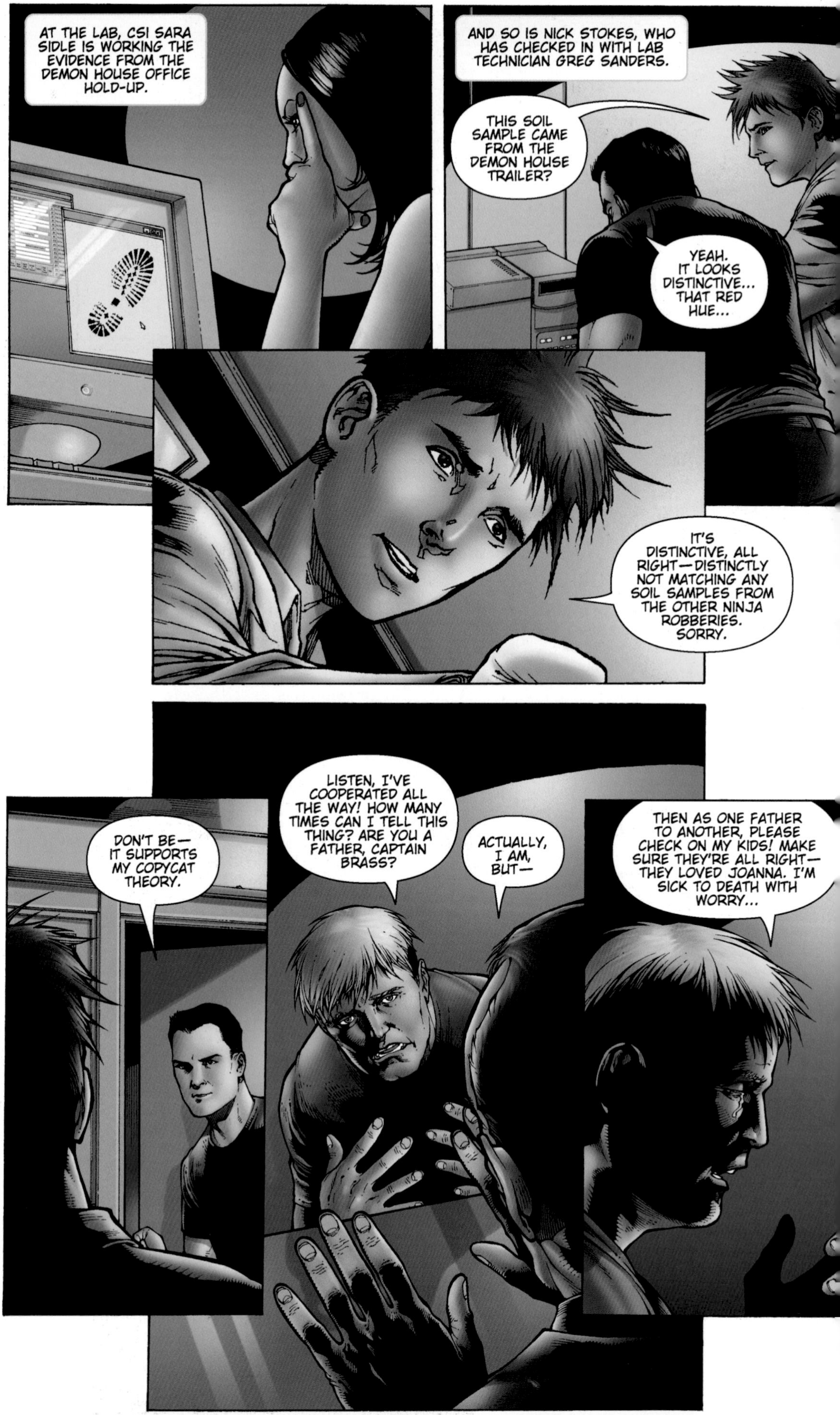
AT THE LAB, CSI SARA SIDLE IS WORKING THE EVIDENCE FROM THE DEMON HOUSE OFFICE HOLD-UP.
AND SO IS NICK STOKES, WHO HAS CHECKED IN WITH LAB TECHNICIAN GREG SANDERS.
THIS SOIL SAMPLE CAME FROM THE DEMON HOUSE TRAILER?
YEAH. IT LOOKS DISTINCTIVE... THAT RED HUE...
IT'S DISTINCTIVE, ALL RIGHT—DISTINCTLY NOT MATCHING ANY SOIL SAMPLES FROM THE OTHER NINJA ROBBERIES. SORRY.
DON'T BE— IT SUPPORTS MY COPYCAT THEORY.
LISTEN, I'VE COOPERATED ALL THE WAY! HOW MANY TIMES CAN I TELL THIS THING? ARE YOU A FATHER, CAPTAIN BRASS?
ACTUALLY, I AM, BUT—
THEN AS ONE FATHER TO ANOTHER, PLEASE CHECK ON MY KIDS! MAKE SURE THEY'RE ALL RIGHT— THEY LOVED JOANNA. I'M SICK TO DEATH WITH WORRY...

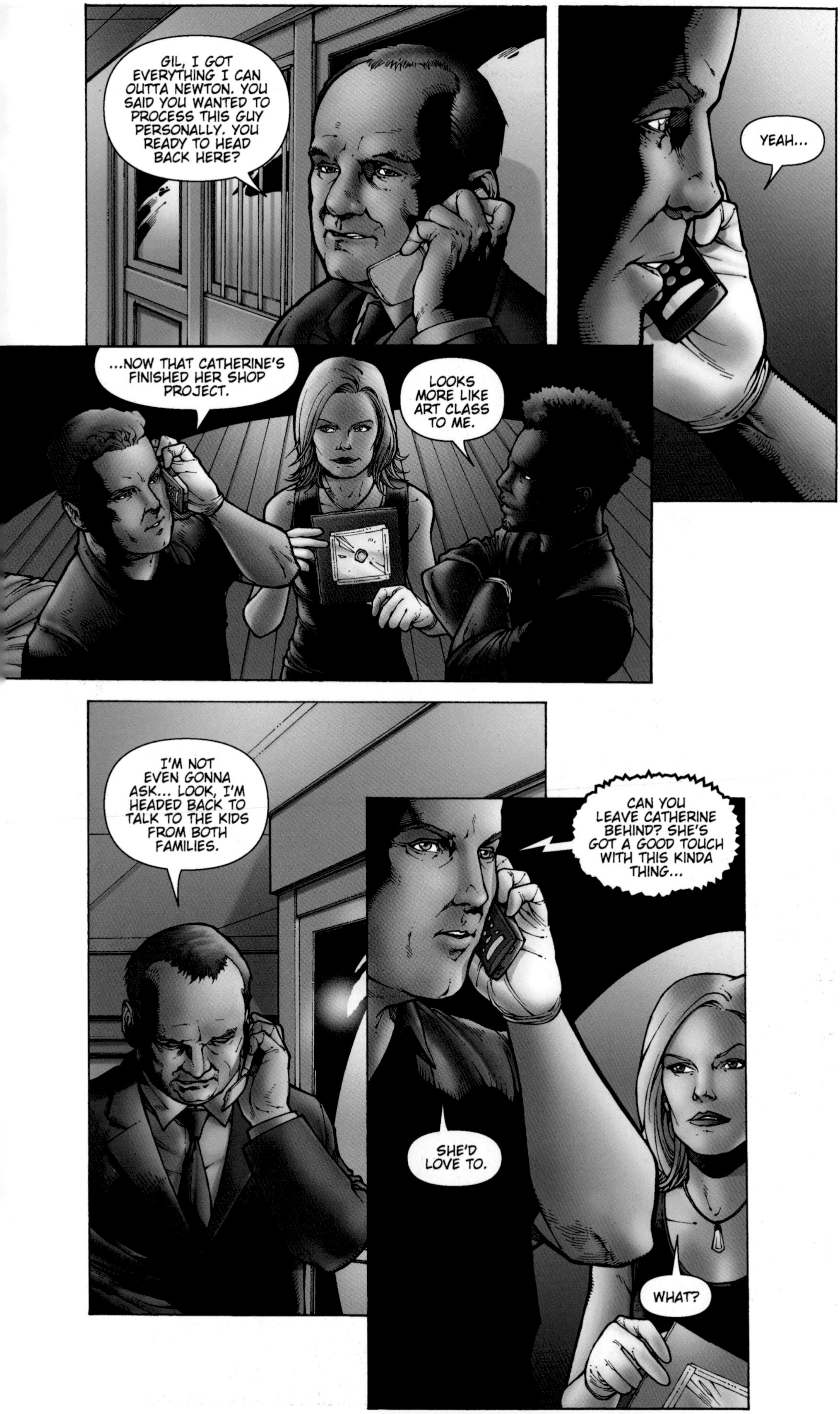
GIL, I GOT EVERYTHING I CAN OUTTA NEWTON. YOU SAID YOU WANTED TO PROCESS THIS GUY PERSONALLY. YOU READY TO HEAD BACK HERE?
YEAH...
...NOW THAT CATHERINE'S FINISHED HER SHOP PROJECT.
LOOKS MORE LIKE ART CLASS TO ME.
I'M NOT EVEN GONNA ASK... LOOK, I'M HEADED BACK TO TALK TO THE KIDS FROM BOTH FAMILIES.
CAN YOU LEAVE CATHERINE BEHIND? SHE'S GOT A GOOD TOUCH WITH THIS KINDA THING...
SHE'D LOVE TO.
WHAT?

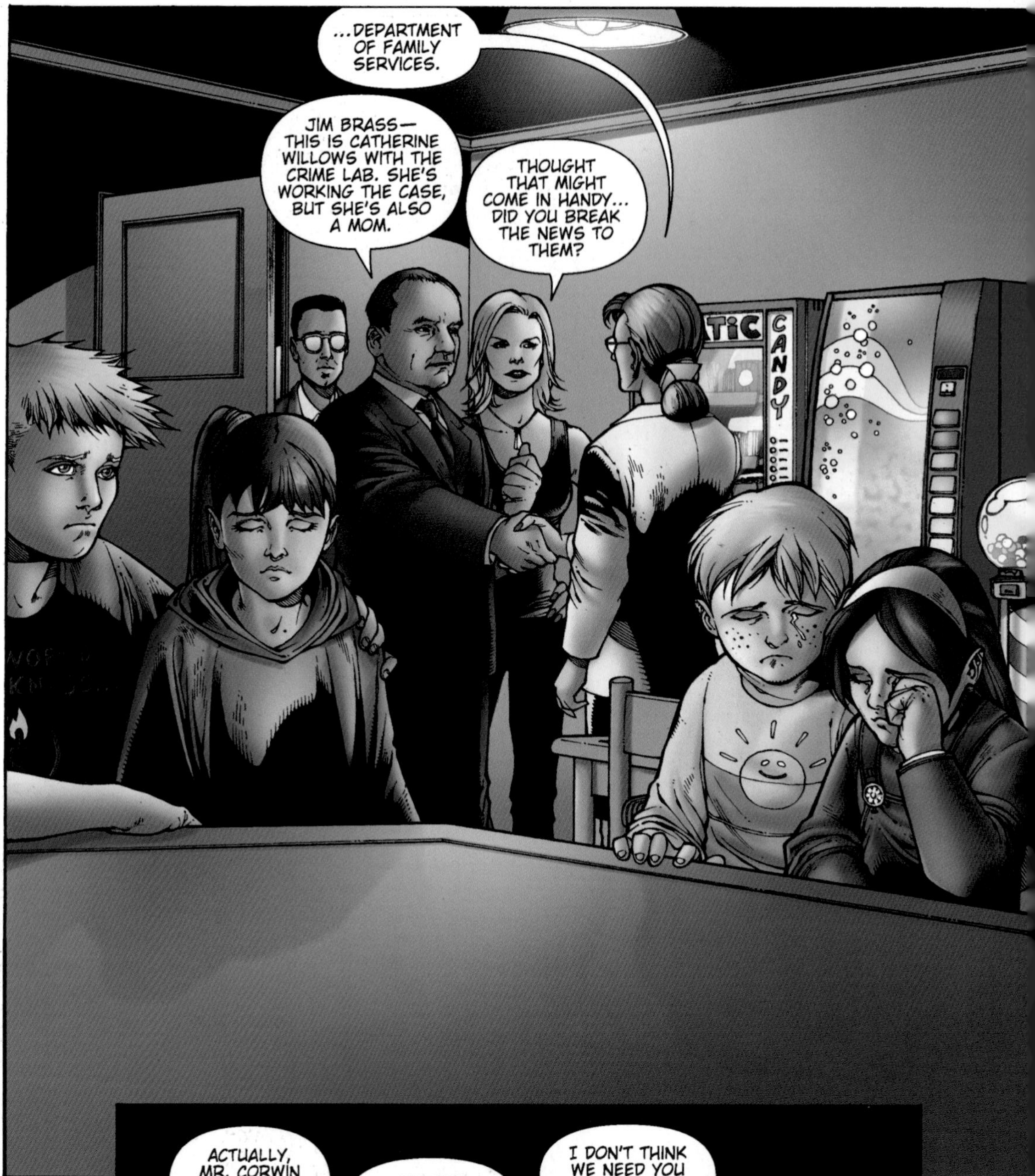
...DEPARTMENT OF FAMILY SERVICES.
JIM BRASS— THIS IS CATHERINE WILLOWS WITH THE CRIME LAB. SHE'S WORKING THE CASE, BUT SHE'S ALSO A MOM.
THOUGHT THAT MIGHT COME IN HANDY... DID YOU BREAK THE NEWS TO THEM?
CANDY

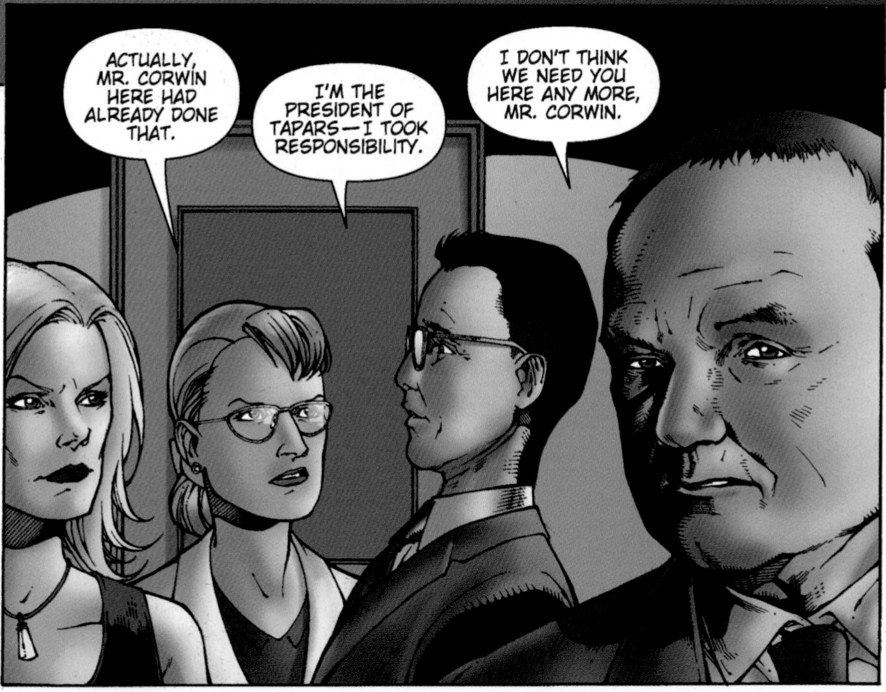
ACTUALLY, MR. CORWIN HERE HAD ALREADY DONE THAT.
I'M THE PRESIDENT OF TAPARS—I TOOK RESPONSIBILITY.
I DON'T THINK WE NEED YOU HERE ANY MORE, MR. CORWIN.

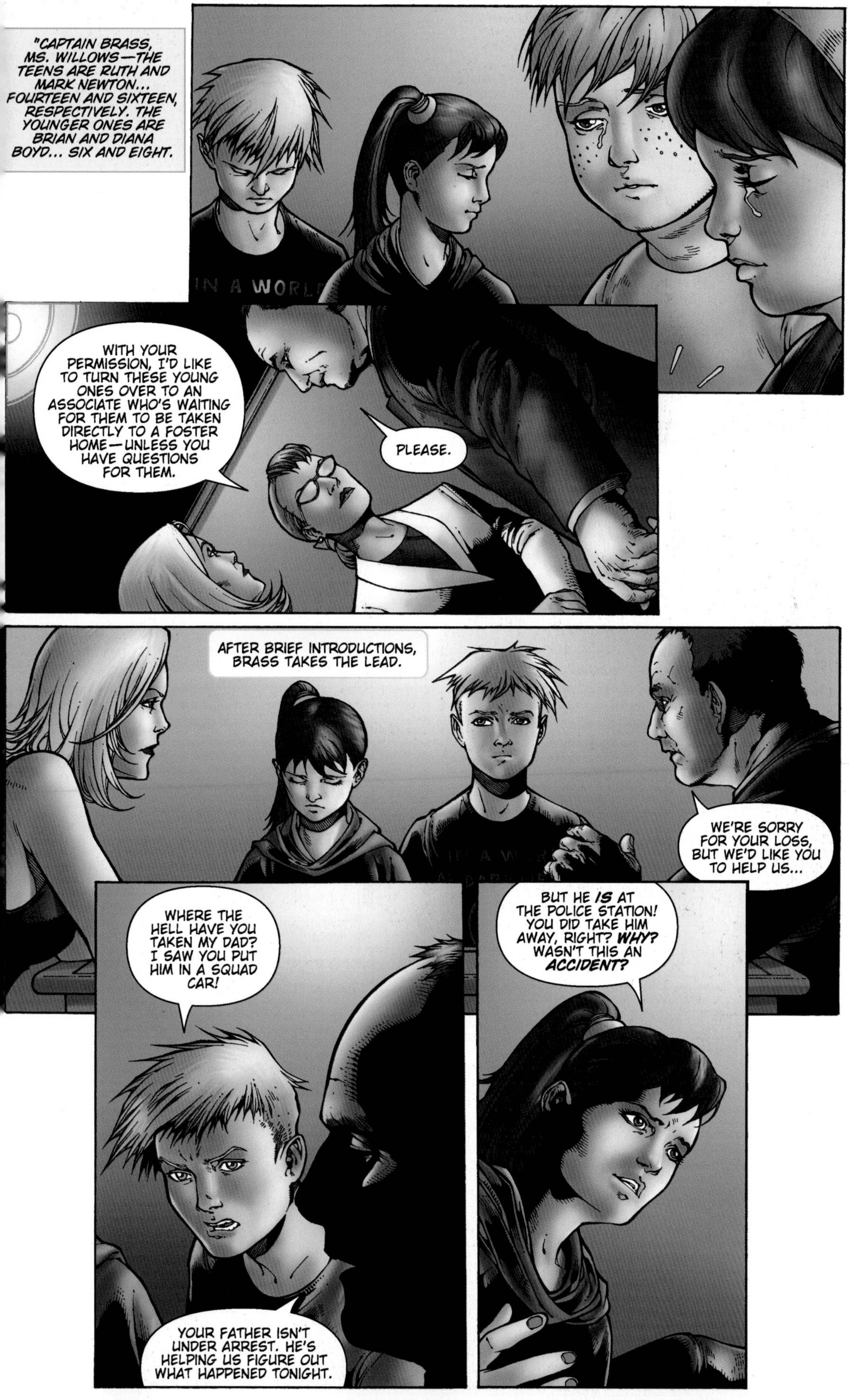
"CAPTAIN BRASS, MS. WILLOWS—THE TEENS ARE RUTH AND MARK NEWTON... FOURTEEN AND SIXTEEN, RESPECTIVELY. THE YOUNGER ONES ARE BRIAN AND DIANA BOYD... SIX AND EIGHT.
WITH YOUR PERMISSION, I'D LIKE TO TURN THESE YOUNG ONES OVER TO AN ASSOCIATE WHO'S WAITING FOR THEM TO BE TAKEN DIRECTLY TO A FOSTER HOME—UNLESS YOU HAVE QUESTIONS FOR THEM.
PLEASE.
AFTER BRIEF INTRODUCTIONS, BRASS TAKES THE LEAD.
WE'RE SORRY FOR YOUR LOSS, BUT WE'D LIKE YOU TO HELP US...
WHERE THE HELL HAVE YOU TAKEN MY DAD? I SAW YOU PUT HIM IN A SQUAD CAR!
YOUR FATHER ISN'T UNDER ARREST. HE'S HELPING US FIGURE OUT WHAT HAPPENED TONIGHT.
BUT HE *IS* AT THE POLICE STATION! YOU DID TAKE HIM AWAY, RIGHT? *WHY?* WASN'T THIS AN *ACCIDENT?*

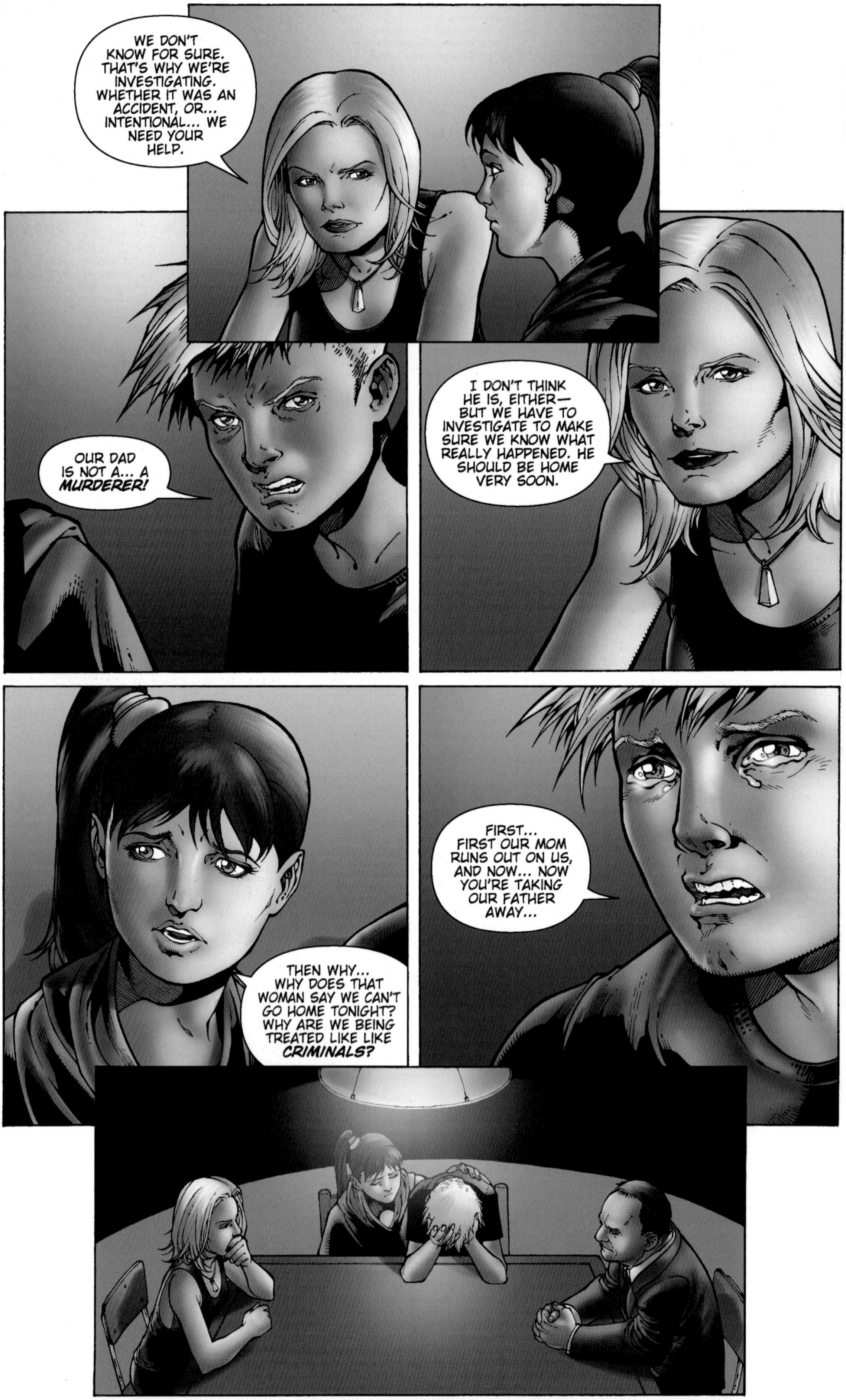
WE DON'T KNOW FOR SURE. THAT'S WHY WE'RE INVESTIGATING. WHETHER IT WAS AN ACCIDENT, OR... INTENTIONAL... WE NEED YOUR HELP.
OUR DAD IS NOT A... A *MURDERER!*
I DON'T THINK HE IS, EITHER— BUT WE HAVE TO INVESTIGATE TO MAKE SURE WE KNOW WHAT REALLY HAPPENED. HE SHOULD BE HOME VERY SOON.
THEN WHY... WHY DOES THAT WOMAN SAY WE CAN'T GO HOME TONIGHT? WHY ARE WE BEING TREATED LIKE LIKE *CRIMINALS?*
FIRST... FIRST OUR MOM RUNS OUT ON US, AND NOW... NOW YOU'RE TAKING OUR FATHER AWAY...

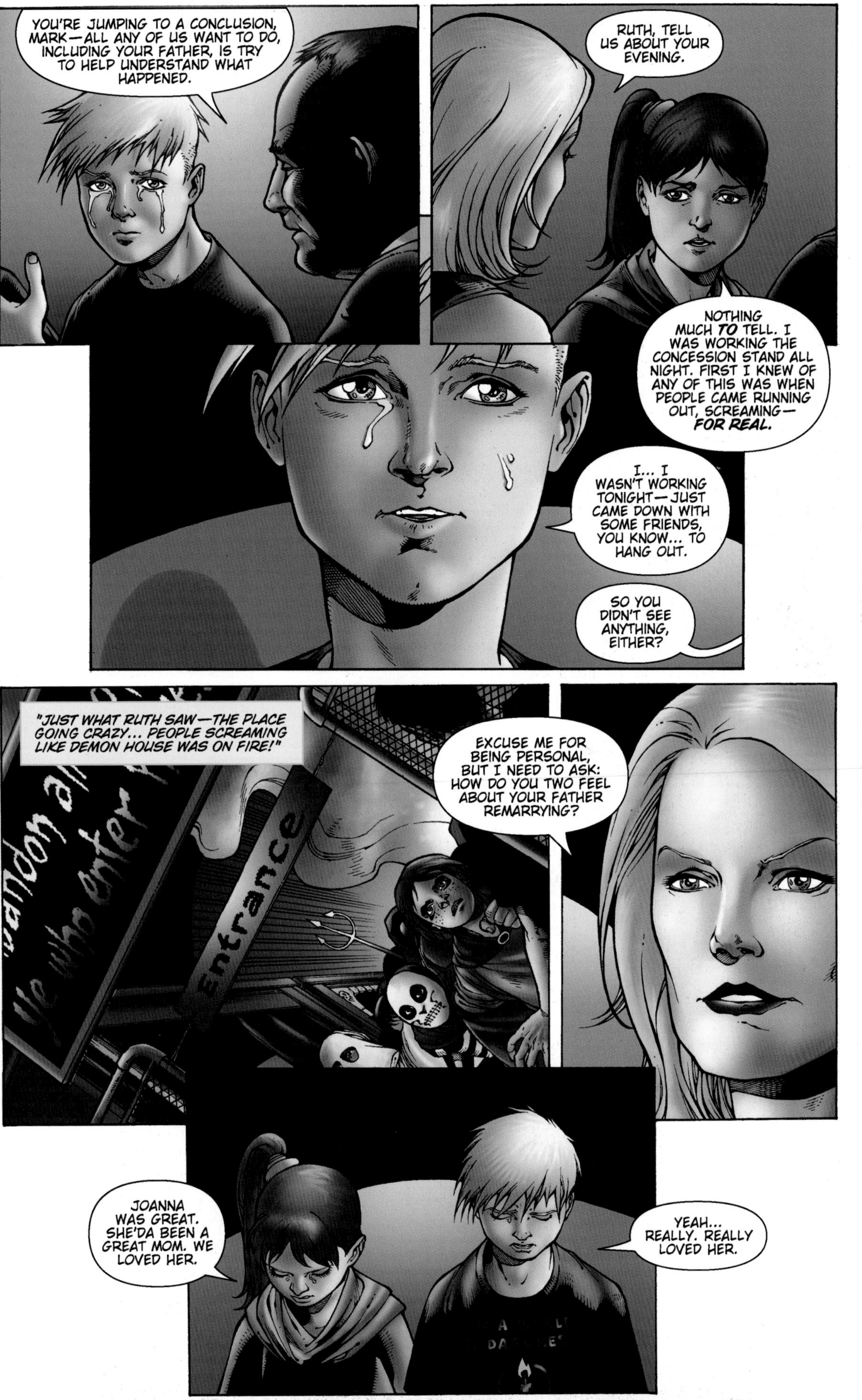
YOU'RE JUMPING TO A CONCLUSION, MARK—ALL ANY OF US WANT TO DO, INCLUDING YOUR FATHER, IS TRY TO HELP UNDERSTAND WHAT HAPPENED.
RUTH, TELL US ABOUT YOUR EVENING.
NOTHING MUCH ***TO*** TELL. I WAS WORKING THE CONCESSION STAND ALL NIGHT. FIRST I KNEW OF ANY OF THIS WAS WHEN PEOPLE CAME RUNNING OUT, SCREAMING—***FOR REAL.***
I... I WASN'T WORKING TONIGHT—JUST CAME DOWN WITH SOME FRIENDS, YOU KNOW... TO HANG OUT.
SO YOU DIDN'T SEE ANYTHING, EITHER?
"JUST WHAT RUTH SAW—THE PLACE GOING CRAZY... PEOPLE SCREAMING LIKE DEMON HOUSE WAS ON FIRE!"
Entrance
EXCUSE ME FOR BEING PERSONAL, BUT I NEED TO ASK: HOW DO YOU TWO FEEL ABOUT YOUR FATHER REMARRYING?
JOANNA WAS GREAT. SHE'DA BEEN A GREAT MOM. WE LOVED HER.
YEAH... REALLY. REALLY LOVED HER.

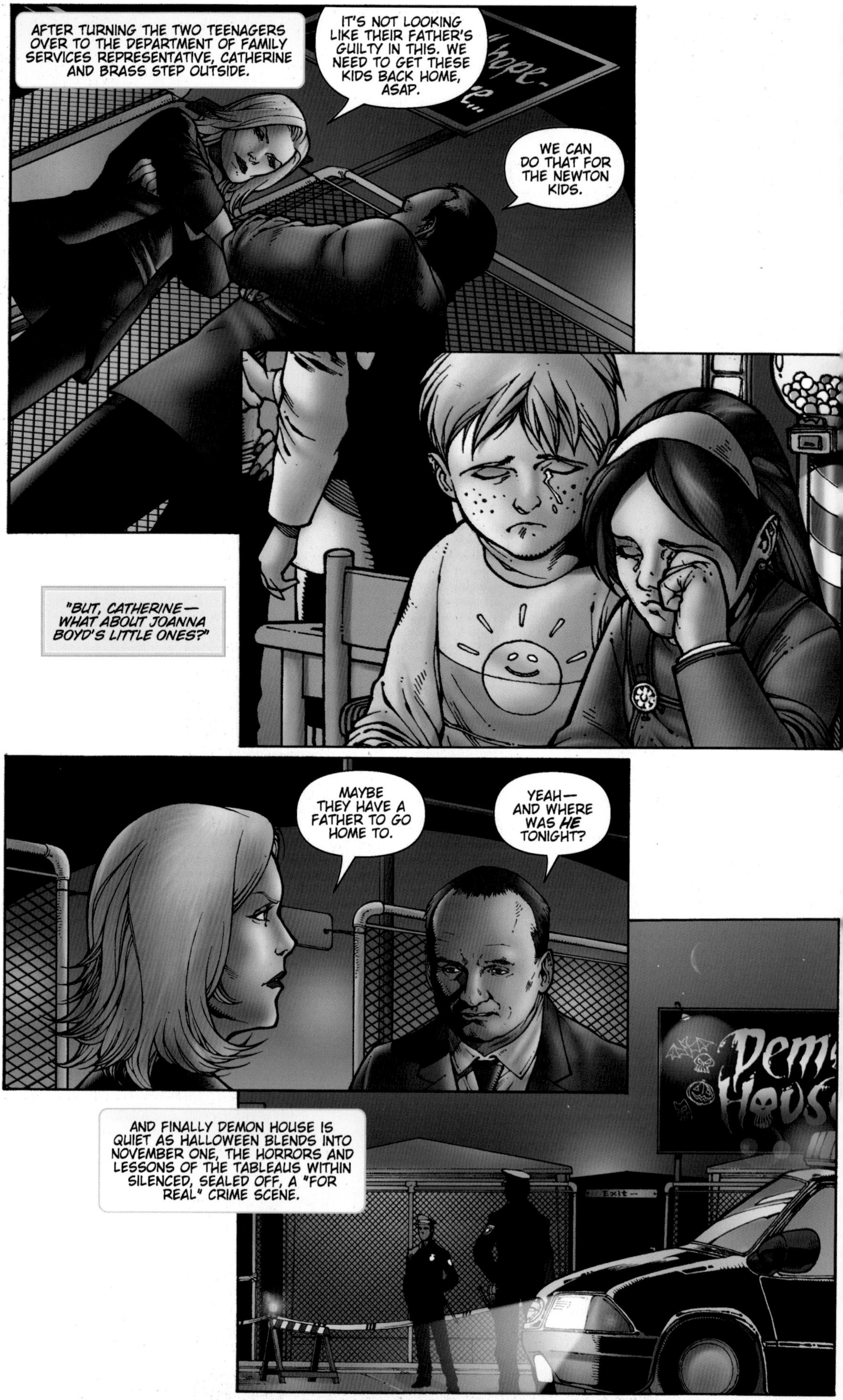
AFTER TURNING THE TWO TEENAGERS OVER TO THE DEPARTMENT OF FAMILY SERVICES REPRESENTATIVE, CATHERINE AND BRASS STEP OUTSIDE.
IT'S NOT LOOKING LIKE THEIR FATHER'S GUILTY IN THIS. WE NEED TO GET THESE KIDS BACK HOME, ASAP.
WE CAN DO THAT FOR THE NEWTON KIDS.
"BUT, CATHERINE— WHAT ABOUT JOANNA BOYD'S LITTLE ONES?"
MAYBE THEY HAVE A FATHER TO GO HOME TO.
YEAH— AND WHERE WAS HE TONIGHT?
AND FINALLY DEMON HOUSE IS QUIET AS HALLOWEEN BLENDS INTO NOVEMBER ONE, THE HORRORS AND LESSONS OF THE TABLEAUS WITHIN SILENCED, SEALED OFF, A "FOR REAL" CRIME SCENE.
Exit

TWENTY-FOUR HOURS LATER, THE CSI'S INVESTIGATING THE TWO CRIMES AT DEMON HOUSE ARE MAKING SLOW IF STEADY PROGRESS. SARA IS RUNNING KARL NEWTON'S FINGERPRINTS THROUGH AFIS...

...WHILE IN A NEARBY LAB WARRICK WORKS THE SHELL CASING.

AFTER APPLYING A LIQUID THAT DRIES QUICKLY INTO A SKIN-LIKE MEMBRANE, GRISSOM IS LIFTING THE THUMBPRINT FROM THE NOW-DRIED BUBBLE GUM ON CATHERINE'S "SHOP PROJECT"...

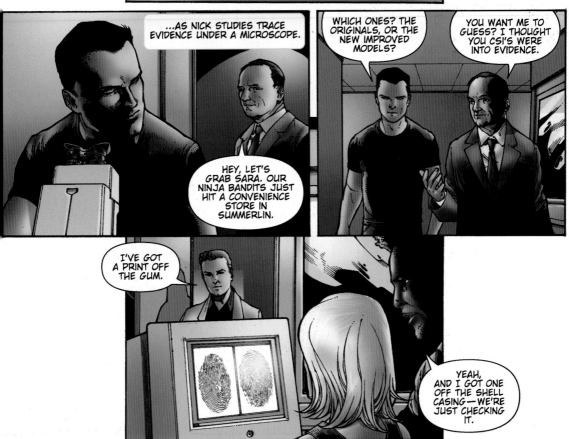

...AS NICK STUDIES TRACE EVIDENCE UNDER A MICROSCOPE.

HEY, LET'S GRAB SARA. OUR NINJA BANDITS JUST HIT A CONVENIENCE STORE IN SUMMERLIN.

WHICH ONES? THE ORIGINALS, OR THE NEW IMPROVED MODELS?

YOU WANT ME TO GUESS? I THOUGHT YOU CSI'S WERE INTO EVIDENCE.

I'VE GOT A PRINT OFF THE GUM.

YEAH, AND I GOT ONE OFF THE SHELL CASING—WE'RE JUST CHECKING IT.

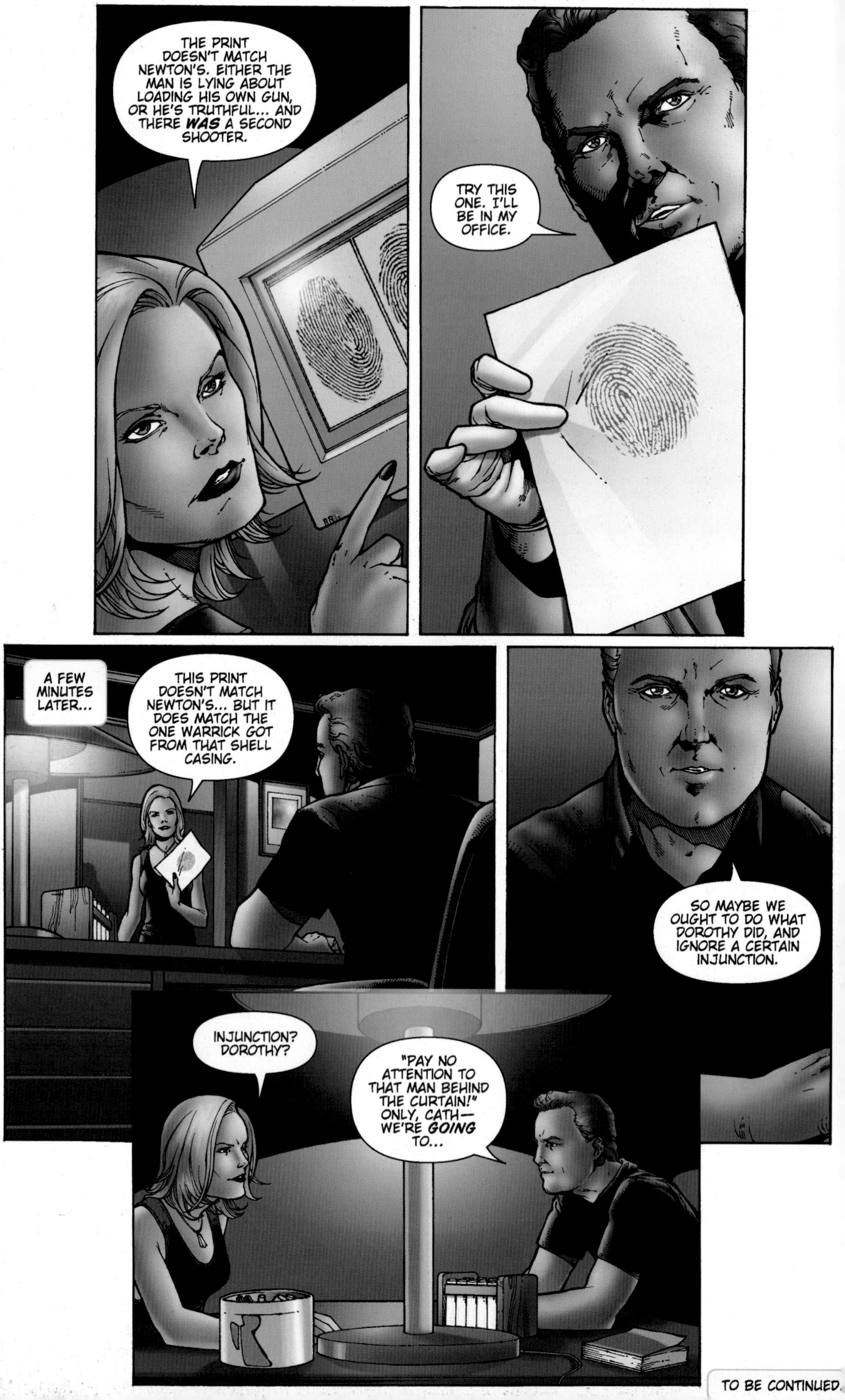
THE PRINT DOESN'T MATCH NEWTON'S. EITHER THE MAN IS LYING ABOUT LOADING HIS OWN GUN, OR HE'S TRUTHFUL... AND THERE **WAS** A SECOND SHOOTER.
TRY THIS ONE. I'LL BE IN MY OFFICE.
A FEW MINUTES LATER...
THIS PRINT DOESN'T MATCH NEWTON'S... BUT IT DOES MATCH THE ONE WARRICK GOT FROM THAT SHELL CASING.
SO MAYBE WE OUGHT TO DO WHAT DOROTHY DID, AND IGNORE A CERTAIN INJUNCTION.
INJUNCTION? DOROTHY?
"PAY NO ATTENTION TO THAT MAN BEHIND THE CURTAIN!" ONLY, CATH— WE'RE **GOING** TO...
TO BE CONTINUED.

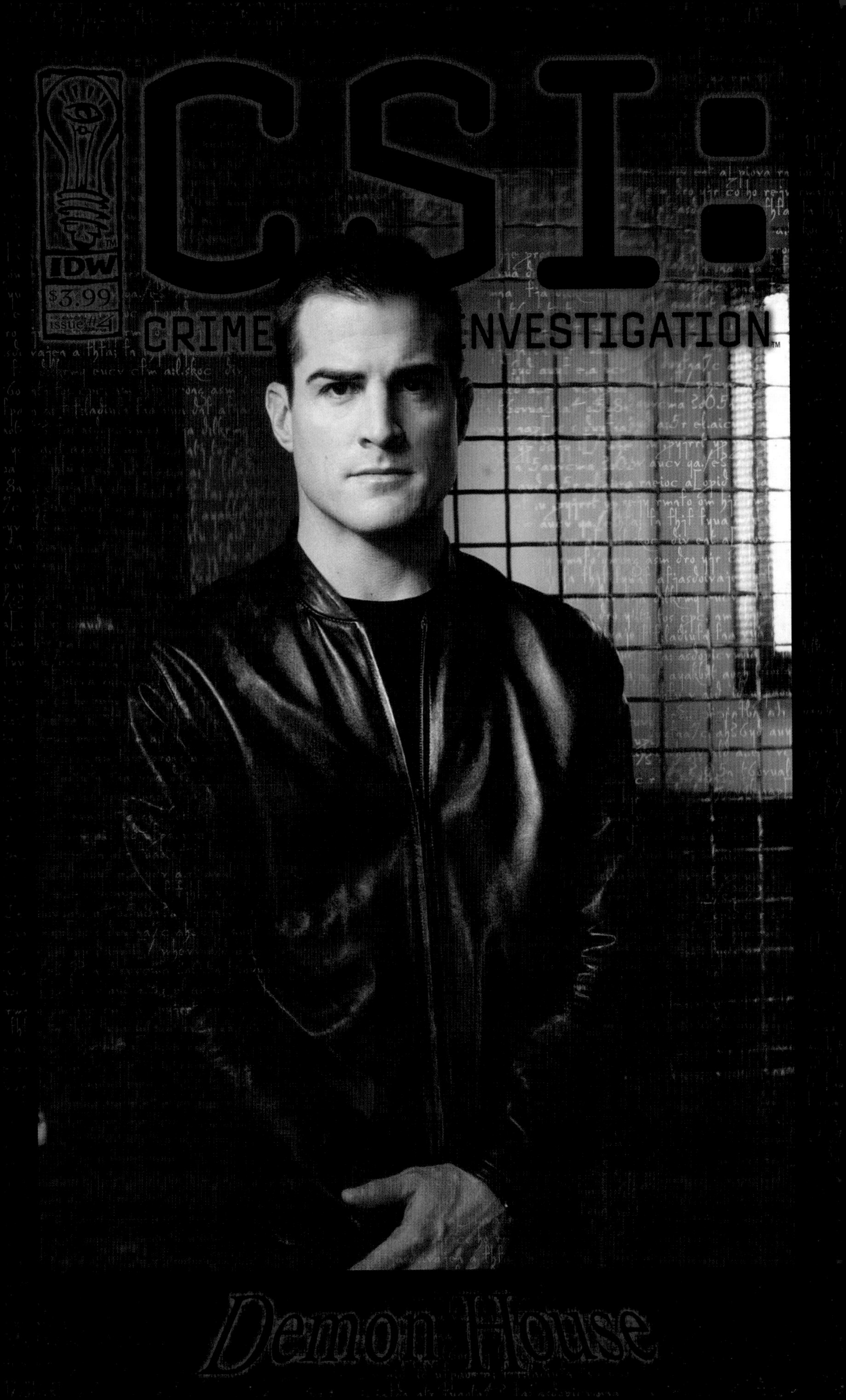
IDW
$3.99
issue #4
C.S.I:
CRIME
INVESTIGATION
Demon House

chapter four

Quarterback Sneak

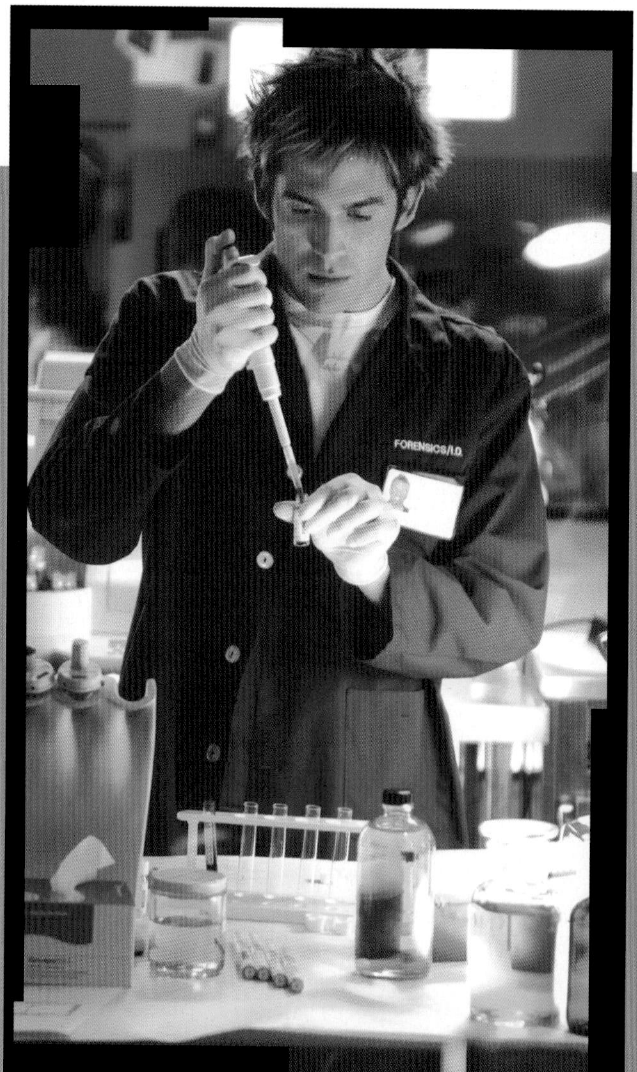
FORENSICS/I.D.

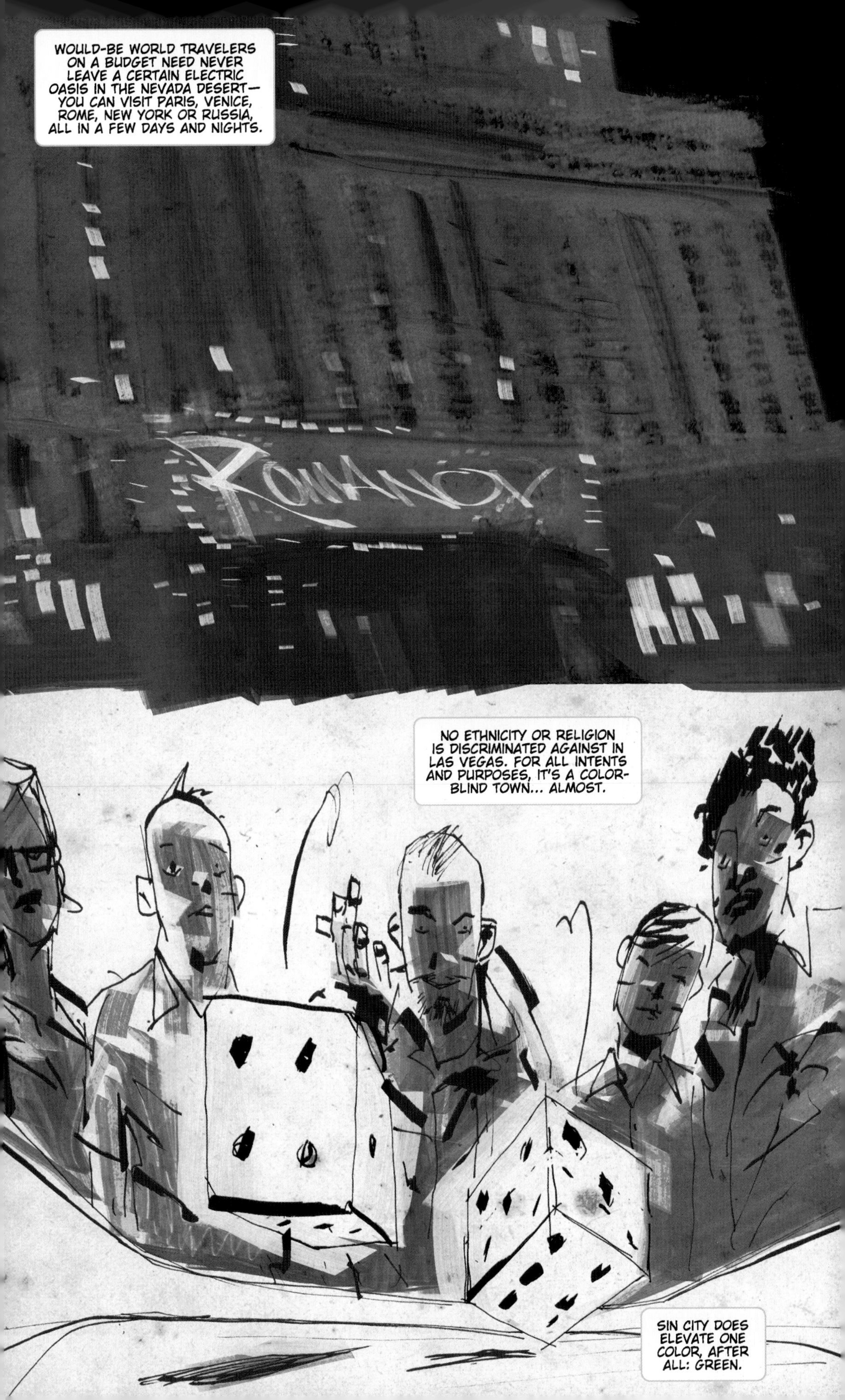
WOULD-BE WORLD TRAVELERS ON A BUDGET NEED NEVER LEAVE A CERTAIN ELECTRIC OASIS IN THE NEVADA DESERT— YOU CAN VISIT PARIS, VENICE, ROME, NEW YORK OR RUSSIA, ALL IN A FEW DAYS AND NIGHTS.
ROMANOV
NO ETHNICITY OR RELIGION IS DISCRIMINATED AGAINST IN LAS VEGAS. FOR ALL INTENTS AND PURPOSES, IT'S A COLOR-BLIND TOWN... ALMOST.
SIN CITY DOES ELEVATE ONE COLOR, AFTER ALL: GREEN.

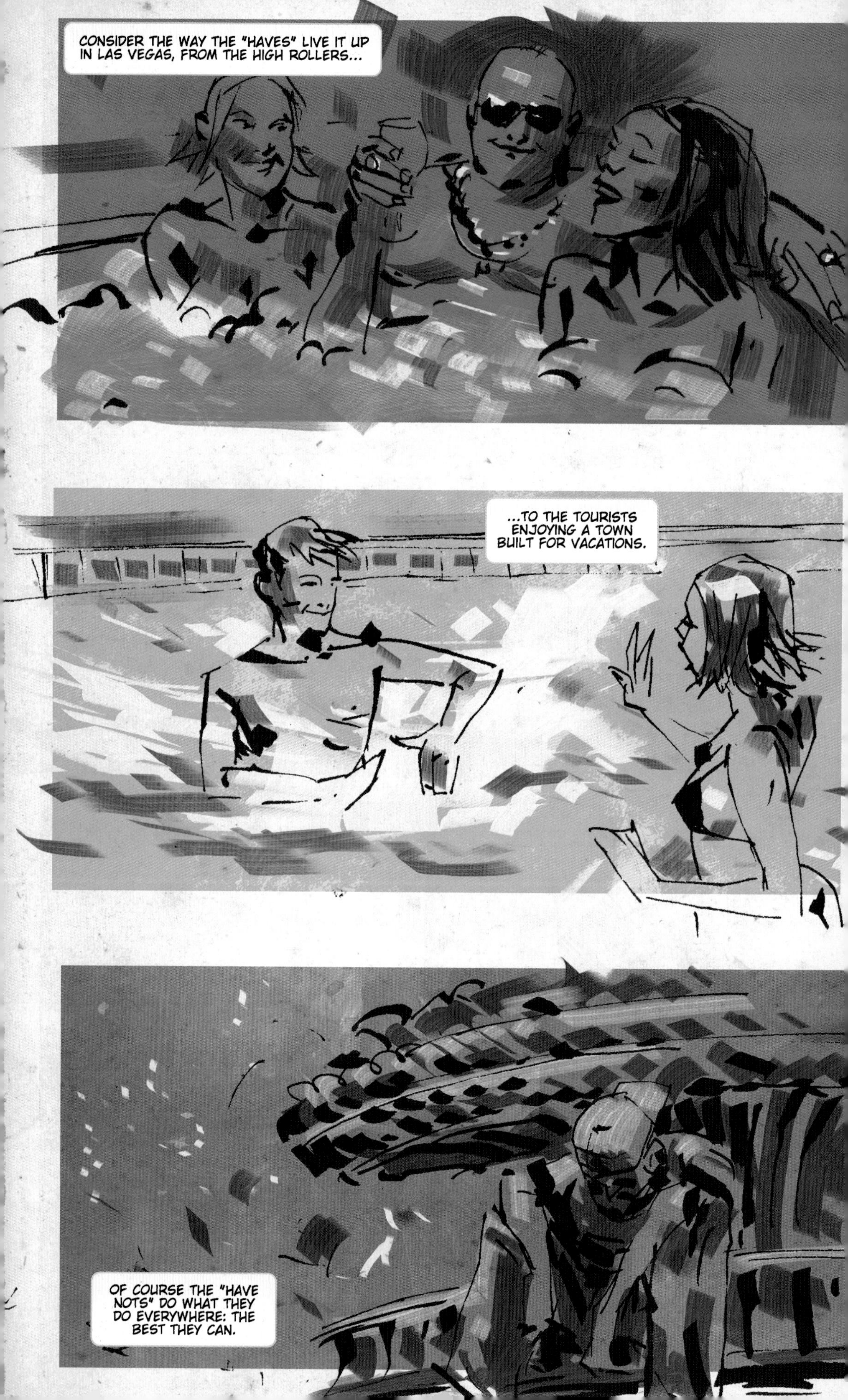
CONSIDER THE WAY THE "HAVES" LIVE IT UP IN LAS VEGAS, FROM THE HIGH ROLLERS...
...TO THE TOURISTS ENJOYING A TOWN BUILT FOR VACATIONS.
OF COURSE THE "HAVE NOTS" DO WHAT THEY DO EVERYWHERE: THE BEST THEY CAN.

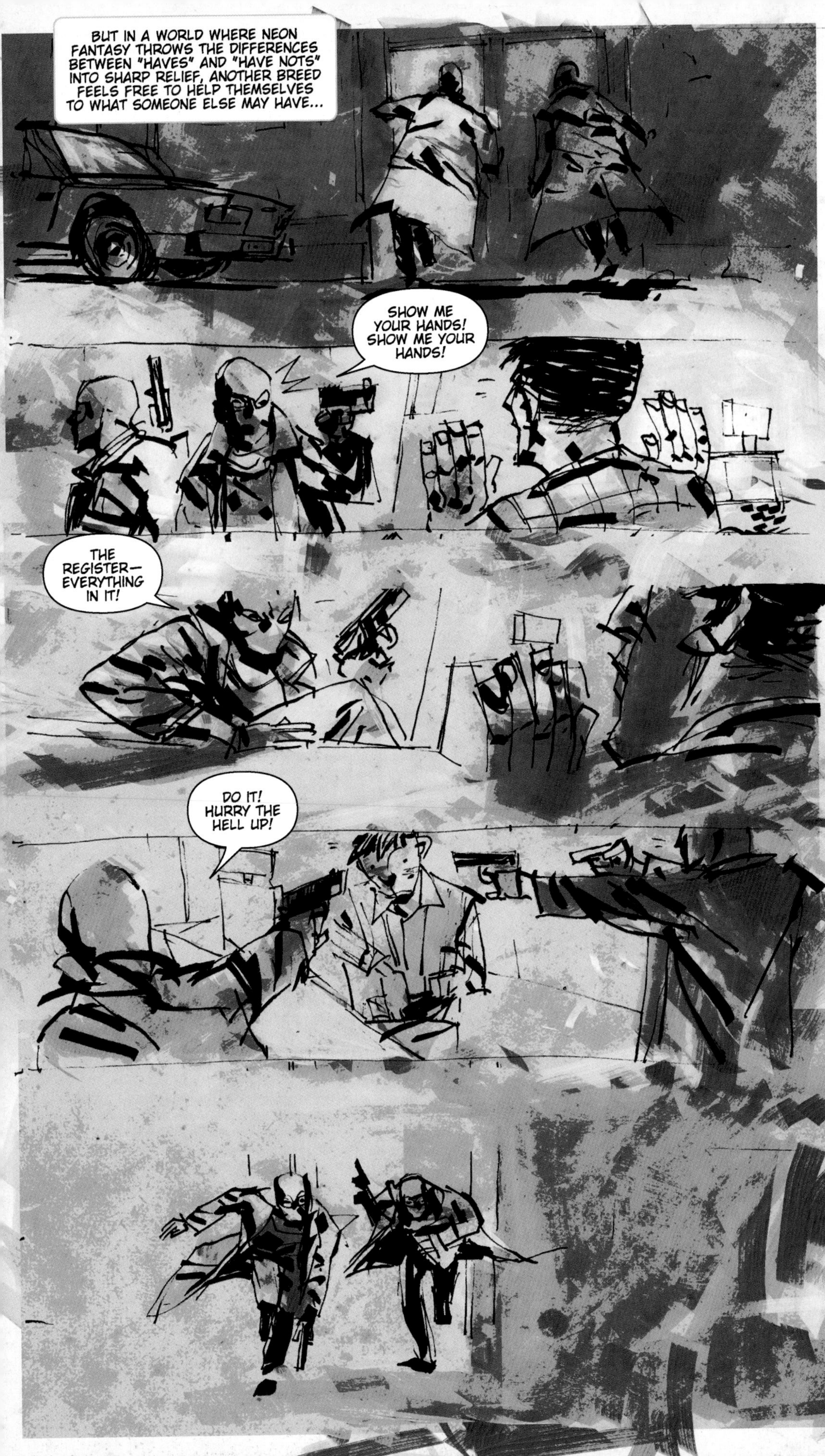
BUT IN A WORLD WHERE NEON FANTASY THROWS THE DIFFERENCES BETWEEN "HAVES" AND "HAVE NOTS" INTO SHARP RELIEF, ANOTHER BREED FEELS FREE TO HELP THEMSELVES TO WHAT SOMEONE ELSE MAY HAVE...
SHOW ME YOUR HANDS! SHOW ME YOUR HANDS!
THE REGISTER— EVERYTHING IN IT!
DO IT! HURRY THE HELL UP!

CSI'S NICK STOKES AND SARA SIDLE, STUDYING THE SECURITY TAPE OF A ROBBERY THAT WENT DOWN JUST HOURS BEFORE, ARE BECOMING CONVINCED THE $40,000 HEIST AT DEMON HOUSE WAS A COPYCAT JOB.

BACK THAT UP! WHERE THE ONE GUY DOES THE DILLINGER LEAP.

THE WHAT?

"JEEZ, SARA, DON'T YOU WATCH THE HISTORY CHANNEL? THE DEPRESSION-ERA BANK ROBBER, JOHN DILLINGER... HE LOVED TO LEAP OVER BANK COUNTERS AND SHAKE UP THE TELLERS."

"A VAULT TO GET TO THE VAULT, NICKY?"

"HEY— FREEZE THAT!"

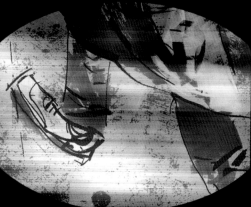

"NOW, ZOOM IN, SARA."

"I'M WITH YOU, NICK— RUNNING SHOES!"

THE PAIR WHO HIT THE DEMON HOUSE BUSINESS OFFICE WORE *BOOTS.*

YEAH, AND THESE NINJAS ARE USING PISTOLS, LIKE IN THE OTHER CONVENIENCE STORE JOBS.

NOT A SHOTGUN IN SIGHT. LET'S CHECK THE OTHER TAPE, WHERE THEY'RE *EXITING...*

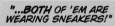
"...BOTH OF 'EM ARE WEARING SNEAKERS!"

LET'S BACK THAT UP AGAIN, AND ZOOM IN.

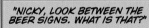
"NICKY, LOOK BETWEEN THE BEER SIGNS. WHAT IS THAT?"

"I THINK IT'S A BUMPER... AND HALF A LICENSE PLATE! WE NEED VIDEO ENHANCEMENT ON THIS."

AN HOUR LATER, AFTER SARA HAS DIGITIZED THE VIDEO INTO A COMPUTER, APPLYING AN ENHANCEMENT PROGRAM TO A CLOSE-UP OF A STILL FRAME, THE RESULT IS...

NOT PRETTY, BUT IT'S READABLE.

761

PARTIAL LICENSE PLATE. A START—A GOOD START.

NOW LET'S CAPTURE A STILL OF THAT PERP JUMPING OVER THE COUNTER...

WHY? WE CAN TELL THEY'RE WEARING SNEAKERS.

I THOUGHT I NOTICED SOMETHING ON THE WRIST OF THE GUY WHEN HIS SLEEVE PULLED BACK. MIGHT BE A BIRTHMARK...

"...OR MAYBE A TATTOO!"

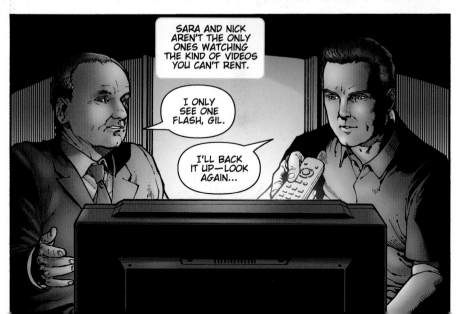

SARA AND NICK AREN'T THE ONLY ONES WATCHING THE KIND OF VIDEOS YOU CAN'T RENT.

I ONLY SEE ONE FLASH, GIL.

I'LL BACK IT UP—LOOK AGAIN...

NIGHTSHIFT SUPERVISOR GIL GRISSOM AND DETECTIVE JIM BRASS GO OVER THE VIDEO OF THE DEMON HOUSE DOMESTIC ABUSE TABLEAU.

THE CAMERA DOESN'T SHOW US KARL NEWTON, OR THE CURTAIN AREA BEHIND HIM... WHERE I SUSPECT THE SHOT CAME FROM...

BUT THE MUZZLE FLASH CREATES A KIND OF WHITE STROBE EFFECT. I SEE THAT... BUT I ONLY SEE IT *ONCE.*

"ALL RIGHT, JIM—WATCH IN SLOW MOTION..."

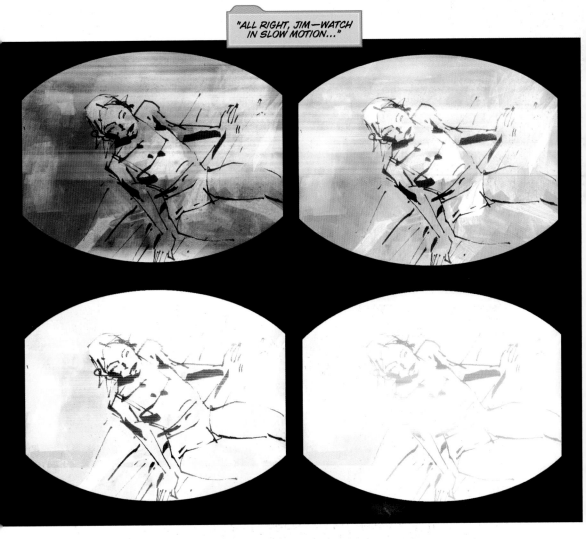

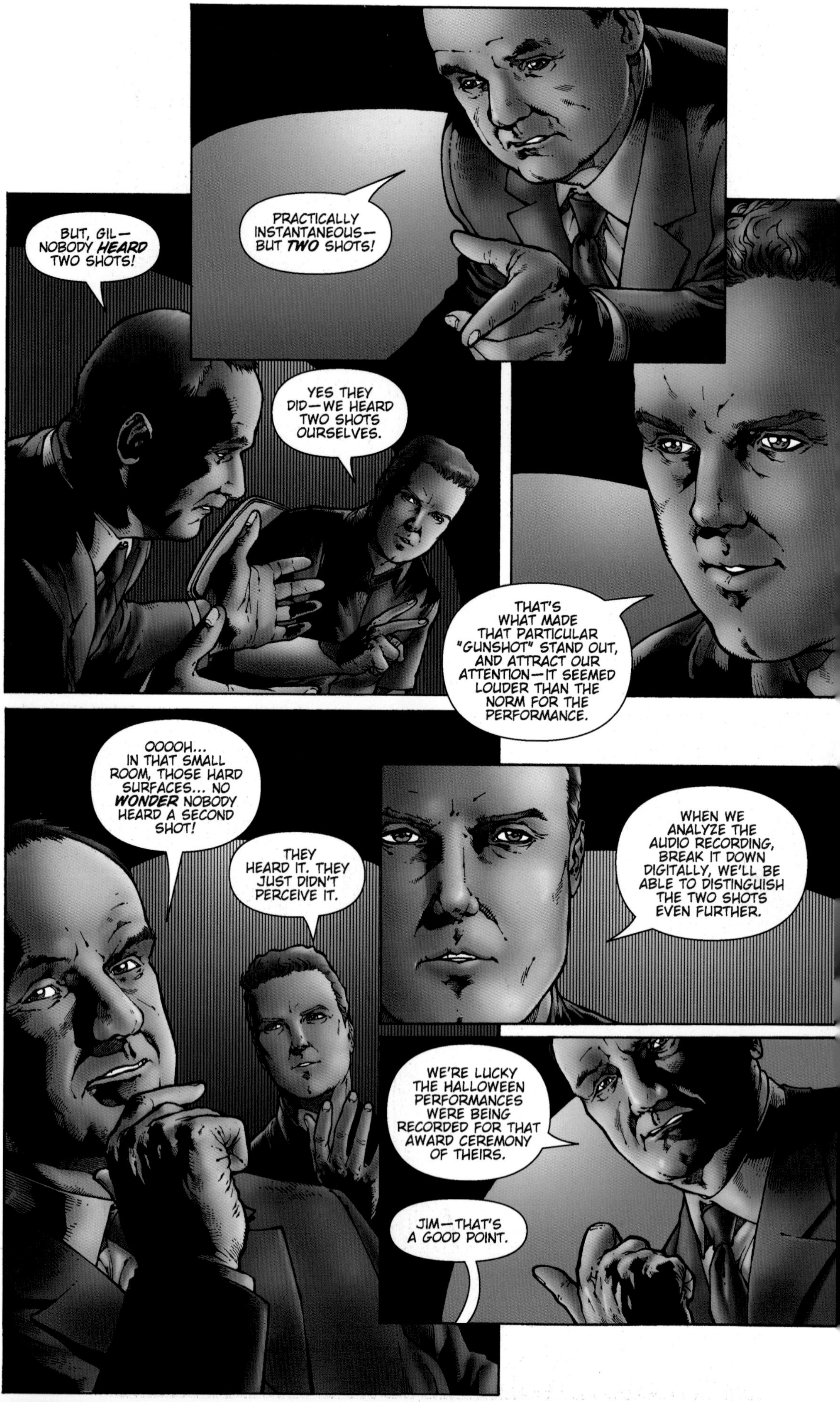
PRACTICALLY INSTANTANEOUS—BUT TWO SHOTS!
BUT, GIL—NOBODY HEARD TWO SHOTS!
YES THEY DID—WE HEARD TWO SHOTS OURSELVES.
THAT'S WHAT MADE THAT PARTICULAR "GUNSHOT" STAND OUT, AND ATTRACT OUR ATTENTION—IT SEEMED LOUDER THAN THE NORM FOR THE PERFORMANCE.
OOOOH... IN THAT SMALL ROOM, THOSE HARD SURFACES... NO WONDER NOBODY HEARD A SECOND SHOT!
THEY HEARD IT. THEY JUST DIDN'T PERCEIVE IT.
WHEN WE ANALYZE THE AUDIO RECORDING, BREAK IT DOWN DIGITALLY, WE'LL BE ABLE TO DISTINGUISH THE TWO SHOTS EVEN FURTHER.
WE'RE LUCKY THE HALLOWEEN PERFORMANCES WERE BEING RECORDED FOR THAT AWARD CEREMONY OF THEIRS.
JIM—THAT'S A GOOD POINT.

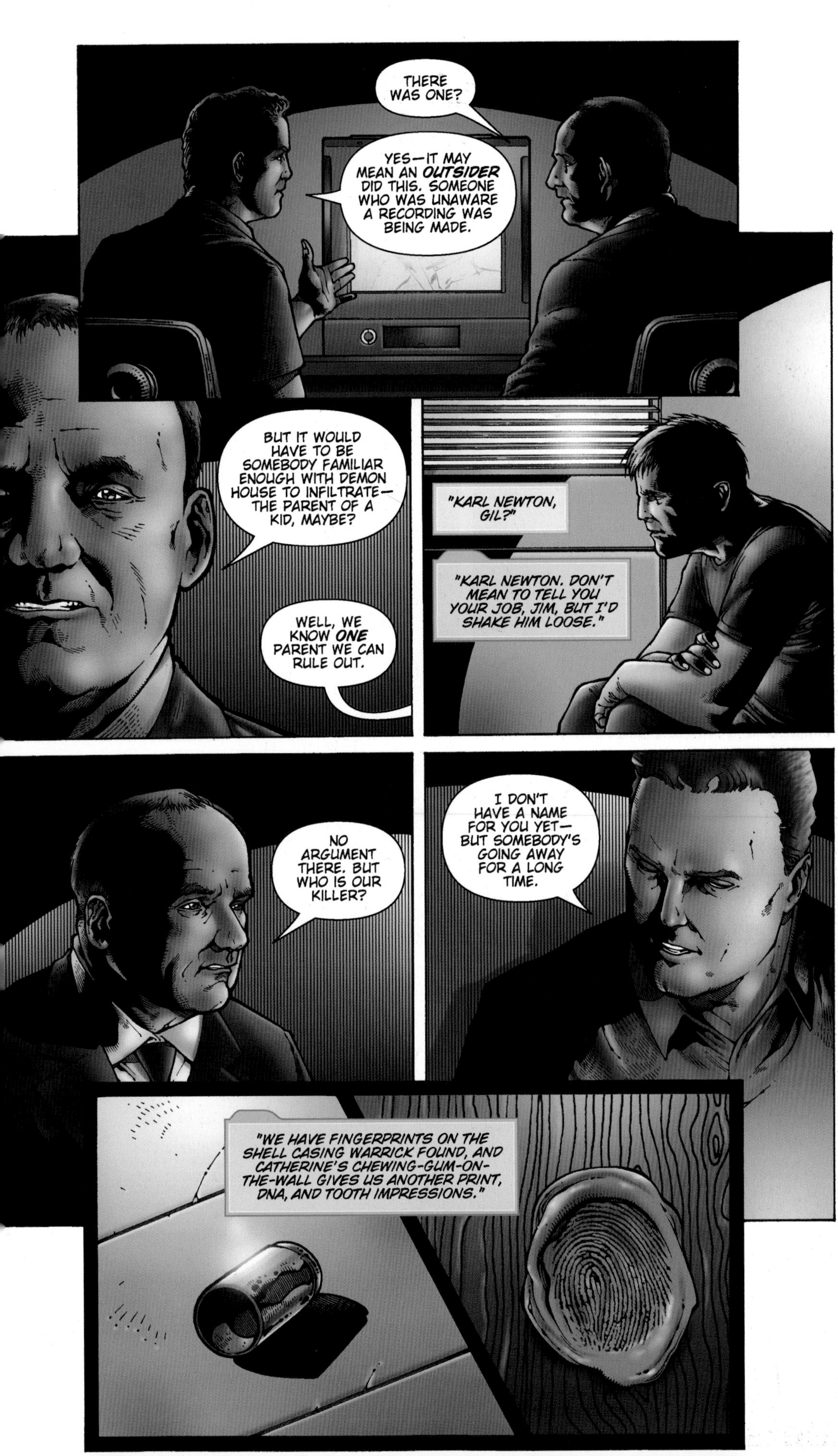

THERE WAS ONE?
YES—IT MAY MEAN AN OUTSIDER DID THIS. SOMEONE WHO WAS UNAWARE A RECORDING WAS BEING MADE.
BUT IT WOULD HAVE TO BE SOMEBODY FAMILIAR ENOUGH WITH DEMON HOUSE TO INFILTRATE—THE PARENT OF A KID, MAYBE?
WELL, WE KNOW ONE PARENT WE CAN RULE OUT.
"KARL NEWTON, GIL?"
"KARL NEWTON. DON'T MEAN TO TELL YOU YOUR JOB, JIM, BUT I'D SHAKE HIM LOOSE."
NO ARGUMENT THERE. BUT WHO IS OUR KILLER?
I DON'T HAVE A NAME FOR YOU YET—BUT SOMEBODY'S GOING AWAY FOR A LONG TIME.
"WE HAVE FINGERPRINTS ON THE SHELL CASING WARRICK FOUND, AND CATHERINE'S CHEWING-GUM-ON-THE-WALL GIVES US ANOTHER PRINT, DNA, AND TOOTH IMPRESSIONS."

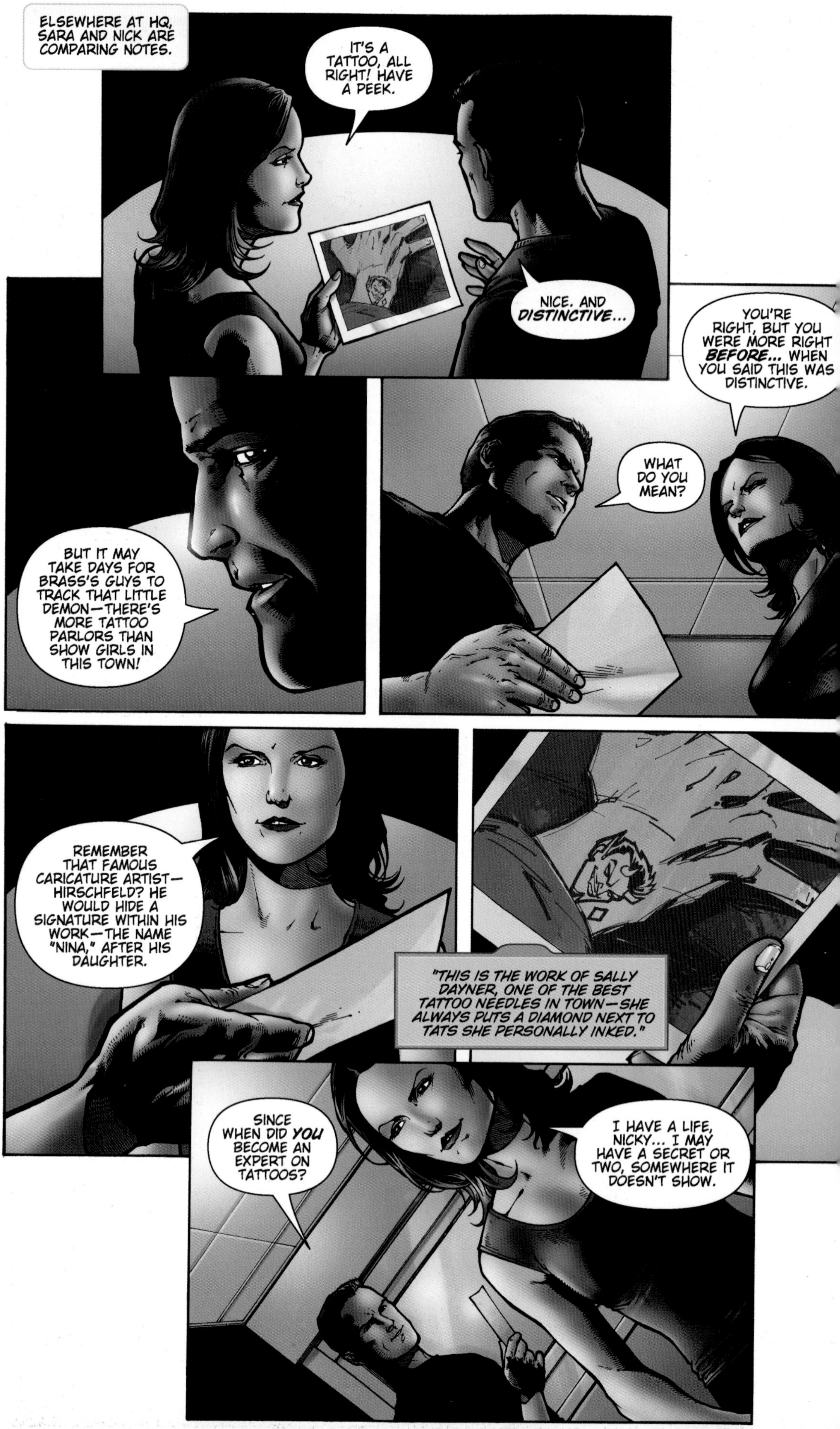
ELSEWHERE AT HQ, SARA AND NICK ARE COMPARING NOTES.
IT'S A TATTOO, ALL RIGHT! HAVE A PEEK.
NICE. AND DISTINCTIVE...
BUT IT MAY TAKE DAYS FOR BRASS'S GUYS TO TRACK THAT LITTLE DEMON—THERE'S MORE TATTOO PARLORS THAN SHOW GIRLS IN THIS TOWN!
YOU'RE RIGHT, BUT YOU WERE MORE RIGHT BEFORE... WHEN YOU SAID THIS WAS DISTINCTIVE.
WHAT DO YOU MEAN?
REMEMBER THAT FAMOUS CARICATURE ARTIST—HIRSCHFELD? HE WOULD HIDE A SIGNATURE WITHIN HIS WORK—THE NAME "NINA," AFTER HIS DAUGHTER.
"THIS IS THE WORK OF SALLY DAYNER, ONE OF THE BEST TATTOO NEEDLES IN TOWN—SHE ALWAYS PUTS A DIAMOND NEXT TO TATS SHE PERSONALLY INKED."
SINCE WHEN DID YOU BECOME AN EXPERT ON TATTOOS?
I HAVE A LIFE, NICKY... I MAY HAVE A SECRET OR TWO, SOMEWHERE IT DOESN'T SHOW.

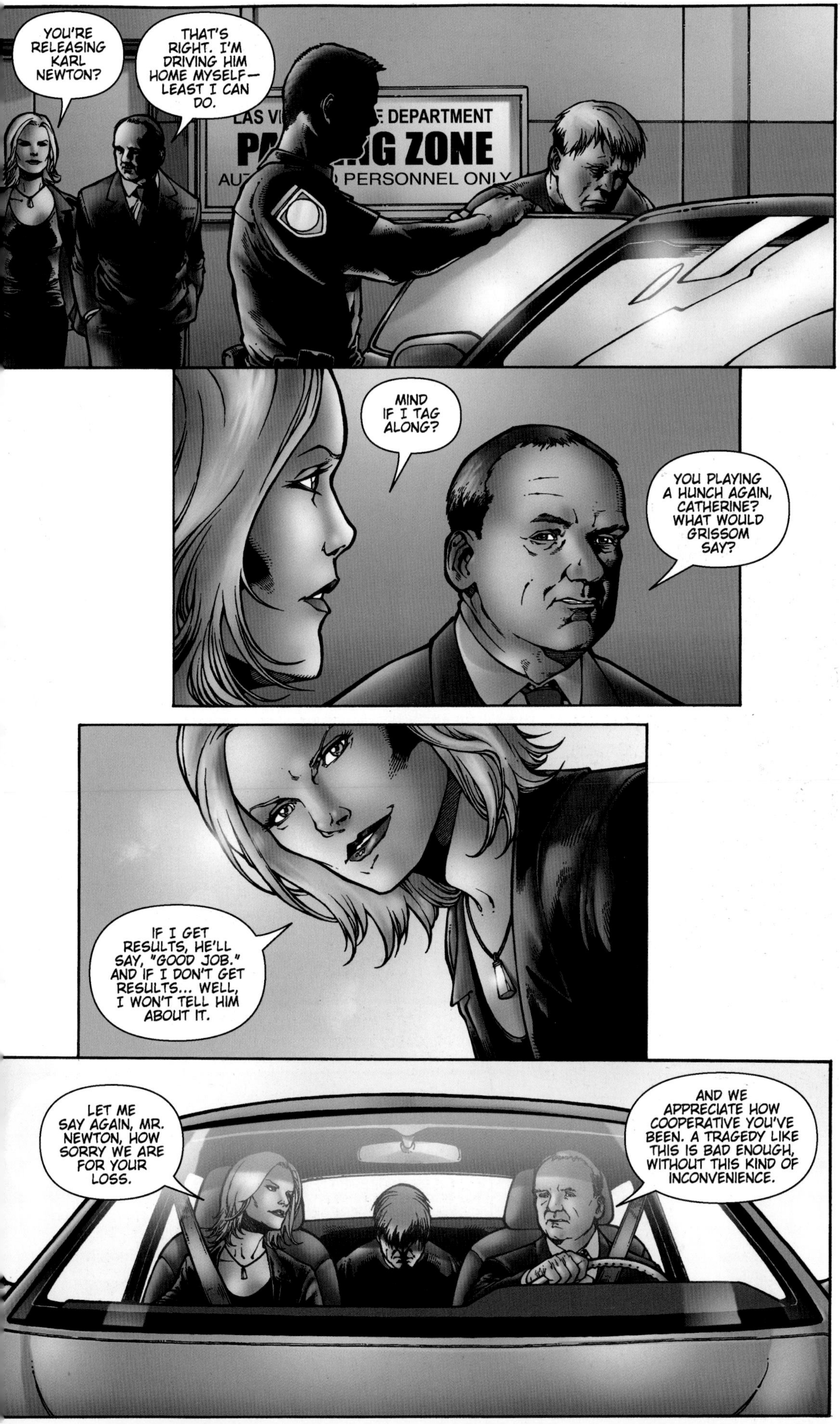
YOU'RE RELEASING KARL NEWTON?
THAT'S RIGHT. I'M DRIVING HIM HOME MYSELF— LEAST I CAN DO.
MIND IF I TAG ALONG?
YOU PLAYING A HUNCH AGAIN, CATHERINE? WHAT WOULD GRISSOM SAY?
IF I GET RESULTS, HE'LL SAY, "GOOD JOB." AND IF I DON'T GET RESULTS... WELL, I WON'T TELL HIM ABOUT IT.
LET ME SAY AGAIN, MR. NEWTON, HOW SORRY WE ARE FOR YOUR LOSS.
AND WE APPRECIATE HOW COOPERATIVE YOU'VE BEEN. A TRAGEDY LIKE THIS IS BAD ENOUGH, WITHOUT THIS KIND OF INCONVENIENCE.

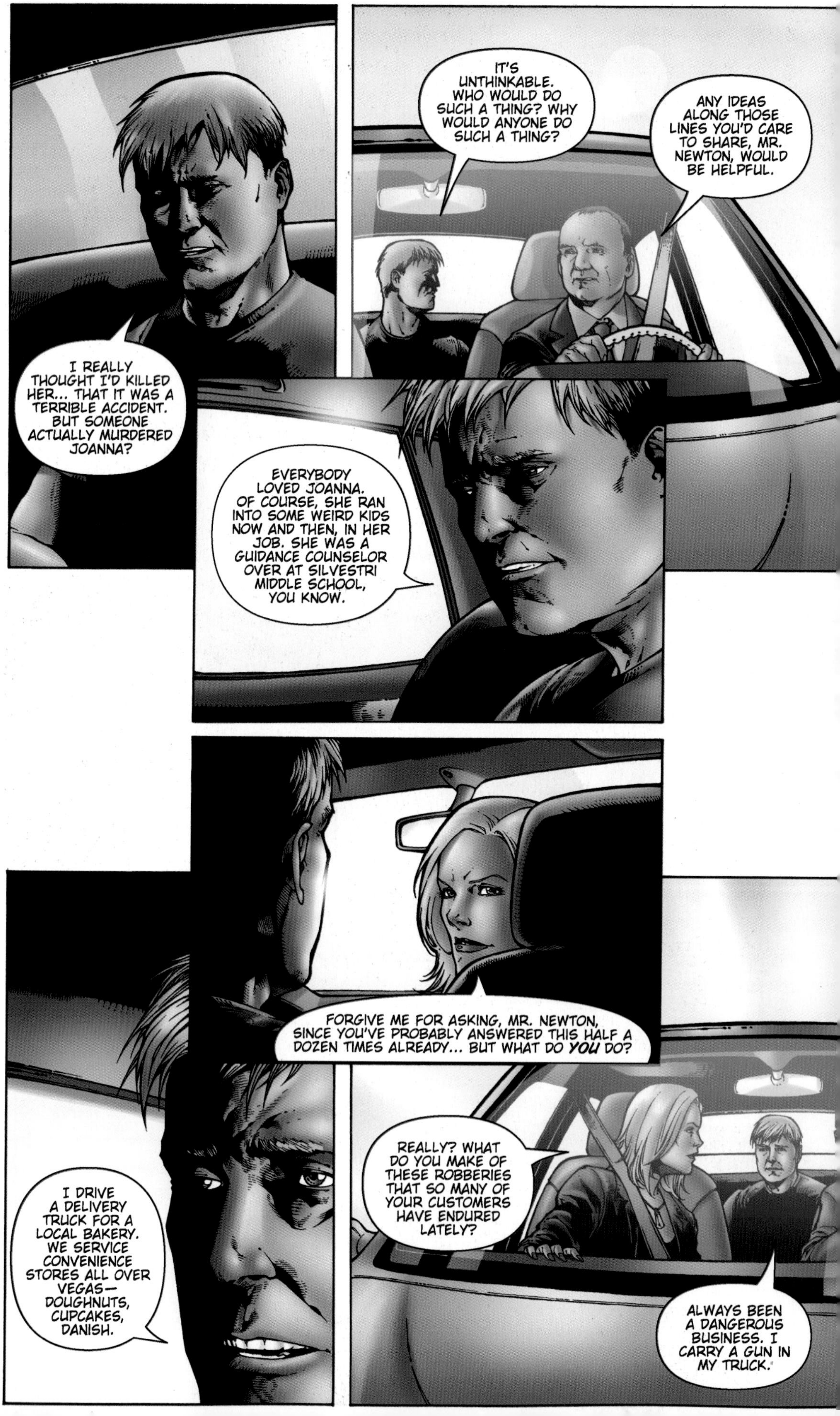

I REALLY THOUGHT I'D KILLED HER... THAT IT WAS A TERRIBLE ACCIDENT. BUT SOMEONE ACTUALLY MURDERED JOANNA?
IT'S UNTHINKABLE. WHO WOULD DO SUCH A THING? WHY WOULD ANYONE DO SUCH A THING?
ANY IDEAS ALONG THOSE LINES YOU'D CARE TO SHARE, MR. NEWTON, WOULD BE HELPFUL.
EVERYBODY LOVED JOANNA. OF COURSE, SHE RAN INTO SOME WEIRD KIDS NOW AND THEN, IN HER JOB. SHE WAS A GUIDANCE COUNSELOR OVER AT SILVESTRI MIDDLE SCHOOL, YOU KNOW.
FORGIVE ME FOR ASKING, MR. NEWTON, SINCE YOU'VE PROBABLY ANSWERED THIS HALF A DOZEN TIMES ALREADY... BUT WHAT DO *YOU* DO?
I DRIVE A DELIVERY TRUCK FOR A LOCAL BAKERY. WE SERVICE CONVENIENCE STORES ALL OVER VEGAS— DOUGHNUTS, CUPCAKES, DANISH.
REALLY? WHAT DO YOU MAKE OF THESE ROBBERIES THAT SO MANY OF YOUR CUSTOMERS HAVE ENDURED LATELY?
ALWAYS BEEN A DANGEROUS BUSINESS. I CARRY A GUN IN MY TRUCK.

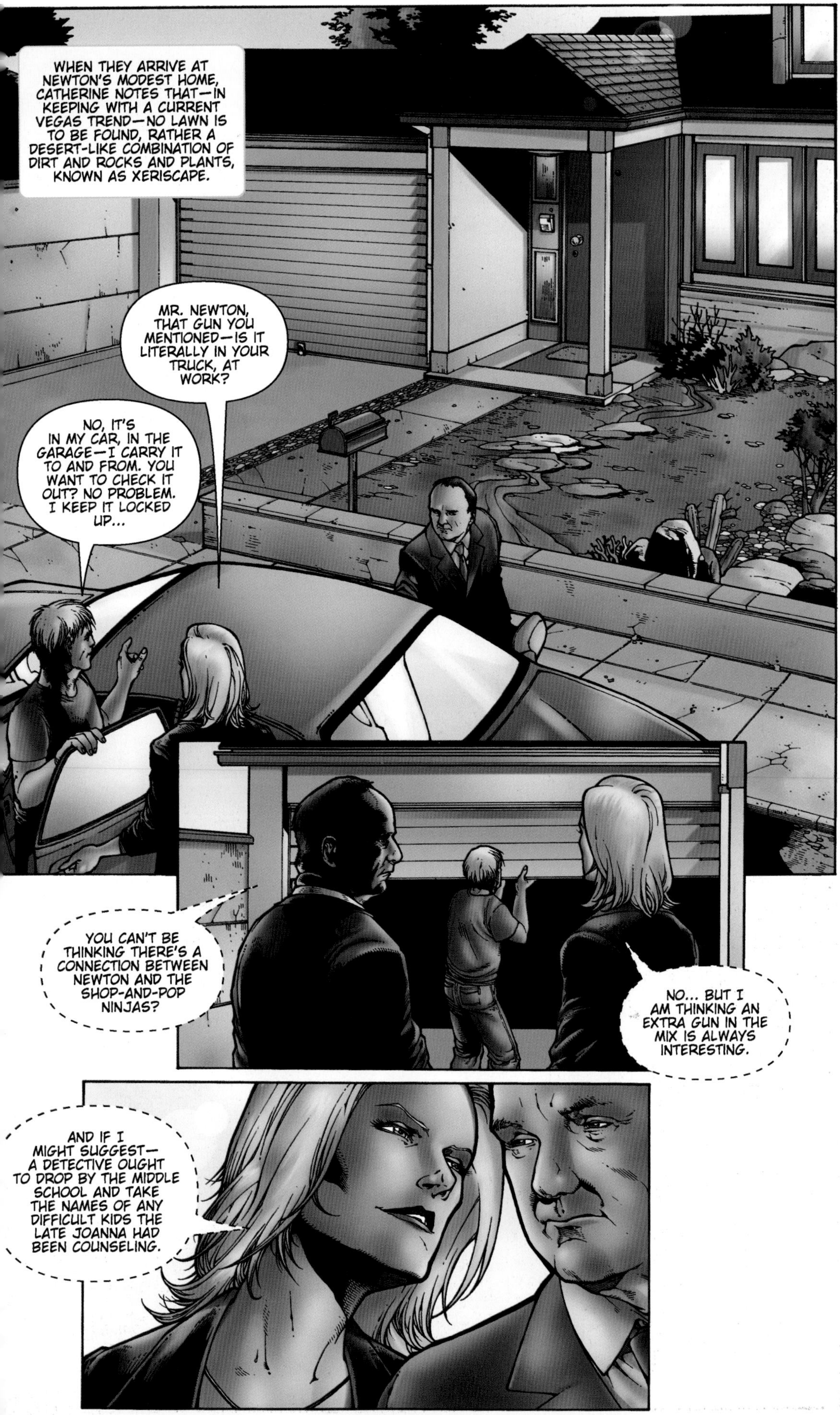
WHEN THEY ARRIVE AT NEWTON'S MODEST HOME, CATHERINE NOTES THAT—IN KEEPING WITH A CURRENT VEGAS TREND—NO LAWN IS TO BE FOUND, RATHER A DESERT-LIKE COMBINATION OF DIRT AND ROCKS AND PLANTS, KNOWN AS XERISCAPE.
MR. NEWTON, THAT GUN YOU MENTIONED—IS IT LITERALLY IN YOUR TRUCK, AT WORK?
NO, IT'S IN MY CAR, IN THE GARAGE—I CARRY IT TO AND FROM. YOU WANT TO CHECK IT OUT? NO PROBLEM. I KEEP IT LOCKED UP...
YOU CAN'T BE THINKING THERE'S A CONNECTION BETWEEN NEWTON AND THE SHOP-AND-POP NINJAS?
NO... BUT I AM THINKING AN EXTRA GUN IN THE MIX IS ALWAYS INTERESTING.
AND IF I MIGHT SUGGEST—A DETECTIVE OUGHT TO DROP BY THE MIDDLE SCHOOL AND TAKE THE NAMES OF ANY DIFFICULT KIDS THE LATE JOANNA HAD BEEN COUNSELING.

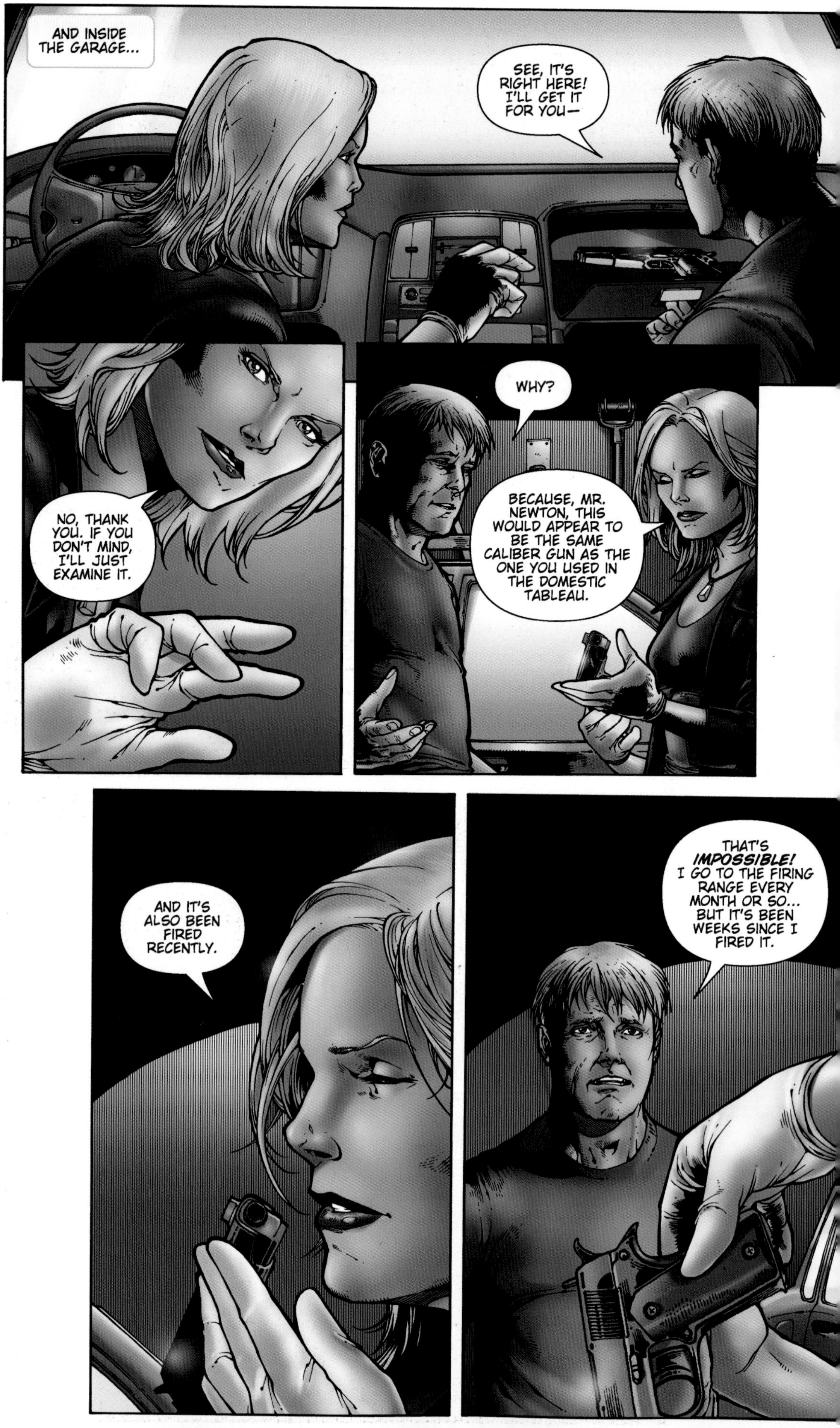
AND INSIDE THE GARAGE...
SEE, IT'S RIGHT HERE! I'LL GET IT FOR YOU—
NO, THANK YOU. IF YOU DON'T MIND, I'LL JUST EXAMINE IT.
WHY?
BECAUSE, MR. NEWTON, THIS WOULD APPEAR TO BE THE SAME CALIBER GUN AS THE ONE YOU USED IN THE DOMESTIC TABLEAU.
AND IT'S ALSO BEEN FIRED RECENTLY.
THAT'S *IMPOSSIBLE!* I GO TO THE FIRING RANGE EVERY MONTH OR SO... BUT IT'S BEEN WEEKS SINCE I FIRED IT.

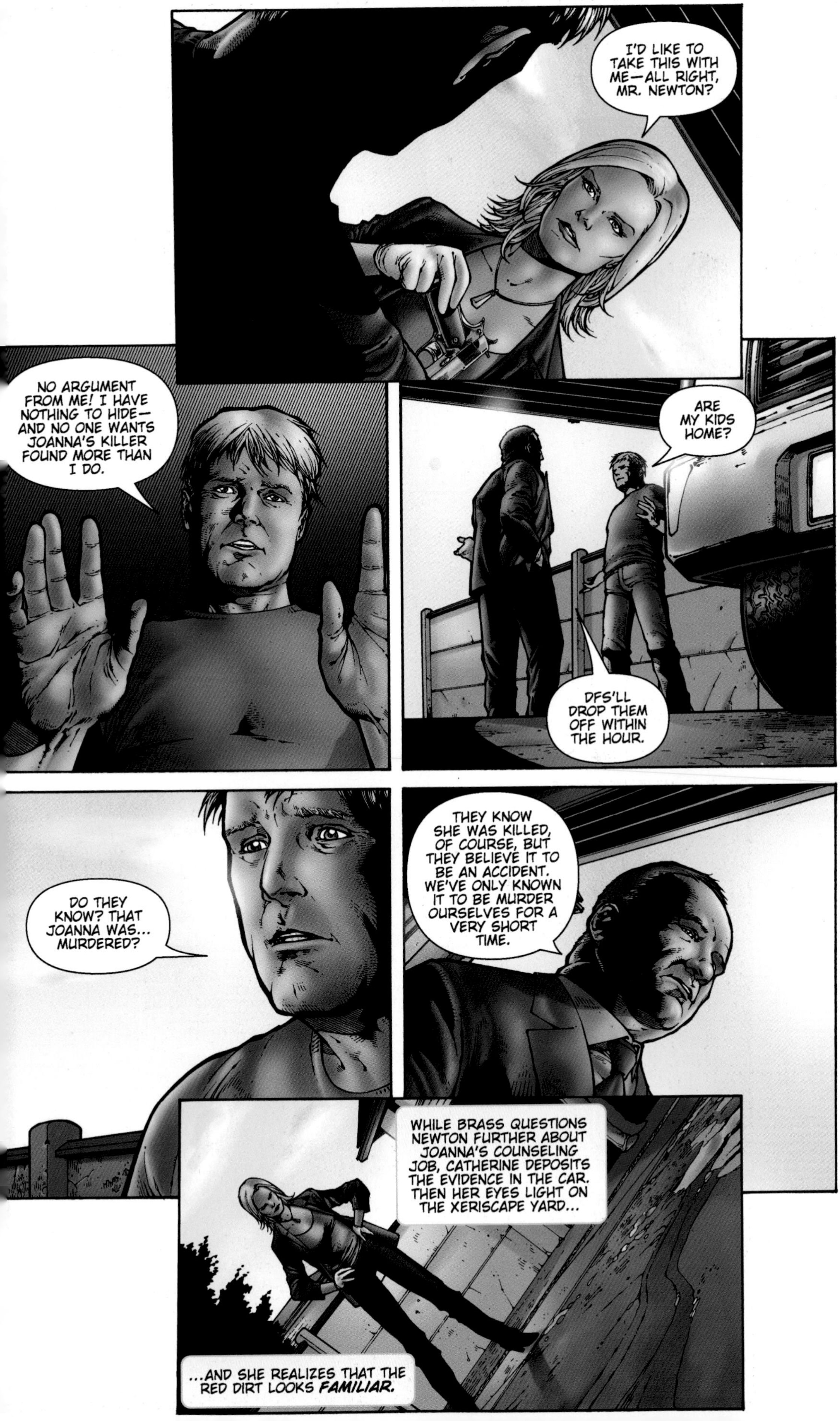
I'D LIKE TO TAKE THIS WITH ME—ALL RIGHT, MR. NEWTON?
NO ARGUMENT FROM ME! I HAVE NOTHING TO HIDE—AND NO ONE WANTS JOANNA'S KILLER FOUND MORE THAN I DO.
ARE MY KIDS HOME?
DFS'LL DROP THEM OFF WITHIN THE HOUR.
DO THEY KNOW? THAT JOANNA WAS... MURDERED?
THEY KNOW SHE WAS KILLED, OF COURSE, BUT THEY BELIEVE IT TO BE AN ACCIDENT. WE'VE ONLY KNOWN IT TO BE MURDER OURSELVES FOR A VERY SHORT TIME.
WHILE BRASS QUESTIONS NEWTON FURTHER ABOUT JOANNA'S COUNSELING JOB, CATHERINE DEPOSITS THE EVIDENCE IN THE CAR. THEN HER EYES LIGHT ON THE XERISCAPE YARD...
...AND SHE REALIZES THAT THE RED DIRT LOOKS *FAMILIAR.*

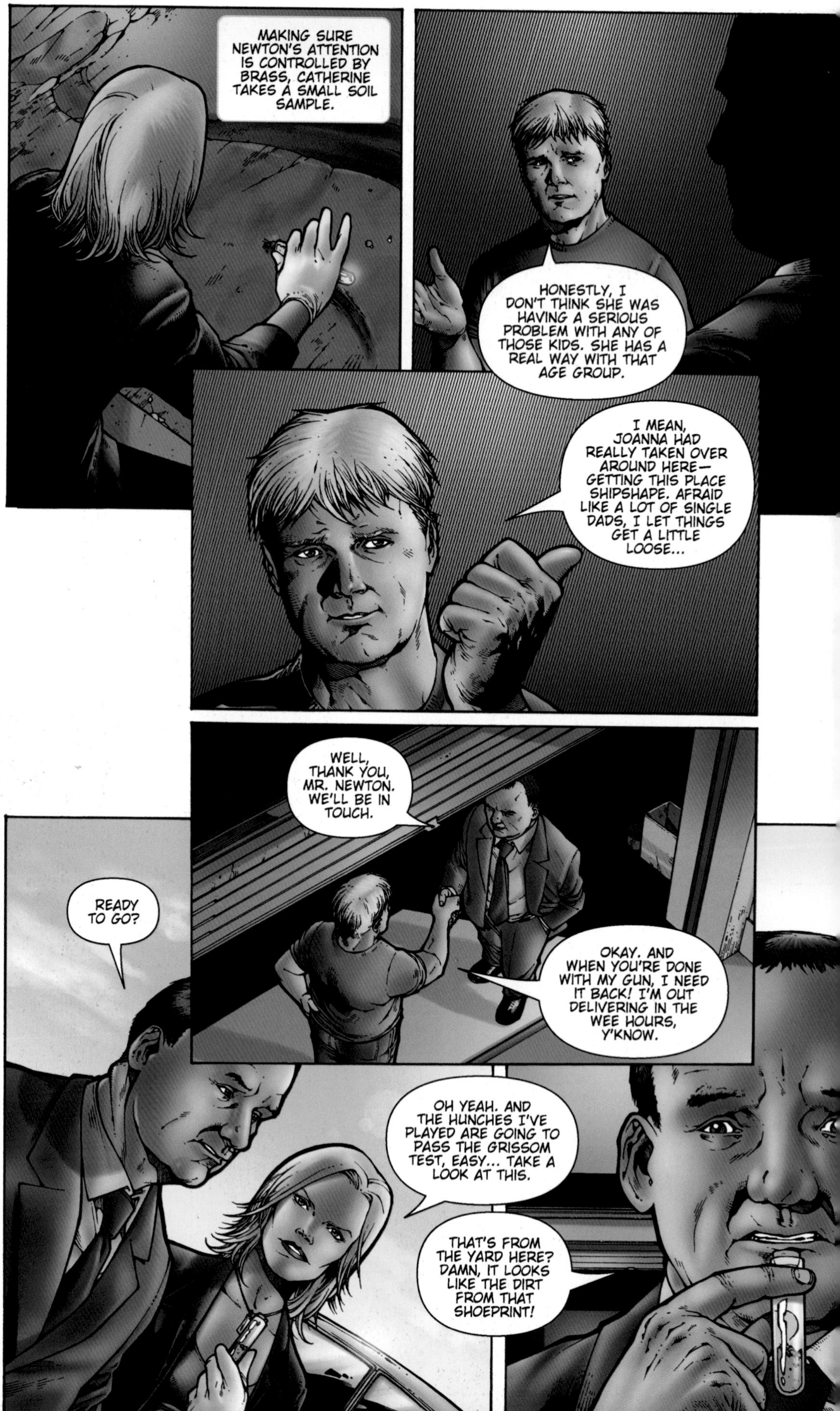
MAKING SURE NEWTON'S ATTENTION IS CONTROLLED BY BRASS, CATHERINE TAKES A SMALL SOIL SAMPLE.
HONESTLY, I DON'T THINK SHE WAS HAVING A SERIOUS PROBLEM WITH ANY OF THOSE KIDS. SHE HAS A REAL WAY WITH THAT AGE GROUP.
I MEAN, JOANNA HAD REALLY TAKEN OVER AROUND HERE— GETTING THIS PLACE SHIPSHAPE. AFRAID LIKE A LOT OF SINGLE DADS, I LET THINGS GET A LITTLE LOOSE...
WELL, THANK YOU, MR. NEWTON. WE'LL BE IN TOUCH.
OKAY. AND WHEN YOU'RE DONE WITH MY GUN, I NEED IT BACK! I'M OUT DELIVERING IN THE WEE HOURS, Y'KNOW.
READY TO GO?
OH YEAH. AND THE HUNCHES I'VE PLAYED ARE GOING TO PASS THE GRISSOM TEST, EASY... TAKE A LOOK AT THIS.
THAT'S FROM THE YARD HERE? DAMN, IT LOOKS LIKE THE DIRT FROM THAT SHOEPRINT!

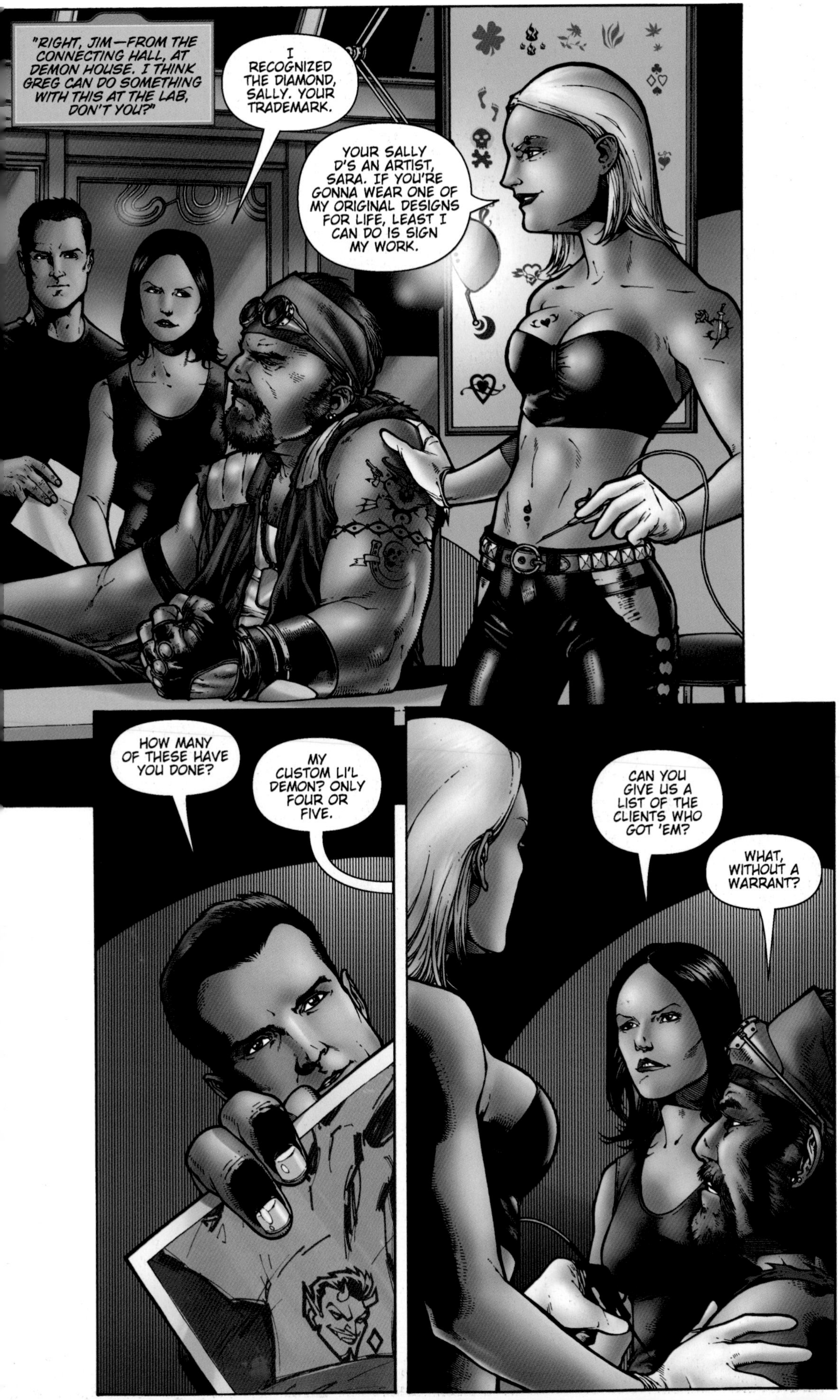
"RIGHT, JIM—FROM THE CONNECTING HALL, AT DEMON HOUSE. I THINK GREG CAN DO SOMETHING WITH THIS AT THE LAB, DON'T YOU?"
I RECOGNIZED THE DIAMOND, SALLY. YOUR TRADEMARK.
YOUR SALLY D'S AN ARTIST, SARA. IF YOU'RE GONNA WEAR ONE OF MY ORIGINAL DESIGNS FOR LIFE, LEAST I CAN DO IS SIGN MY WORK.
HOW MANY OF THESE HAVE YOU DONE?
MY CUSTOM LI'L DEMON? ONLY FOUR OR FIVE.
CAN YOU GIVE US A LIST OF THE CLIENTS WHO GOT 'EM?
WHAT, WITHOUT A WARRANT?

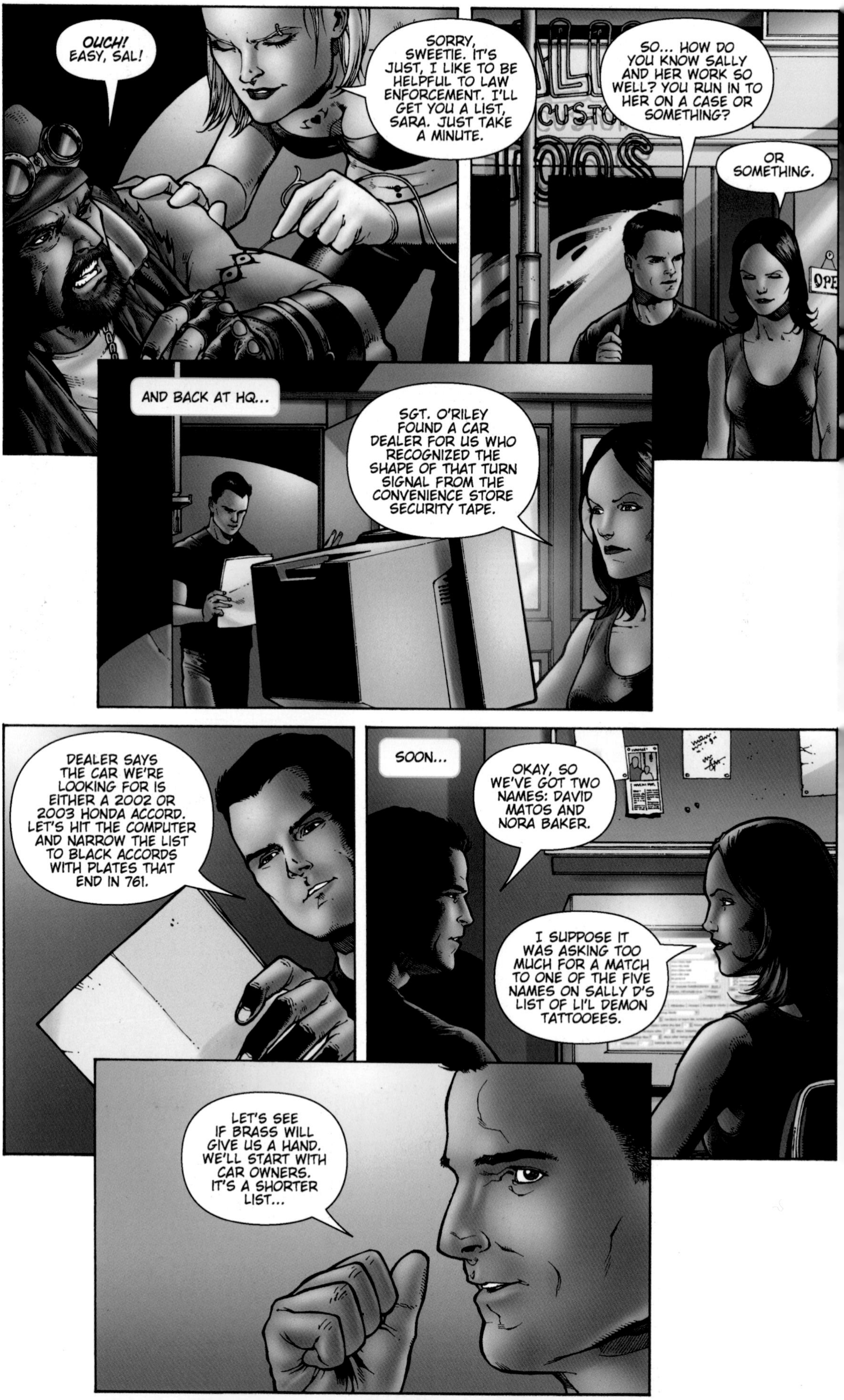
OUCH! EASY, SAL!
SORRY, SWEETIE. IT'S JUST, I LIKE TO BE HELPFUL TO LAW ENFORCEMENT. I'LL GET YOU A LIST, SARA. JUST TAKE A MINUTE.
SO... HOW DO YOU KNOW SALLY AND HER WORK SO WELL? YOU RUN IN TO HER ON A CASE OR SOMETHING?
OR SOMETHING.
AND BACK AT HQ...
SGT. O'RILEY FOUND A CAR DEALER FOR US WHO RECOGNIZED THE SHAPE OF THAT TURN SIGNAL FROM THE CONVENIENCE STORE SECURITY TAPE.
DEALER SAYS THE CAR WE'RE LOOKING FOR IS EITHER A 2002 OR 2003 HONDA ACCORD. LET'S HIT THE COMPUTER AND NARROW THE LIST TO BLACK ACCORDS WITH PLATES THAT END IN 761.
SOON...
OKAY, SO WE'VE GOT TWO NAMES: DAVID MATOS AND NORA BAKER.
I SUPPOSE IT WAS ASKING TOO MUCH FOR A MATCH TO ONE OF THE FIVE NAMES ON SALLY D'S LIST OF LI'L DEMON TATTOOEES.
LET'S SEE IF BRASS WILL GIVE US A HAND. WE'LL START WITH CAR OWNERS. IT'S A SHORTER LIST...

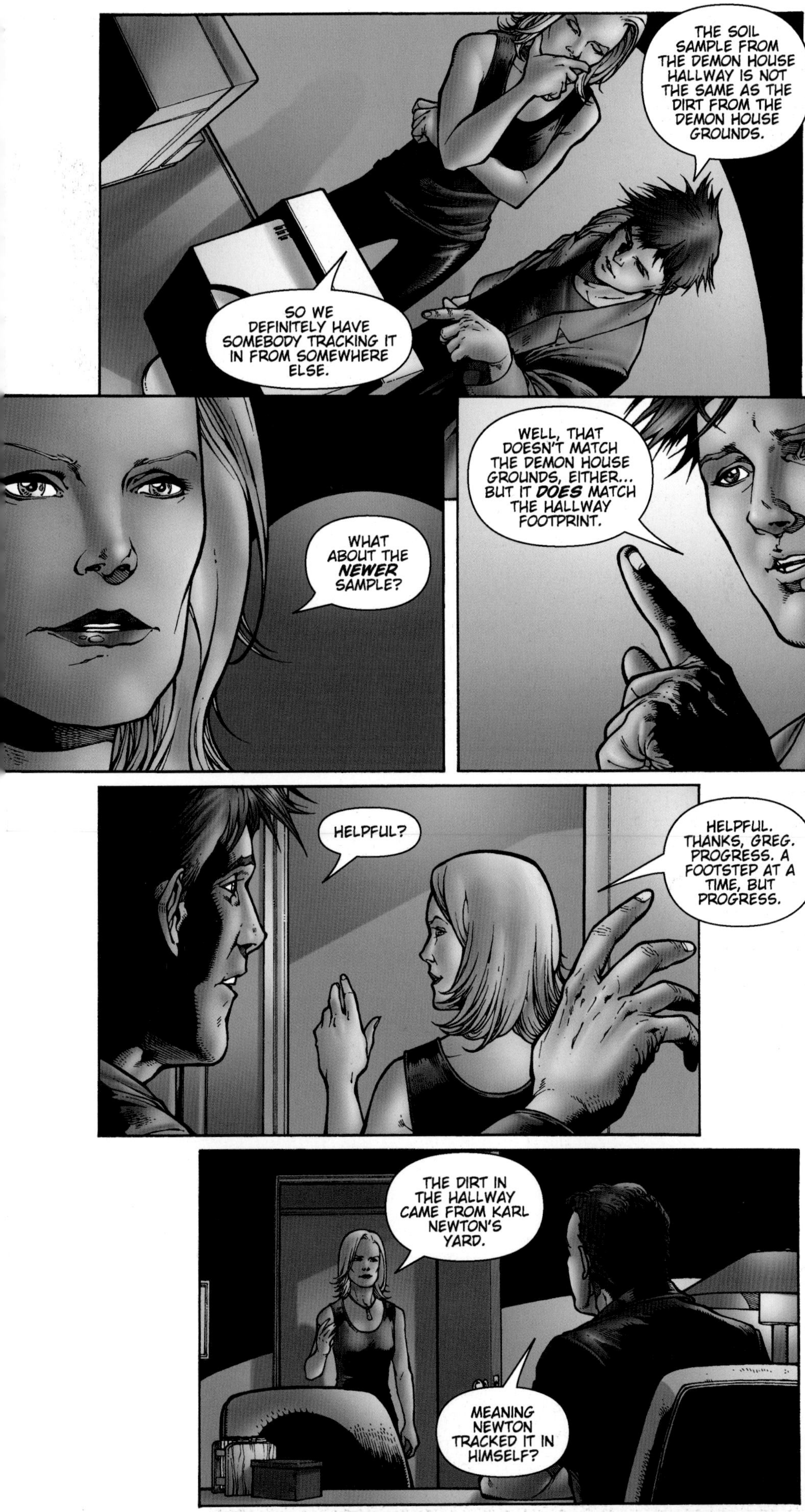
THE SOIL SAMPLE FROM THE DEMON HOUSE HALLWAY IS NOT THE SAME AS THE DIRT FROM THE DEMON HOUSE GROUNDS.
SO WE DEFINITELY HAVE SOMEBODY TRACKING IT IN FROM SOMEWHERE ELSE.
WHAT ABOUT THE *NEWER* SAMPLE?
WELL, THAT DOESN'T MATCH THE DEMON HOUSE GROUNDS, EITHER... BUT IT *DOES* MATCH THE HALLWAY FOOTPRINT.
HELPFUL?
HELPFUL. THANKS, GREG. PROGRESS. A FOOTSTEP AT A TIME, BUT PROGRESS.
THE DIRT IN THE HALLWAY CAME FROM KARL NEWTON'S YARD.
MEANING NEWTON TRACKED IT IN HIMSELF?

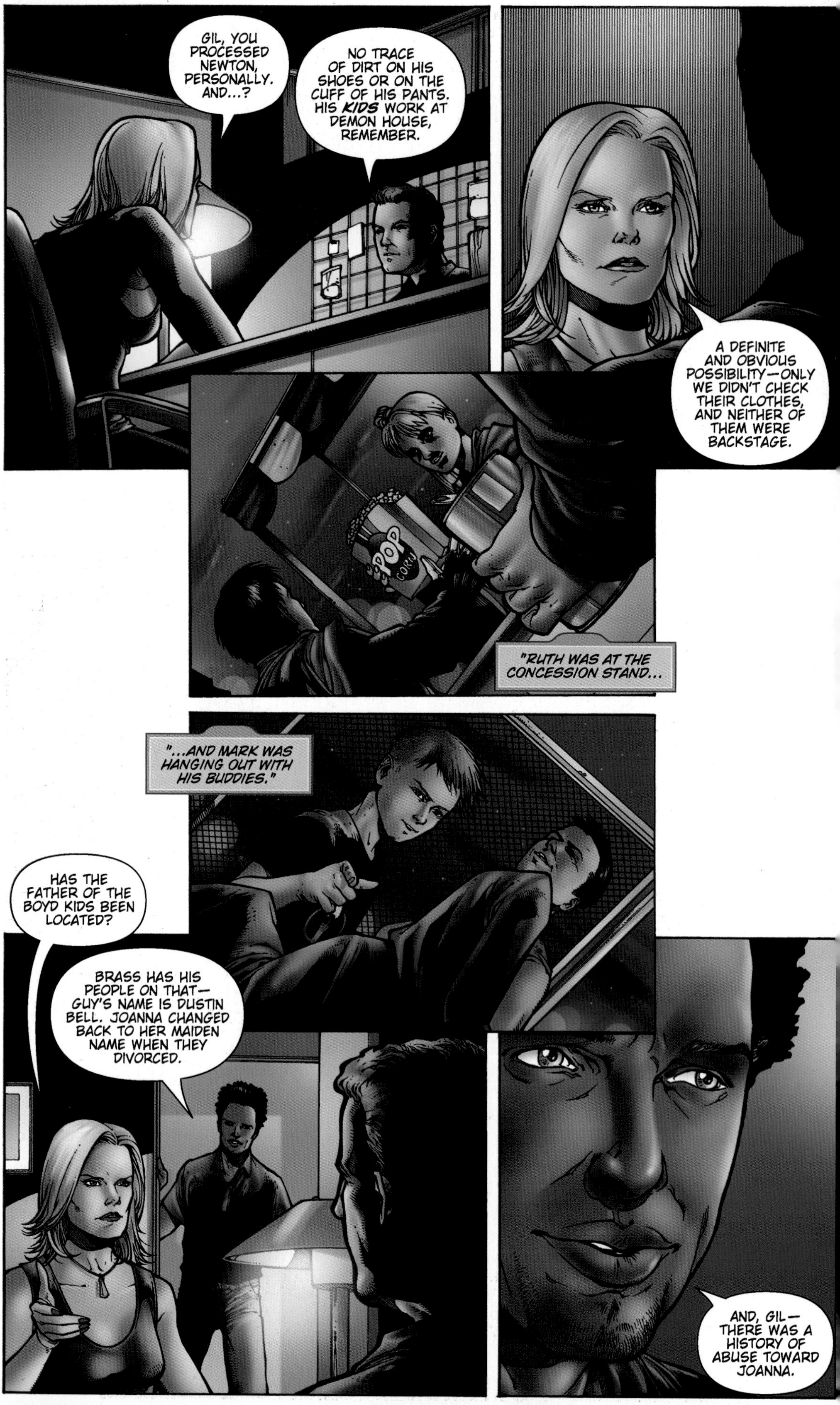
GIL, YOU PROCESSED NEWTON, PERSONALLY. AND...?
NO TRACE OF DIRT ON HIS SHOES OR ON THE CUFF OF HIS PANTS. HIS KIDS WORK AT DEMON HOUSE, REMEMBER.
A DEFINITE AND OBVIOUS POSSIBILITY—ONLY WE DIDN'T CHECK THEIR CLOTHES, AND NEITHER OF THEM WERE BACKSTAGE.
"RUTH WAS AT THE CONCESSION STAND...
"...AND MARK WAS HANGING OUT WITH HIS BUDDIES."
HAS THE FATHER OF THE BOYD KIDS BEEN LOCATED?
BRASS HAS HIS PEOPLE ON THAT—GUY'S NAME IS DUSTIN BELL. JOANNA CHANGED BACK TO HER MAIDEN NAME WHEN THEY DIVORCED.
AND, GIL—THERE WAS A HISTORY OF ABUSE TOWARD JOANNA.

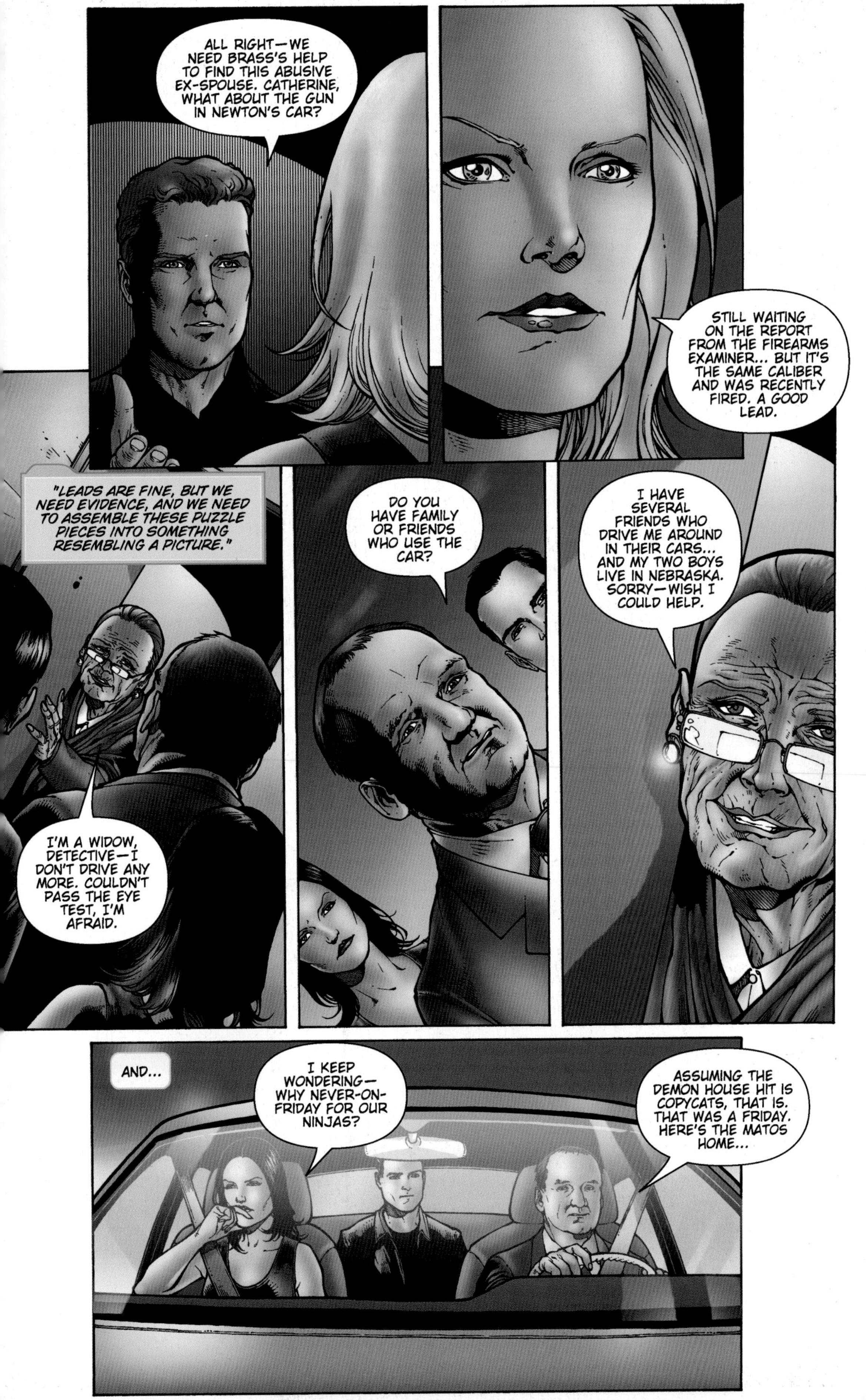
ALL RIGHT—WE NEED BRASS'S HELP TO FIND THIS ABUSIVE EX-SPOUSE. CATHERINE, WHAT ABOUT THE GUN IN NEWTON'S CAR?
STILL WAITING ON THE REPORT FROM THE FIREARMS EXAMINER... BUT IT'S THE SAME CALIBER AND WAS RECENTLY FIRED. A GOOD LEAD.
"LEADS ARE FINE, BUT WE NEED EVIDENCE, AND WE NEED TO ASSEMBLE THESE PUZZLE PIECES INTO SOMETHING RESEMBLING A PICTURE."
I'M A WIDOW, DETECTIVE—I DON'T DRIVE ANY MORE. COULDN'T PASS THE EYE TEST, I'M AFRAID.
DO YOU HAVE FAMILY OR FRIENDS WHO USE THE CAR?
I HAVE SEVERAL FRIENDS WHO DRIVE ME AROUND IN THEIR CARS... AND MY TWO BOYS LIVE IN NEBRASKA. SORRY—WISH I COULD HELP.
AND...
I KEEP WONDERING—WHY NEVER-ON-FRIDAY FOR OUR NINJAS?
ASSUMING THE DEMON HOUSE HIT IS COPYCATS, THAT IS. THAT WAS A FRIDAY. HERE'S THE MATOS HOME...

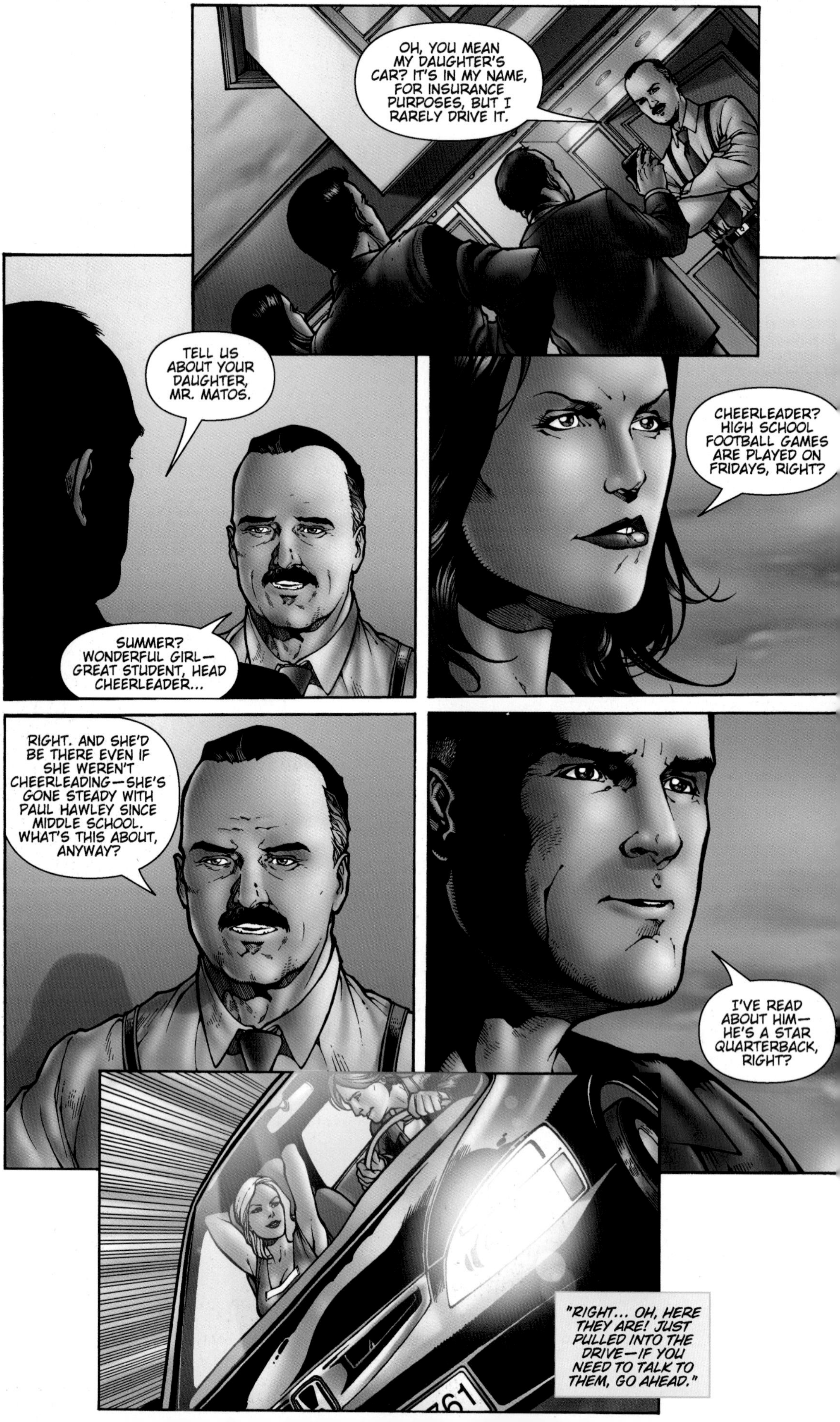
OH, YOU MEAN MY DAUGHTER'S CAR? IT'S IN MY NAME, FOR INSURANCE PURPOSES, BUT I RARELY DRIVE IT.
TELL US ABOUT YOUR DAUGHTER, MR. MATOS.
SUMMER? WONDERFUL GIRL— GREAT STUDENT, HEAD CHEERLEADER...
CHEERLEADER? HIGH SCHOOL FOOTBALL GAMES ARE PLAYED ON FRIDAYS, RIGHT?
RIGHT. AND SHE'D BE THERE EVEN IF SHE WEREN'T CHEERLEADING—SHE'S GONE STEADY WITH PAUL HAWLEY SINCE MIDDLE SCHOOL. WHAT'S THIS ABOUT, ANYWAY?
I'VE READ ABOUT HIM— HE'S A STAR QUARTERBACK, RIGHT?
"RIGHT... OH, HERE THEY ARE! JUST PULLED INTO THE DRIVE—IF YOU NEED TO TALK TO THEM, GO AHEAD."

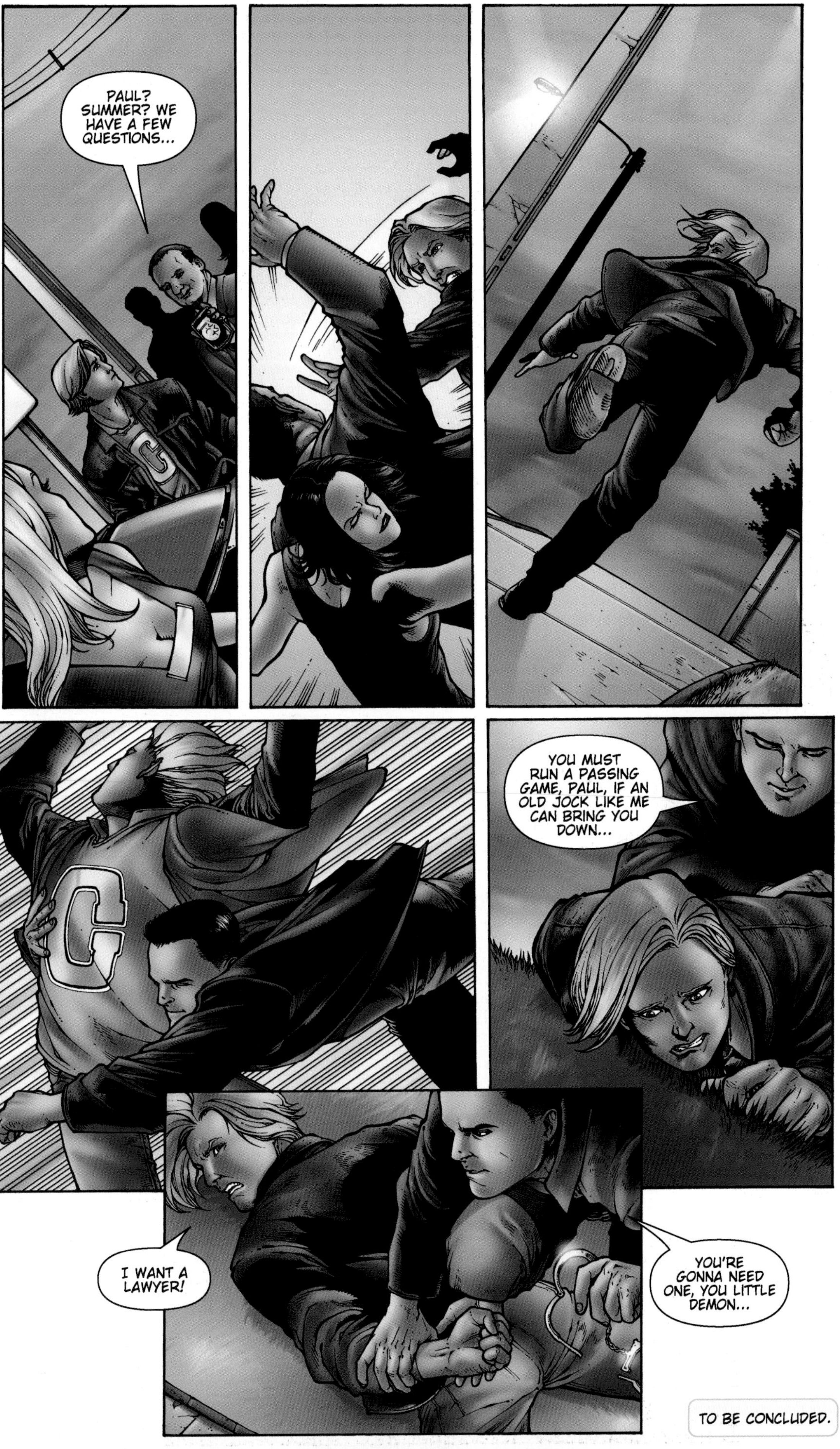
PAUL? SUMMER? WE HAVE A FEW QUESTIONS...
YOU MUST RUN A PASSING GAME, PAUL, IF AN OLD JOCK LIKE ME CAN BRING YOU DOWN...
I WANT A LAWYER!
YOU'RE GONNA NEED ONE, YOU LITTLE DEMON...
TO BE CONCLUDED.

chapter five

Just Say No

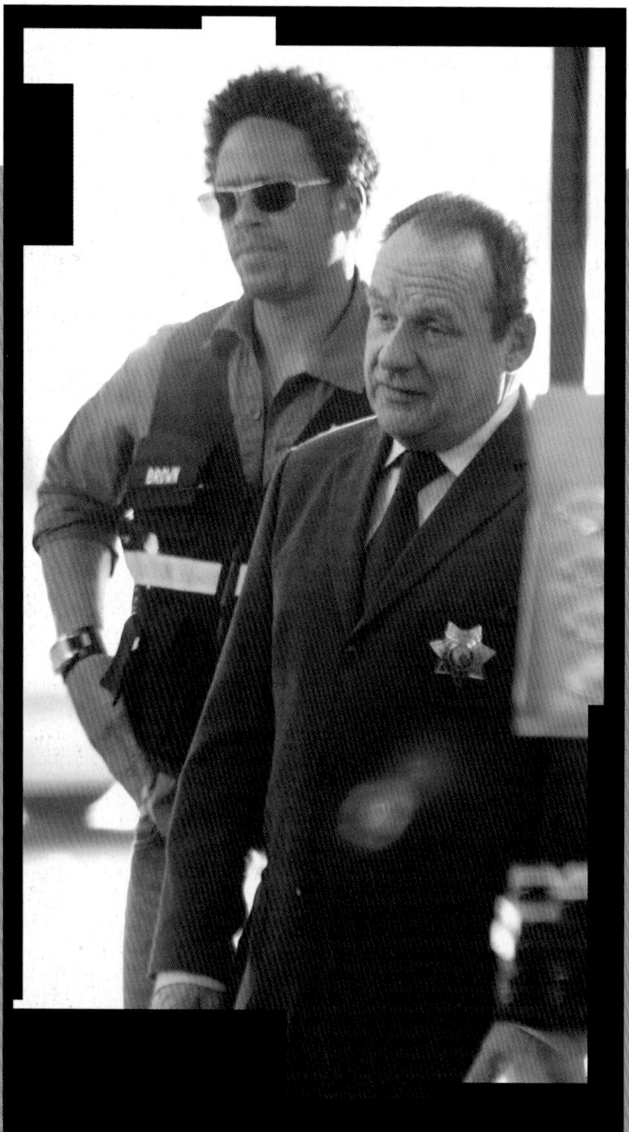

BROWN

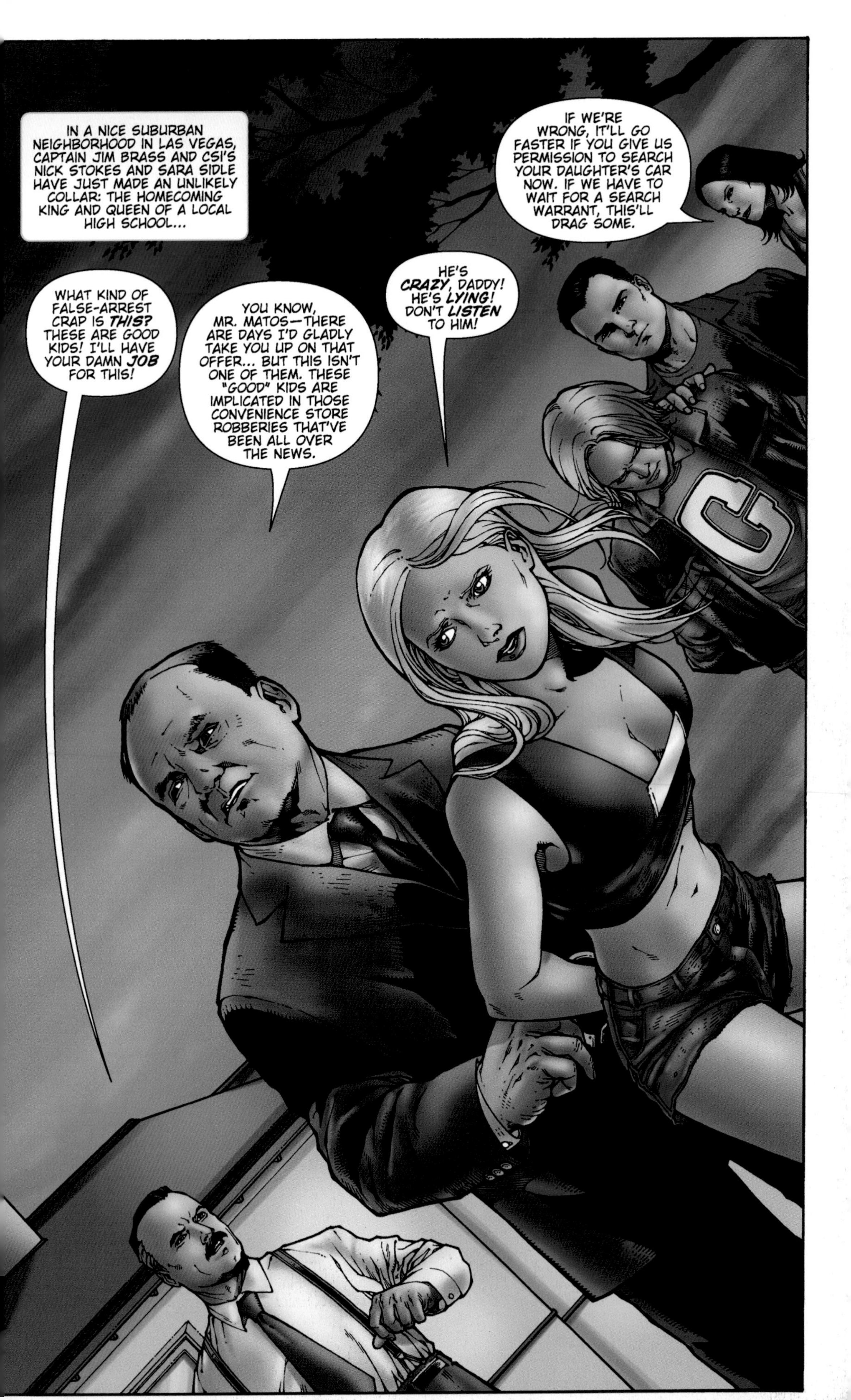
IN A NICE SUBURBAN NEIGHBORHOOD IN LAS VEGAS, CAPTAIN JIM BRASS AND CSI'S NICK STOKES AND SARA SIDLE HAVE JUST MADE AN UNLIKELY COLLAR: THE HOMECOMING KING AND QUEEN OF A LOCAL HIGH SCHOOL...
WHAT KIND OF FALSE-ARREST CRAP IS *THIS?* THESE ARE GOOD KIDS! I'LL HAVE YOUR DAMN *JOB* FOR THIS!
YOU KNOW, MR. MATOS—THERE ARE DAYS I'D GLADLY TAKE YOU UP ON THAT OFFER... BUT THIS ISN'T ONE OF THEM. THESE "GOOD" KIDS ARE IMPLICATED IN THOSE CONVENIENCE STORE ROBBERIES THAT'VE BEEN ALL OVER THE NEWS.
HE'S *CRAZY*, DADDY! HE'S *LYING!* DON'T *LISTEN* TO HIM!
IF WE'RE WRONG, IT'LL GO FASTER IF YOU GIVE US PERMISSION TO SEARCH YOUR DAUGHTER'S CAR NOW. IF WE HAVE TO WAIT FOR A SEARCH WARRANT, THIS'LL DRAG SOME.

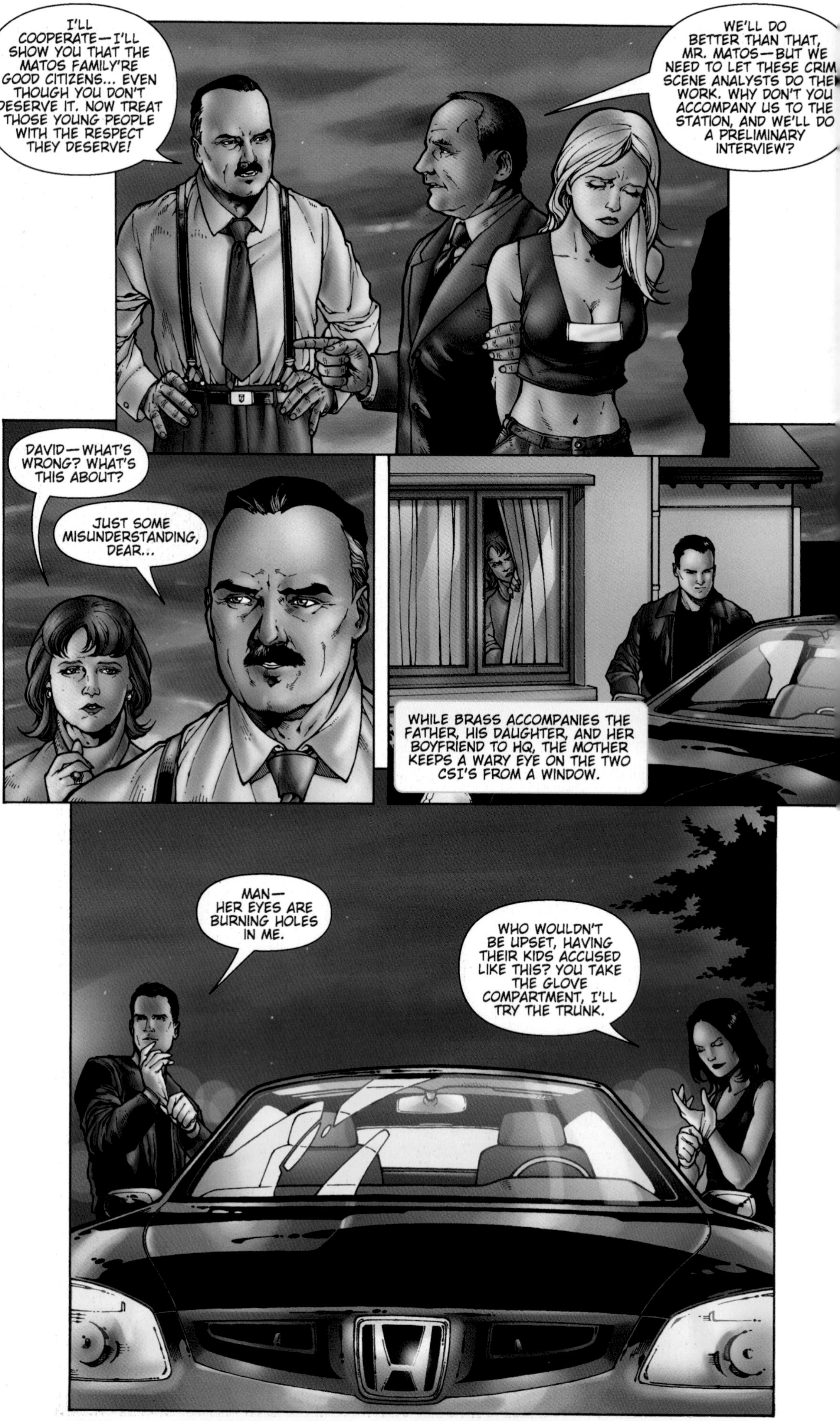
I'LL COOPERATE—I'LL SHOW YOU THAT THE MATOS FAMILY'RE GOOD CITIZENS... EVEN THOUGH YOU DON'T DESERVE IT. NOW TREAT THOSE YOUNG PEOPLE WITH THE RESPECT THEY DESERVE!
WE'LL DO BETTER THAN THAT, MR. MATOS—BUT WE NEED TO LET THESE CRIM SCENE ANALYSTS DO THE WORK. WHY DON'T YOU ACCOMPANY US TO THE STATION, AND WE'LL DO A PRELIMINARY INTERVIEW?
DAVID—WHAT'S WRONG? WHAT'S THIS ABOUT?
JUST SOME MISUNDERSTANDING, DEAR...
WHILE BRASS ACCOMPANIES THE FATHER, HIS DAUGHTER, AND HER BOYFRIEND TO HQ, THE MOTHER KEEPS A WARY EYE ON THE TWO CSI'S FROM A WINDOW.
MAN— HER EYES ARE BURNING HOLES IN ME.
WHO WOULDN'T BE UPSET, HAVING THEIR KIDS ACCUSED LIKE THIS? YOU TAKE THE GLOVE COMPARTMENT, I'LL TRY THE TRUNK.

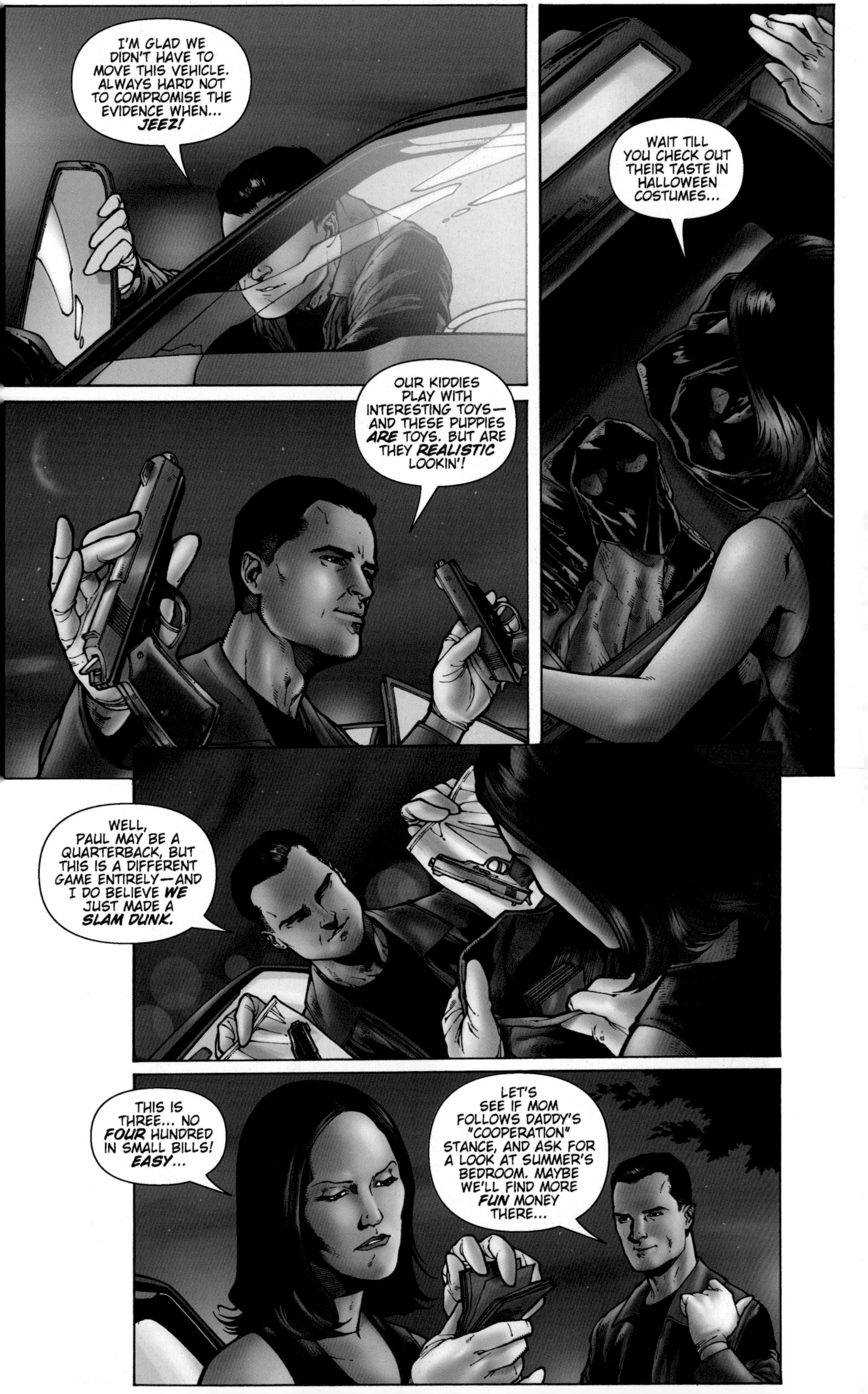
I'M GLAD WE DIDN'T HAVE TO MOVE THIS VEHICLE. ALWAYS HARD NOT TO COMPROMISE THE EVIDENCE WHEN... JEEZ!
WAIT TILL YOU CHECK OUT THEIR TASTE IN HALLOWEEN COSTUMES...
OUR KIDDIES PLAY WITH INTERESTING TOYS— AND THESE PUPPIES ARE TOYS. BUT ARE THEY REALISTIC LOOKIN'!
WELL, PAUL MAY BE A QUARTERBACK, BUT THIS IS A DIFFERENT GAME ENTIRELY—AND I DO BELIEVE WE JUST MADE A SLAM DUNK.
THIS IS THREE... NO FOUR HUNDRED IN SMALL BILLS! EASY...
LET'S SEE IF MOM FOLLOWS DADDY'S "COOPERATION" STANCE, AND ASK FOR A LOOK AT SUMMER'S BEDROOM. MAYBE WE'LL FIND MORE FUN MONEY THERE...

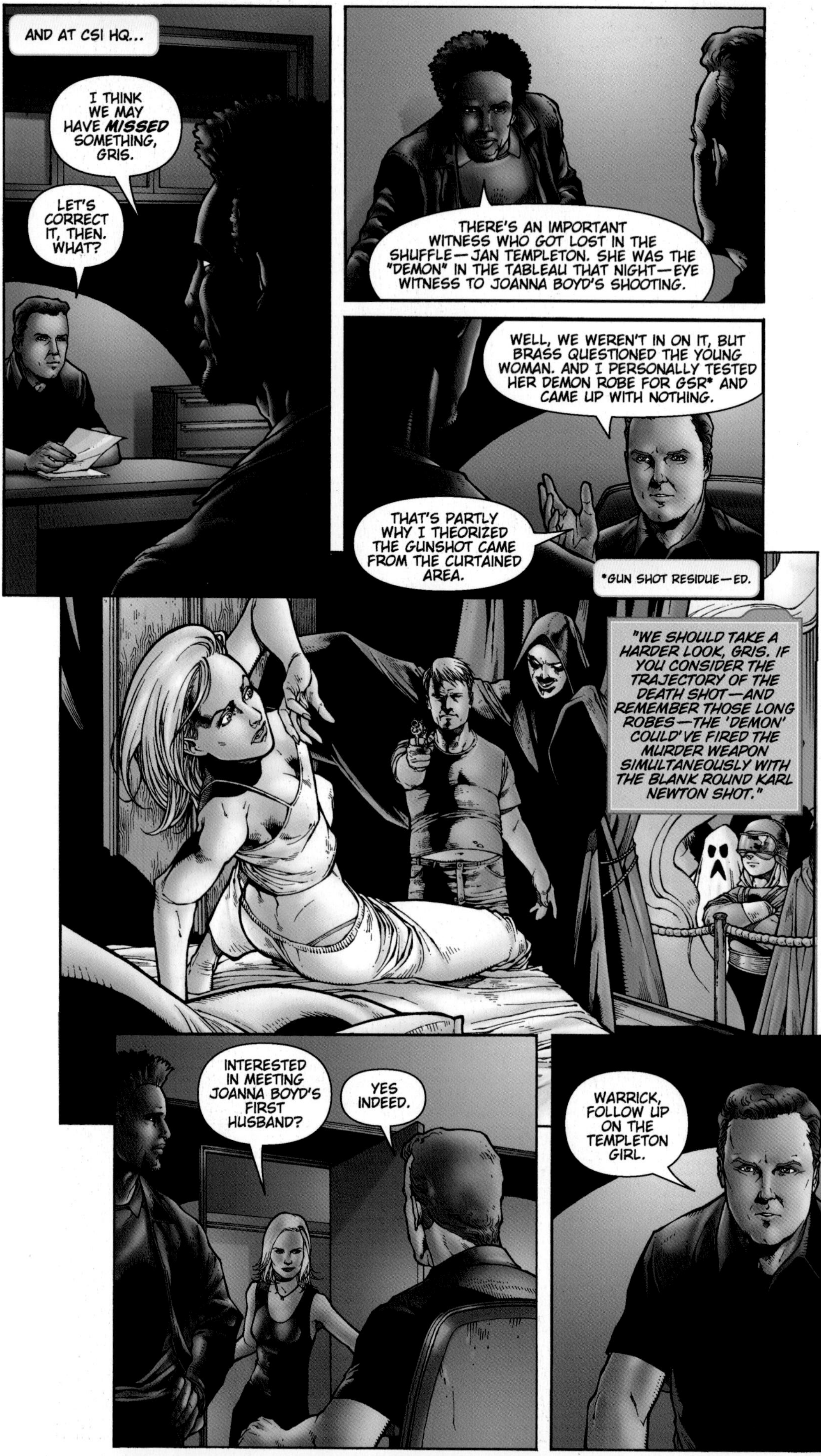
AND AT CSI HQ...
I THINK WE MAY HAVE MISSED SOMETHING, GRIS.
LET'S CORRECT IT, THEN. WHAT?
THERE'S AN IMPORTANT WITNESS WHO GOT LOST IN THE SHUFFLE—JAN TEMPLETON. SHE WAS THE "DEMON" IN THE TABLEAU THAT NIGHT—EYE WITNESS TO JOANNA BOYD'S SHOOTING.
WELL, WE WEREN'T IN ON IT, BUT BRASS QUESTIONED THE YOUNG WOMAN. AND I PERSONALLY TESTED HER DEMON ROBE FOR GSR* AND CAME UP WITH NOTHING.
THAT'S PARTLY WHY I THEORIZED THE GUNSHOT CAME FROM THE CURTAINED AREA.
*GUN SHOT RESIDUE—ED.
"WE SHOULD TAKE A HARDER LOOK, GRIS. IF YOU CONSIDER THE TRAJECTORY OF THE DEATH SHOT—AND REMEMBER THOSE LONG ROBES—THE 'DEMON' COULD'VE FIRED THE MURDER WEAPON SIMULTANEOUSLY WITH THE BLANK ROUND KARL NEWTON SHOT."
INTERESTED IN MEETING JOANNA BOYD'S FIRST HUSBAND?
YES INDEED.
WARRICK, FOLLOW UP ON THE TEMPLETON GIRL.

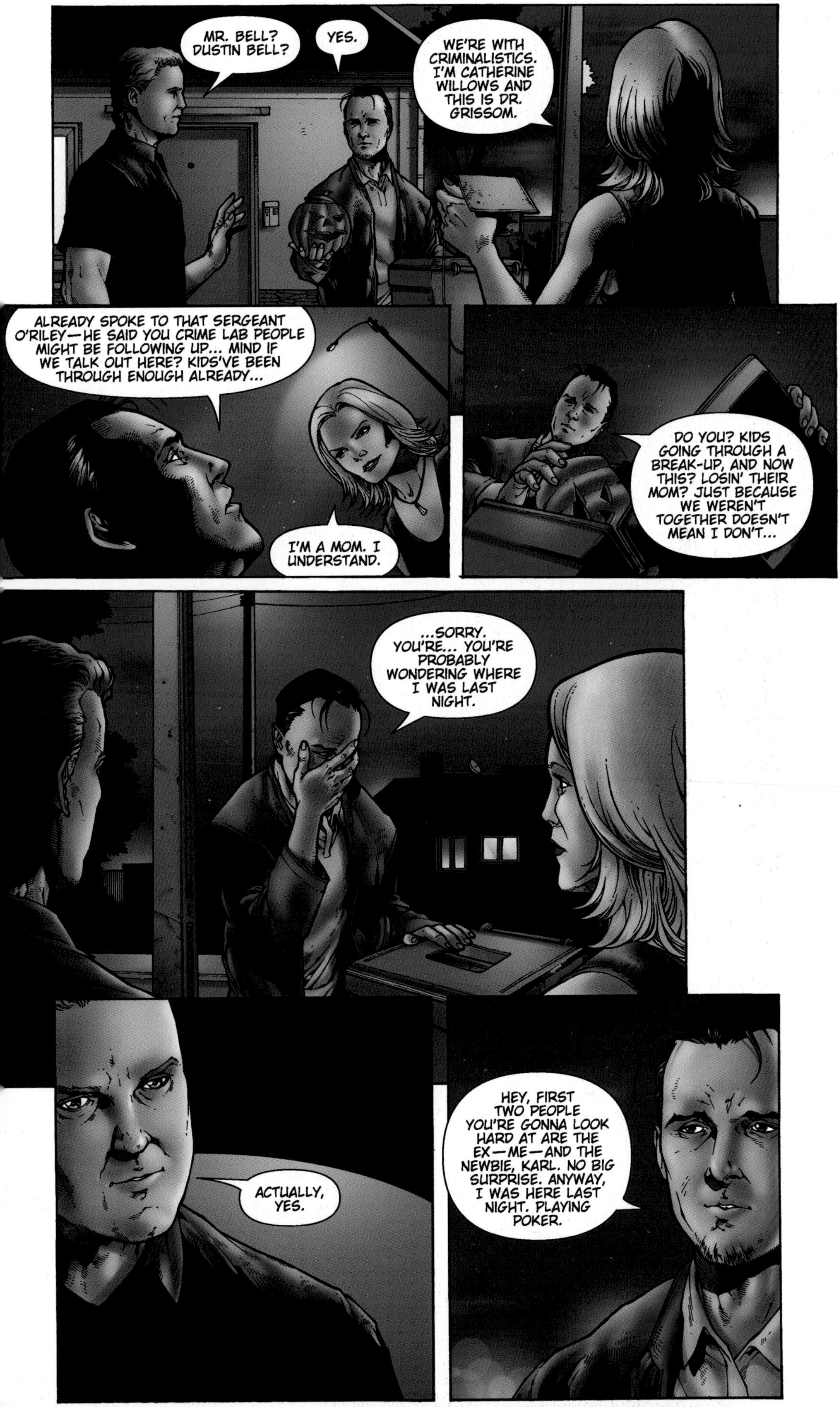
MR. BELL? DUSTIN BELL?
YES.
WE'RE WITH CRIMINALISTICS. I'M CATHERINE WILLOWS AND THIS IS DR. GRISSOM.
ALREADY SPOKE TO THAT SERGEANT O'RILEY—HE SAID YOU CRIME LAB PEOPLE MIGHT BE FOLLOWING UP... MIND IF WE TALK OUT HERE? KIDS'VE BEEN THROUGH ENOUGH ALREADY...
I'M A MOM. I UNDERSTAND.
DO YOU? KIDS GOING THROUGH A BREAK-UP, AND NOW THIS? LOSIN' THEIR MOM? JUST BECAUSE WE WEREN'T TOGETHER DOESN'T MEAN I DON'T...
...SORRY. YOU'RE... YOU'RE PROBABLY WONDERING WHERE I WAS LAST NIGHT.
ACTUALLY, YES.
HEY, FIRST TWO PEOPLE YOU'RE GONNA LOOK HARD AT ARE THE EX—ME—AND THE NEWBIE, KARL. NO BIG SURPRISE. ANYWAY, I WAS HERE LAST NIGHT. PLAYING POKER.

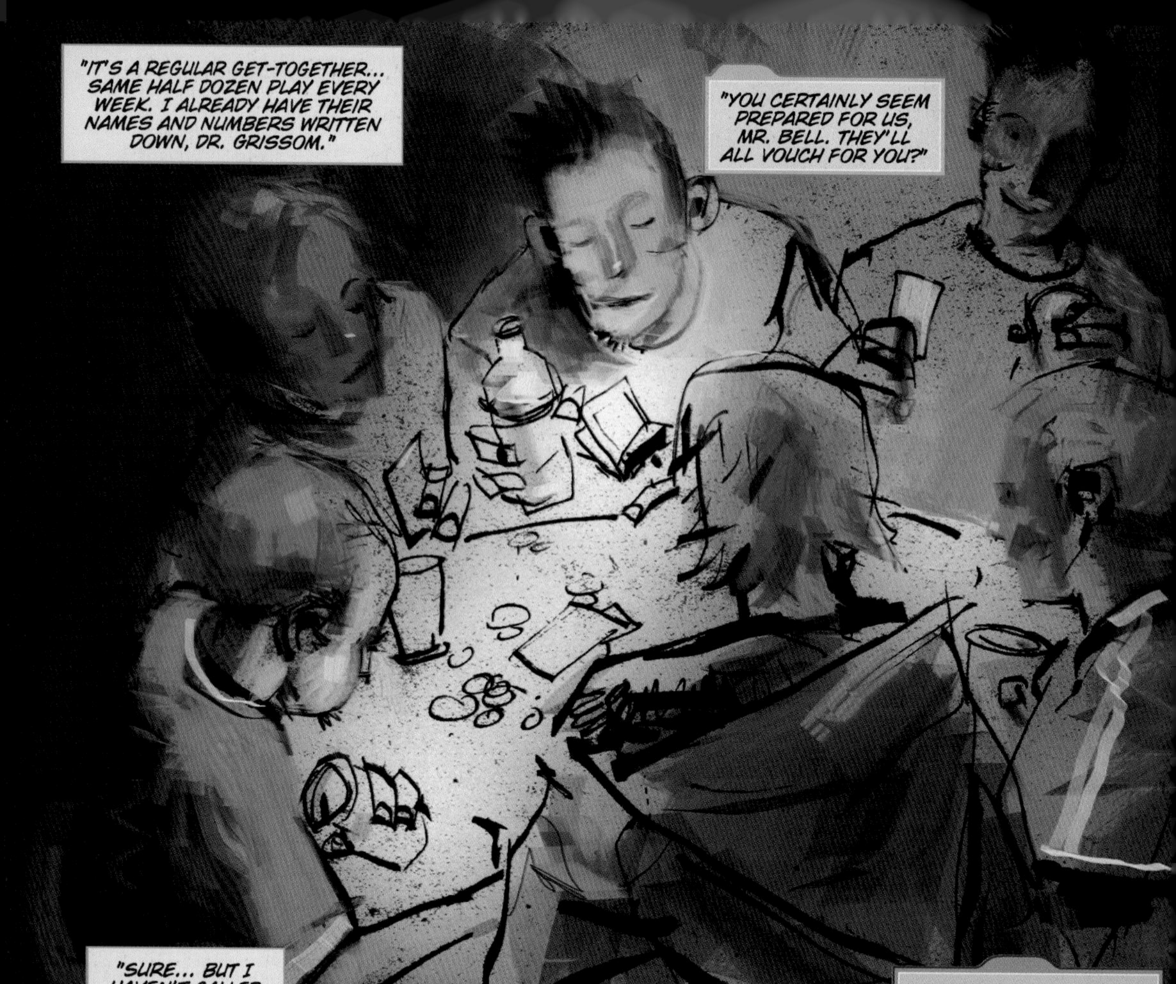
"IT'S A REGULAR GET-TOGETHER... SAME HALF DOZEN PLAY EVERY WEEK. I ALREADY HAVE THEIR NAMES AND NUMBERS WRITTEN DOWN, DR. GRISSOM."
"YOU CERTAINLY SEEM PREPARED FOR US, MR. BELL. THEY'LL ALL VOUCH FOR YOU?"
"SURE... BUT I HAVEN'T CALLED AND PRIMED THEM OR ANYTHING."
"WHAT TIME DID YOUR GUESTS START ARRIVING? AND DO YOU REMEMBER WHEN THEY LEFT?"

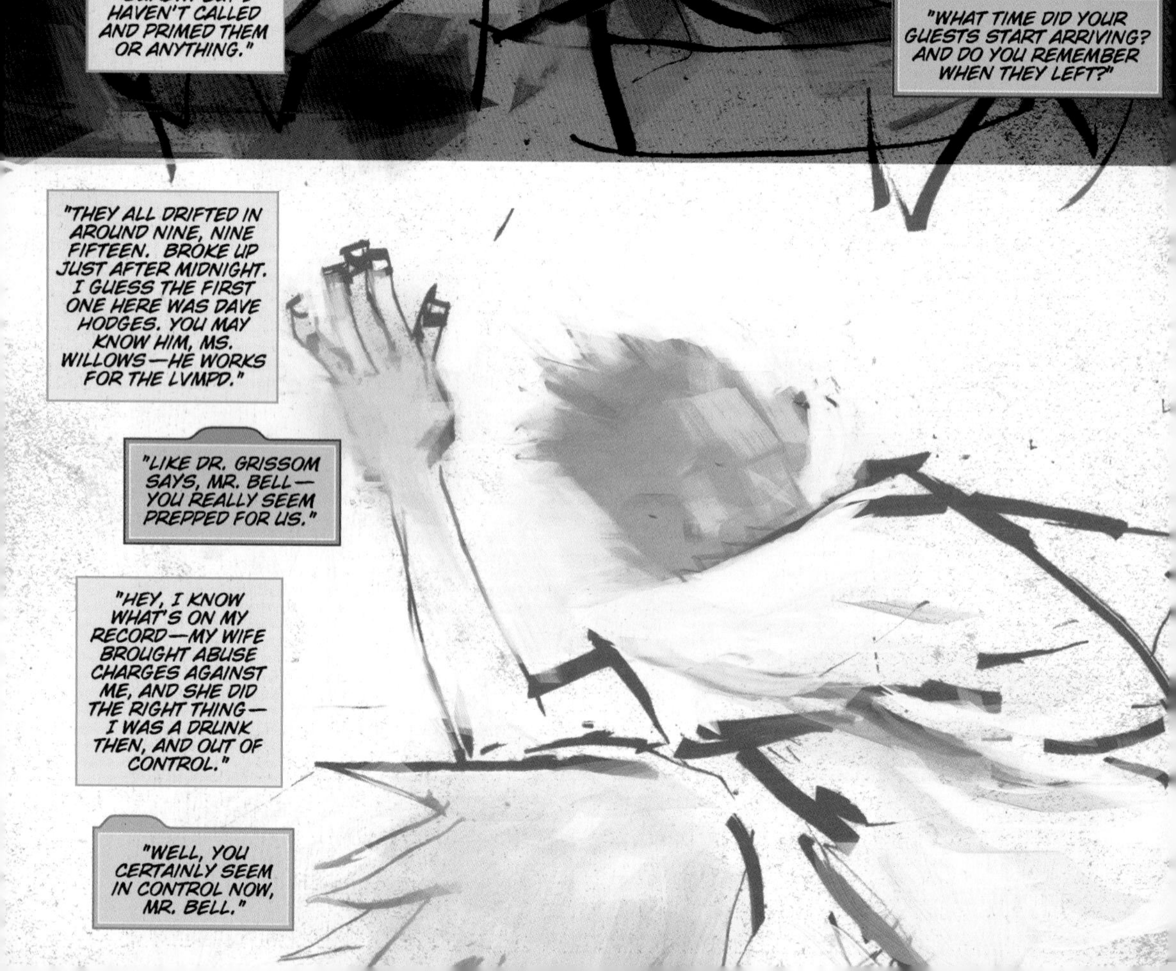
"THEY ALL DRIFTED IN AROUND NINE, NINE FIFTEEN. BROKE UP JUST AFTER MIDNIGHT. I GUESS THE FIRST ONE HERE WAS DAVE HODGES. YOU MAY KNOW HIM, MS. WILLOWS—HE WORKS FOR THE LVMPD."
"LIKE DR. GRISSOM SAYS, MR. BELL—YOU REALLY SEEM PREPPED FOR US."
"HEY, I KNOW WHAT'S ON MY RECORD—MY WIFE BROUGHT ABUSE CHARGES AGAINST ME, AND SHE DID THE RIGHT THING—I WAS A DRUNK THEN, AND OUT OF CONTROL."
"WELL, YOU CERTAINLY SEEM IN CONTROL NOW, MR. BELL."

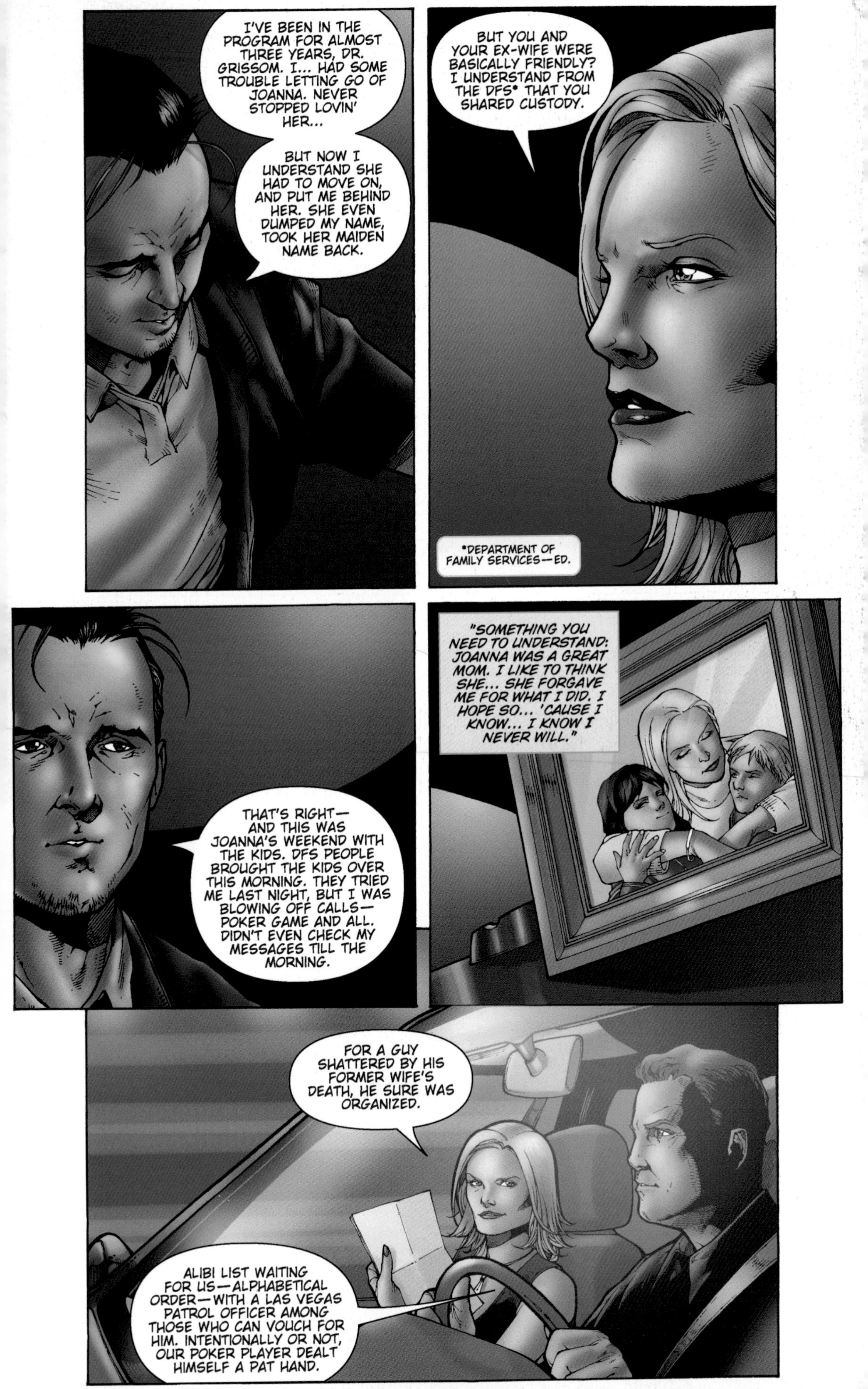
I'VE BEEN IN THE PROGRAM FOR ALMOST THREE YEARS, DR. GRISSOM. I... HAD SOME TROUBLE LETTING GO OF JOANNA. NEVER STOPPED LOVIN' HER...
BUT NOW I UNDERSTAND SHE HAD TO MOVE ON, AND PUT ME BEHIND HER. SHE EVEN DUMPED MY NAME, TOOK HER MAIDEN NAME BACK.
BUT YOU AND YOUR EX-WIFE WERE BASICALLY FRIENDLY? I UNDERSTAND FROM THE DFS* THAT YOU SHARED CUSTODY.
*DEPARTMENT OF FAMILY SERVICES—ED.
THAT'S RIGHT— AND THIS WAS JOANNA'S WEEKEND WITH THE KIDS. DFS PEOPLE BROUGHT THE KIDS OVER THIS MORNING. THEY TRIED ME LAST NIGHT, BUT I WAS BLOWING OFF CALLS— POKER GAME AND ALL. DIDN'T EVEN CHECK MY MESSAGES TILL THE MORNING.
"SOMETHING YOU NEED TO UNDERSTAND: JOANNA WAS A GREAT MOM. I LIKE TO THINK SHE... SHE FORGAVE ME FOR WHAT I DID. I HOPE SO... 'CAUSE I KNOW... I KNOW I NEVER WILL."
FOR A GUY SHATTERED BY HIS FORMER WIFE'S DEATH, HE SURE WAS ORGANIZED.
ALIBI LIST WAITING FOR US—ALPHABETICAL ORDER—WITH A LAS VEGAS PATROL OFFICER AMONG THOSE WHO CAN VOUCH FOR HIM. INTENTIONALLY OR NOT, OUR POKER PLAYER DEALT HIMSELF A PAT HAND.

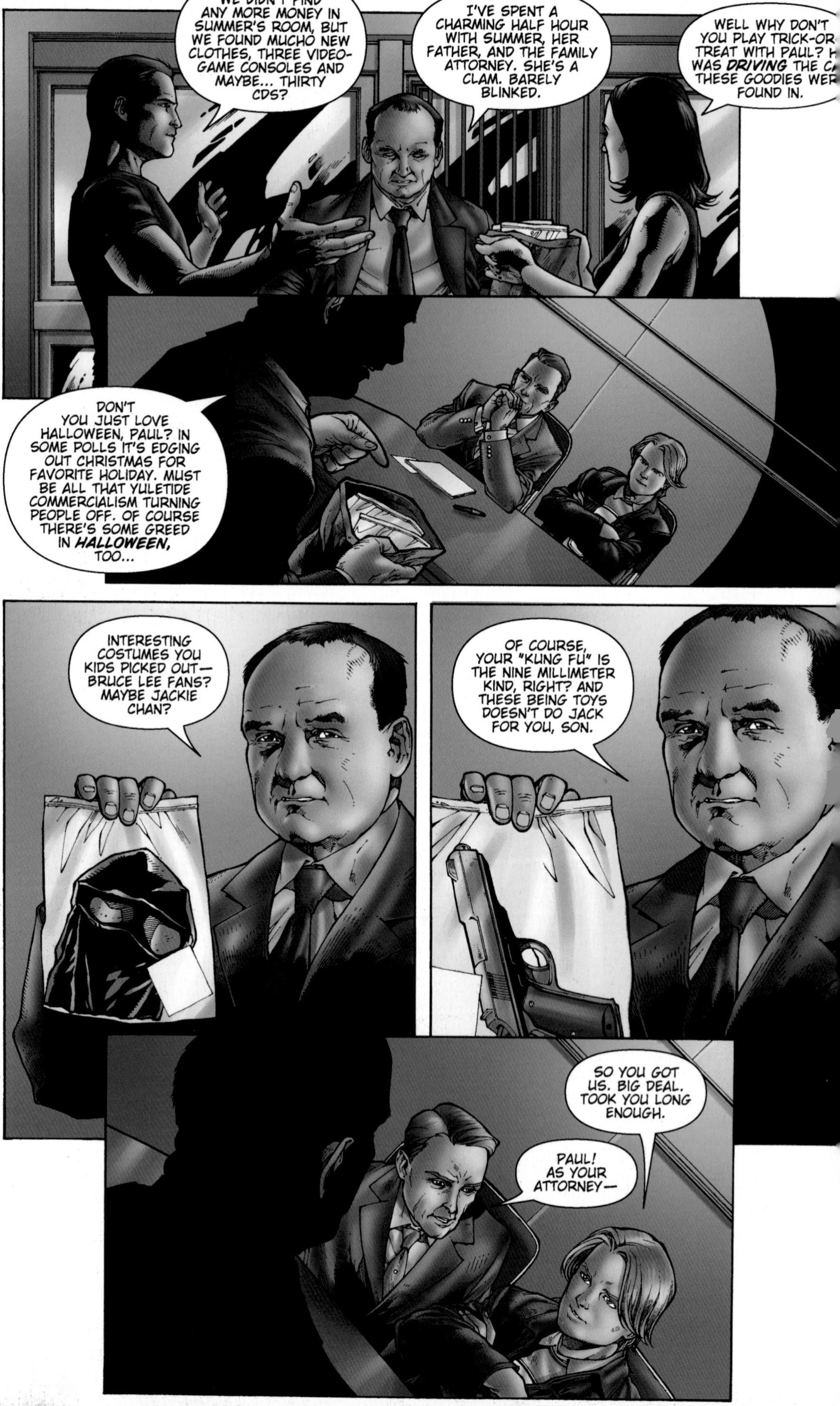
WE DIDN'T FIND ANY MORE MONEY IN SUMMER'S ROOM, BUT WE FOUND MUCHO NEW CLOTHES, THREE VIDEO-GAME CONSOLES AND MAYBE... THIRTY CDS?
I'VE SPENT A CHARMING HALF HOUR WITH SUMMER, HER FATHER, AND THE FAMILY ATTORNEY. SHE'S A CLAM. BARELY BLINKED.
WELL WHY DON'T YOU PLAY TRICK-OR-TREAT WITH PAUL? H WAS DRIVING THE C THESE GOODIES WER FOUND IN.
DON'T YOU JUST LOVE HALLOWEEN, PAUL? IN SOME POLLS IT'S EDGING OUT CHRISTMAS FOR FAVORITE HOLIDAY. MUST BE ALL THAT YULETIDE COMMERCIALISM TURNING PEOPLE OFF. OF COURSE THERE'S SOME GREED IN HALLOWEEN, TOO...
INTERESTING COSTUMES YOU KIDS PICKED OUT— BRUCE LEE FANS? MAYBE JACKIE CHAN?
OF COURSE, YOUR "KUNG FU" IS THE NINE MILLIMETER KIND, RIGHT? AND THESE BEING TOYS DOESN'T DO JACK FOR YOU, SON.
SO YOU GOT US. BIG DEAL. TOOK YOU LONG ENOUGH.
PAUL! AS YOUR ATTORNEY—

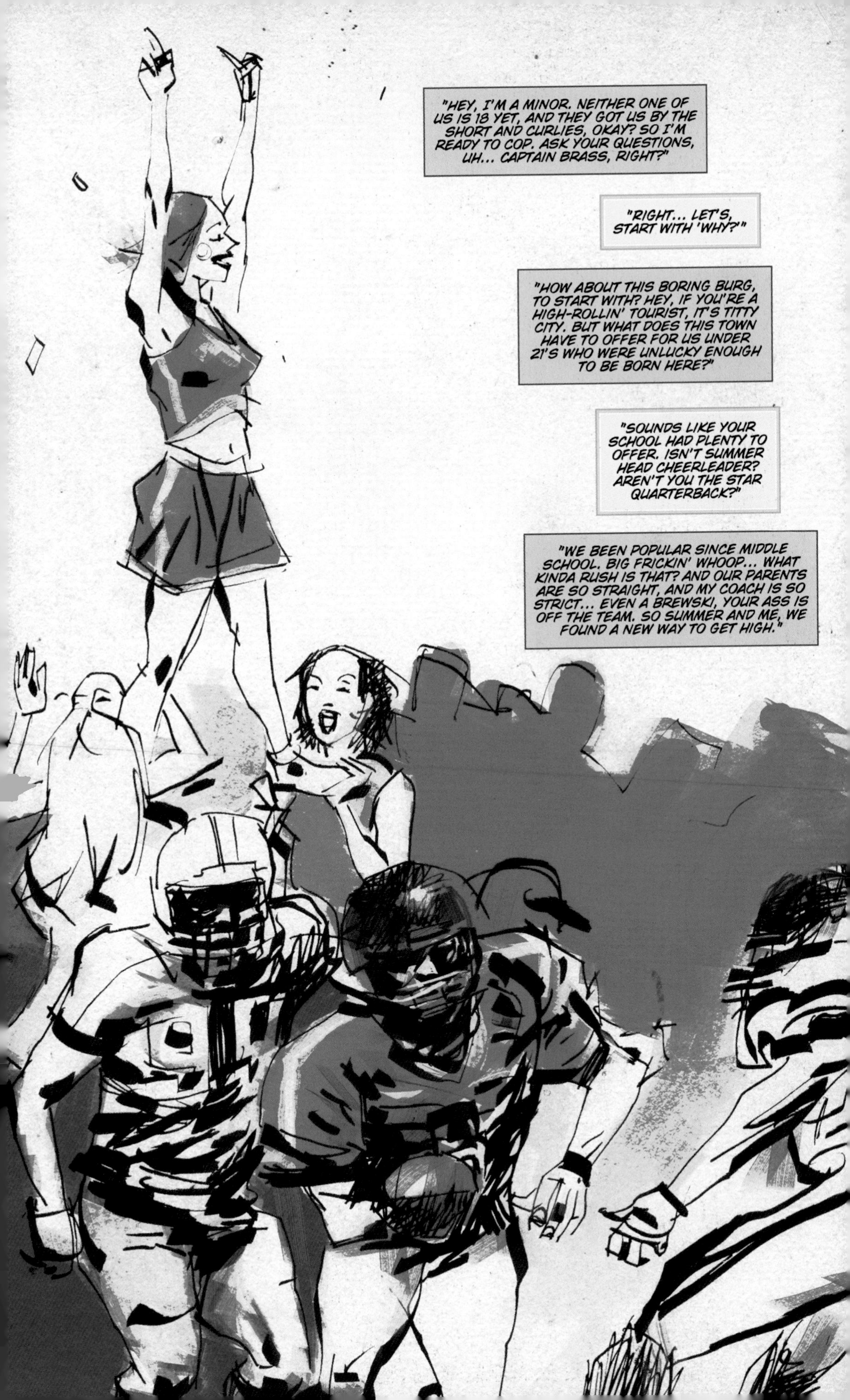
"HEY, I'M A MINOR. NEITHER ONE OF US IS 18 YET, AND THEY GOT US BY THE SHORT AND CURLIES, OKAY? SO I'M READY TO COP. ASK YOUR QUESTIONS, UH... CAPTAIN BRASS, RIGHT?"
"RIGHT... LET'S, START WITH 'WHY?'"
"HOW ABOUT THIS BORING BURG, TO START WITH? HEY, IF YOU'RE A HIGH-ROLLIN' TOURIST, IT'S TITTY CITY. BUT WHAT DOES THIS TOWN HAVE TO OFFER FOR US UNDER 21'S WHO WERE UNLUCKY ENOUGH TO BE BORN HERE?"
"SOUNDS LIKE YOUR SCHOOL HAD PLENTY TO OFFER. ISN'T SUMMER HEAD CHEERLEADER? AREN'T YOU THE STAR QUARTERBACK?"
"WE BEEN POPULAR SINCE MIDDLE SCHOOL. BIG FRICKIN' WHOOP... WHAT KINDA RUSH IS THAT? AND OUR PARENTS ARE SO STRAIGHT, AND MY COACH IS SO STRICT... EVEN A BREWSKI, YOUR ASS IS OFF THE TEAM. SO SUMMER AND ME, WE FOUND A NEW WAY TO GET HIGH."

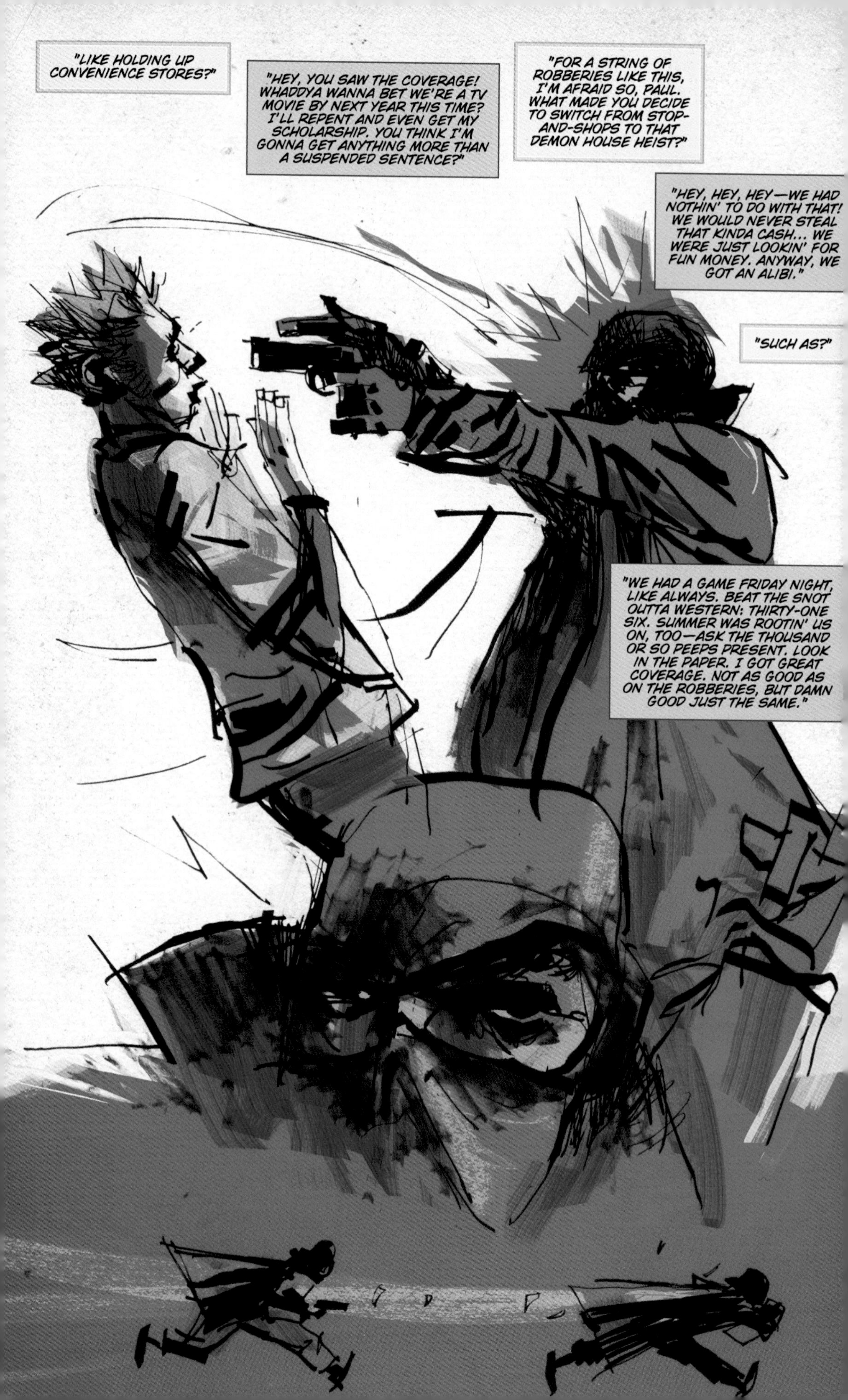
"LIKE HOLDING UP CONVENIENCE STORES?"
"HEY, YOU SAW THE COVERAGE! WHADDYA WANNA BET WE'RE A TV MOVIE BY NEXT YEAR THIS TIME? I'LL REPENT AND EVEN GET MY SCHOLARSHIP. YOU THINK I'M GONNA GET ANYTHING MORE THAN A SUSPENDED SENTENCE?"
"FOR A STRING OF ROBBERIES LIKE THIS, I'M AFRAID SO, PAUL. WHAT MADE YOU DECIDE TO SWITCH FROM STOP-AND-SHOPS TO THAT DEMON HOUSE HEIST?"
"HEY, HEY, HEY—WE HAD NOTHIN' TO DO WITH THAT! WE WOULD NEVER STEAL THAT KINDA CASH... WE WERE JUST LOOKIN' FOR FUN MONEY. ANYWAY, WE GOT AN ALIBI."
"SUCH AS?"
"WE HAD A GAME FRIDAY NIGHT, LIKE ALWAYS. BEAT THE SNOT OUTTA WESTERN: THIRTY-ONE SIX. SUMMER WAS ROOTIN' US ON, TOO—ASK THE THOUSAND OR SO PEEPS PRESENT. LOOK IN THE PAPER. I GOT GREAT COVERAGE. NOT AS GOOD AS ON THE ROBBERIES, BUT DAMN GOOD JUST THE SAME."

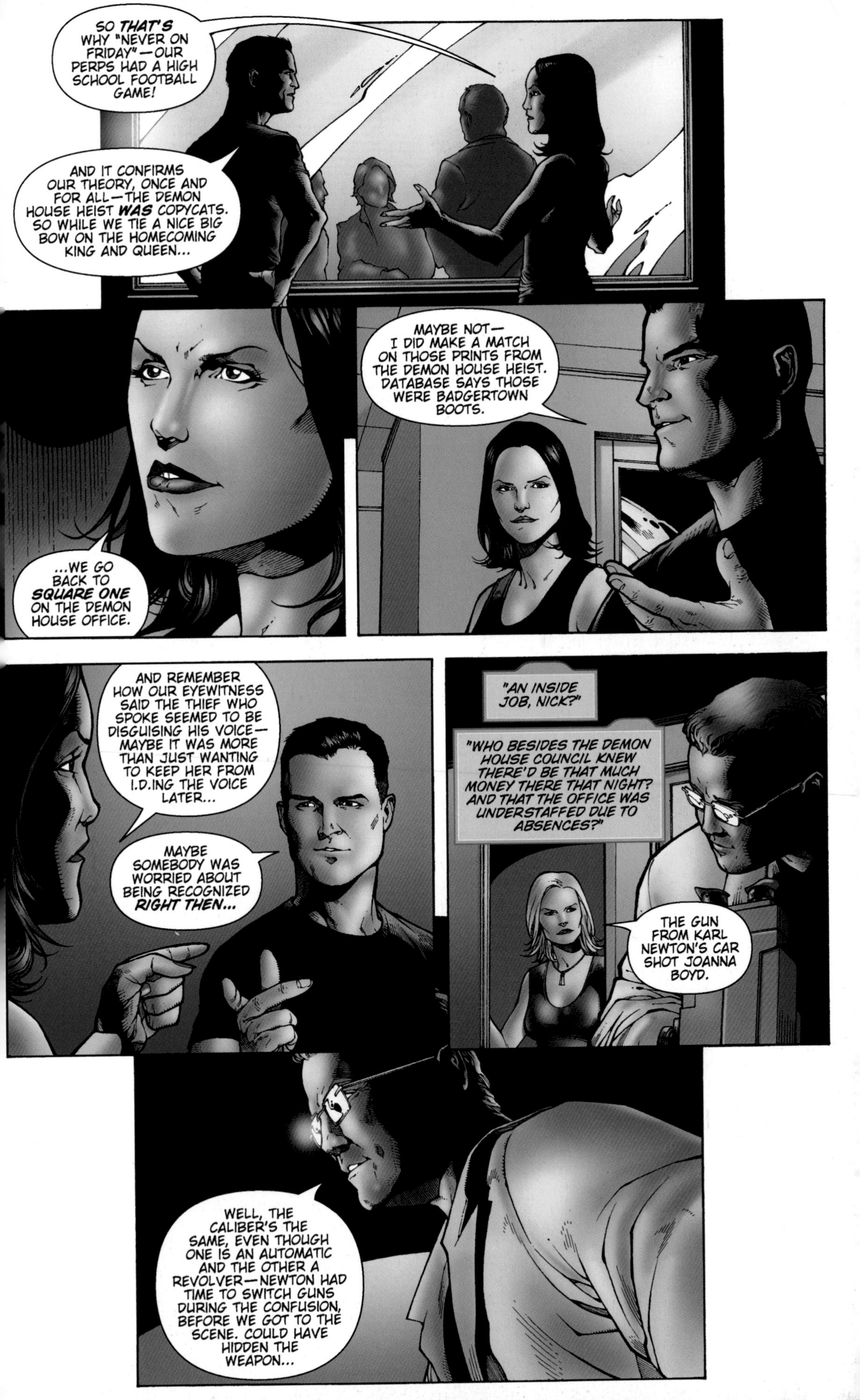
SO *THAT'S* WHY "NEVER ON FRIDAY"—OUR PERPS HAD A HIGH SCHOOL FOOTBALL GAME!
AND IT CONFIRMS OUR THEORY, ONCE AND FOR ALL—THE DEMON HOUSE HEIST *WAS* COPYCATS. SO WHILE WE TIE A NICE BIG BOW ON THE HOMECOMING KING AND QUEEN...
...WE GO BACK TO *SQUARE ONE* ON THE DEMON HOUSE OFFICE.
MAYBE NOT—I DID MAKE A MATCH ON THOSE PRINTS FROM THE DEMON HOUSE HEIST. DATABASE SAYS THOSE WERE BADGERTOWN BOOTS.
AND REMEMBER HOW OUR EYEWITNESS SAID THE THIEF WHO SPOKE SEEMED TO BE DISGUISING HIS VOICE—MAYBE IT WAS MORE THAN JUST WANTING TO KEEP HER FROM I.D.ING THE VOICE LATER...
MAYBE SOMEBODY WAS WORRIED ABOUT BEING RECOGNIZED *RIGHT THEN...*
"AN INSIDE JOB, NICK?"
"WHO BESIDES THE DEMON HOUSE COUNCIL KNEW THERE'D BE THAT MUCH MONEY THERE THAT NIGHT? AND THAT THE OFFICE WAS UNDERSTAFFED DUE TO ABSENCES?"
THE GUN FROM KARL NEWTON'S CAR SHOT JOANNA BOYD.
WELL, THE CALIBER'S THE SAME, EVEN THOUGH ONE IS AN AUTOMATIC AND THE OTHER A REVOLVER—NEWTON HAD TIME TO SWITCH GUNS DURING THE CONFUSION, BEFORE WE GOT TO THE SCENE. COULD HAVE HIDDEN THE WEAPON...

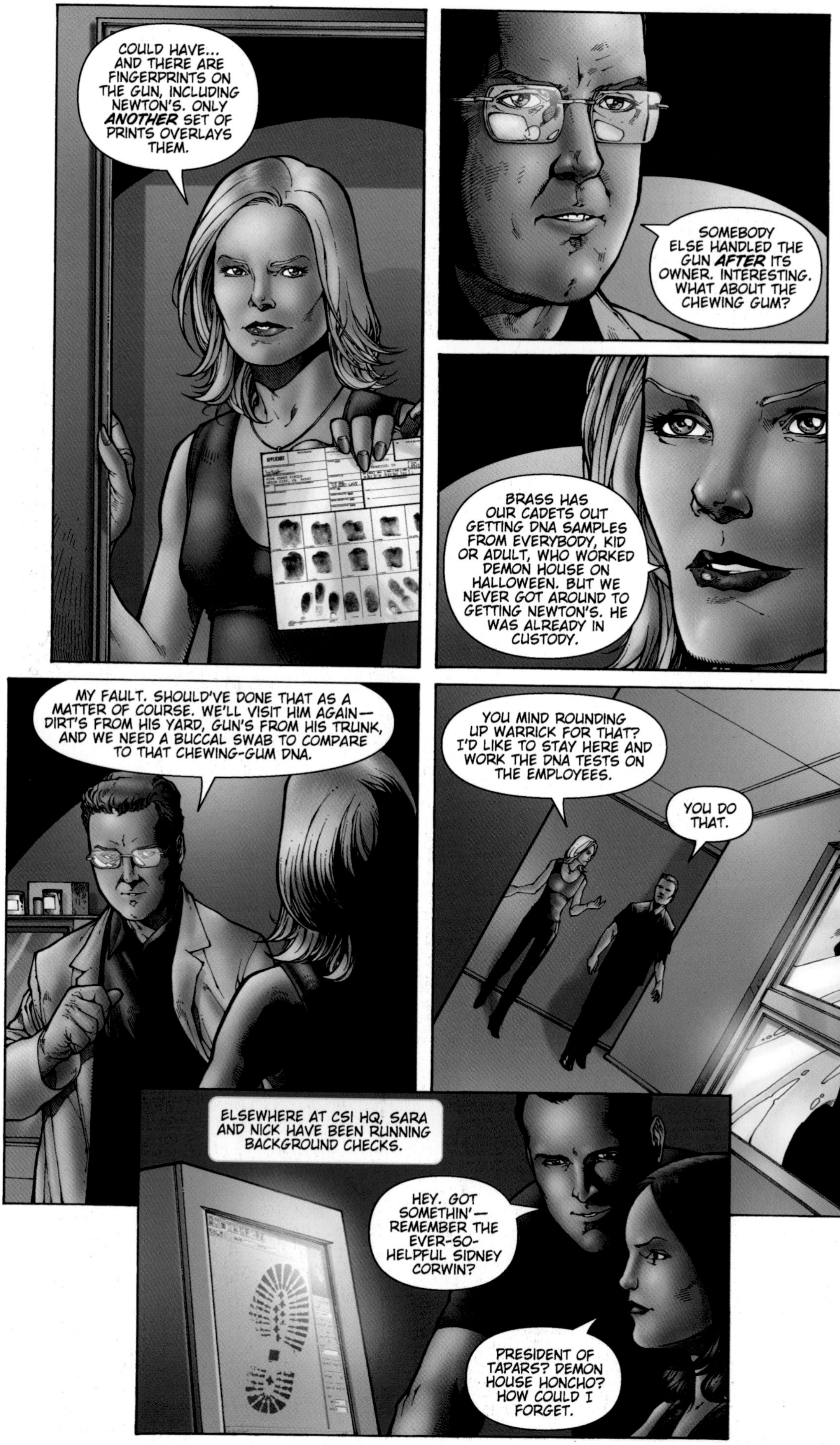

COULD HAVE... AND THERE ARE FINGERPRINTS ON THE GUN, INCLUDING NEWTON'S. ONLY ANOTHER SET OF PRINTS OVERLAYS THEM.
SOMEBODY ELSE HANDLED THE GUN AFTER ITS OWNER. INTERESTING. WHAT ABOUT THE CHEWING GUM?
BRASS HAS OUR CADETS OUT GETTING DNA SAMPLES FROM EVERYBODY, KID OR ADULT, WHO WORKED DEMON HOUSE ON HALLOWEEN. BUT WE NEVER GOT AROUND TO GETTING NEWTON'S. HE WAS ALREADY IN CUSTODY.
MY FAULT. SHOULD'VE DONE THAT AS A MATTER OF COURSE. WE'LL VISIT HIM AGAIN— DIRT'S FROM HIS YARD, GUN'S FROM HIS TRUNK, AND WE NEED A BUCCAL SWAB TO COMPARE TO THAT CHEWING-GUM DNA.
YOU MIND ROUNDING UP WARRICK FOR THAT? I'D LIKE TO STAY HERE AND WORK THE DNA TESTS ON THE EMPLOYEES.
YOU DO THAT.
ELSEWHERE AT CSI HQ, SARA AND NICK HAVE BEEN RUNNING BACKGROUND CHECKS.
HEY. GOT SOMETHIN'— REMEMBER THE EVER-SO-HELPFUL SIDNEY CORWIN?
PRESIDENT OF TAPARS? DEMON HOUSE HONCHO? HOW COULD I FORGET.

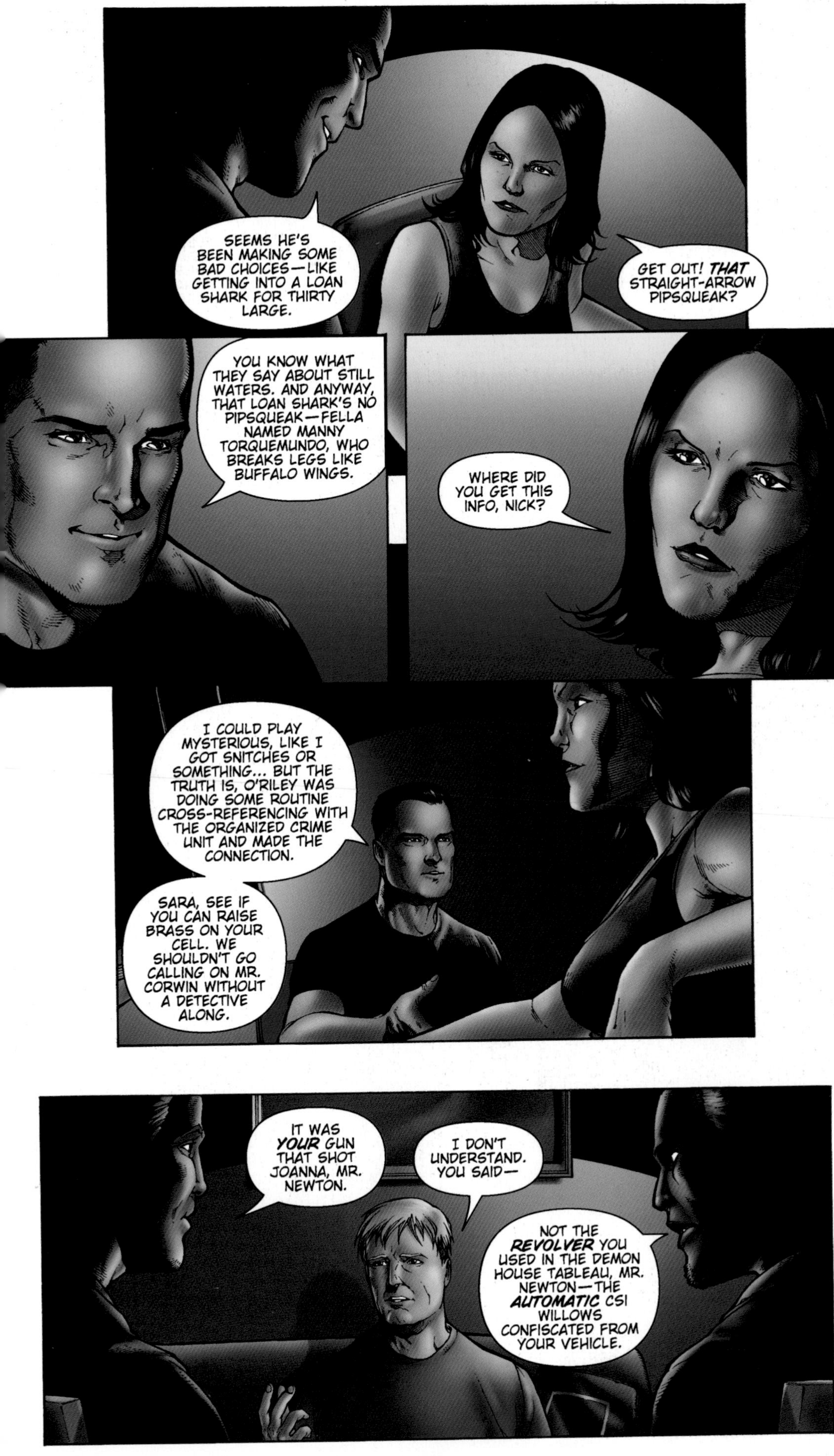
SEEMS HE'S BEEN MAKING SOME BAD CHOICES—LIKE GETTING INTO A LOAN SHARK FOR THIRTY LARGE.
GET OUT! *THAT* STRAIGHT-ARROW PIPSQUEAK?
YOU KNOW WHAT THEY SAY ABOUT STILL WATERS. AND ANYWAY, THAT LOAN SHARK'S NO PIPSQUEAK—FELLA NAMED MANNY TORQUEMUNDO, WHO BREAKS LEGS LIKE BUFFALO WINGS.
WHERE DID YOU GET THIS INFO, NICK?
I COULD PLAY MYSTERIOUS, LIKE I GOT SNITCHES OR SOMETHING... BUT THE TRUTH IS, O'RILEY WAS DOING SOME ROUTINE CROSS-REFERENCING WITH THE ORGANIZED CRIME UNIT AND MADE THE CONNECTION.
SARA, SEE IF YOU CAN RAISE BRASS ON YOUR CELL. WE SHOULDN'T GO CALLING ON MR. CORWIN WITHOUT A DETECTIVE ALONG.
IT WAS *YOUR* GUN THAT SHOT JOANNA, MR. NEWTON.
I DON'T UNDERSTAND. YOU SAID—
NOT THE *REVOLVER* YOU USED IN THE DEMON HOUSE TABLEAU, MR. NEWTON—THE *AUTOMATIC* CSI WILLOWS CONFISCATED FROM YOUR VEHICLE.

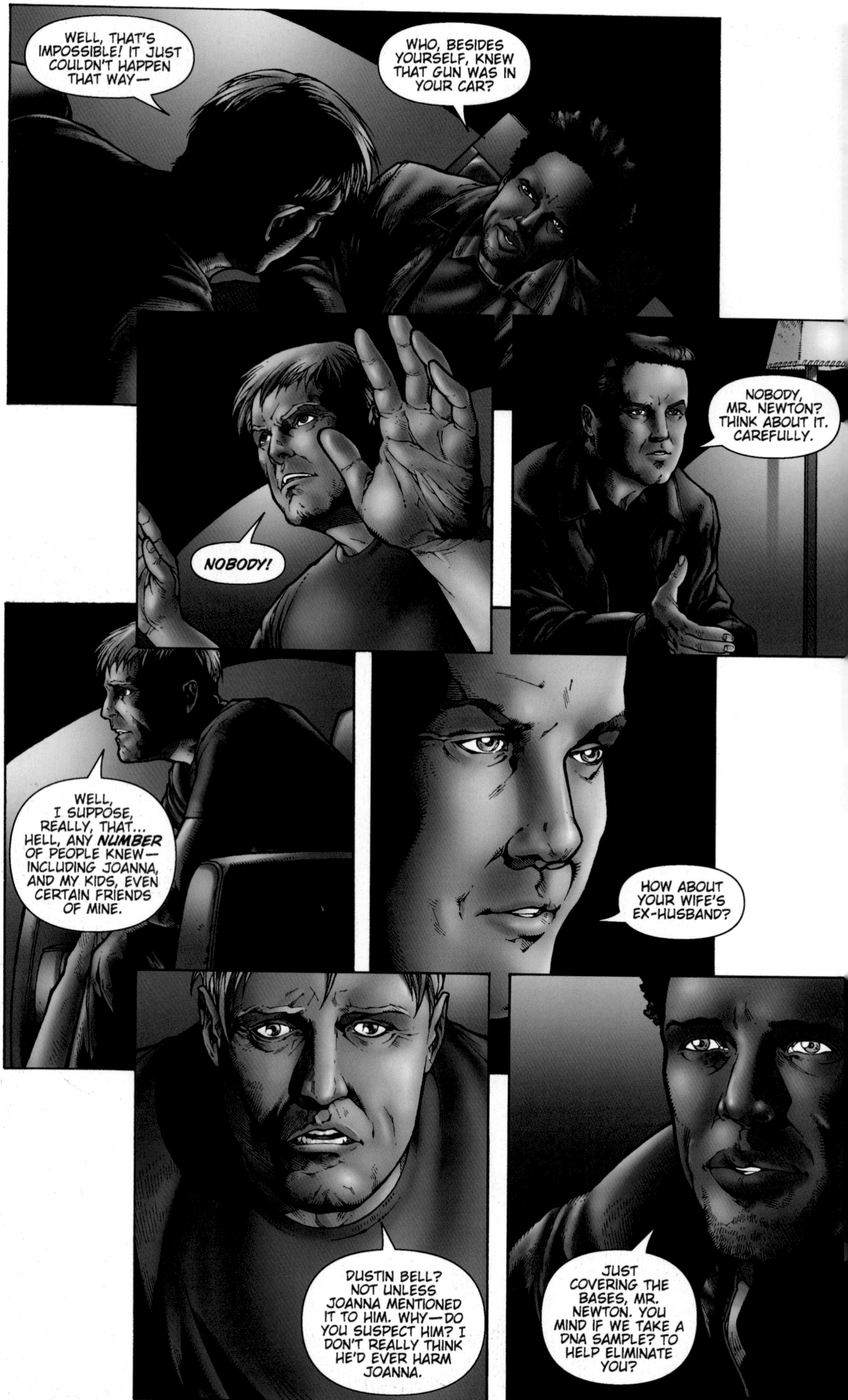

WELL, THAT'S IMPOSSIBLE! IT JUST COULDN'T HAPPEN THAT WAY—
WHO, BESIDES YOURSELF, KNEW THAT GUN WAS IN YOUR CAR?
NOBODY!
NOBODY, MR. NEWTON? THINK ABOUT IT. CAREFULLY.
WELL, I SUPPOSE, REALLY, THAT... HELL, ANY NUMBER OF PEOPLE KNEW— INCLUDING JOANNA, AND MY KIDS, EVEN CERTAIN FRIENDS OF MINE.
HOW ABOUT YOUR WIFE'S EX-HUSBAND?
DUSTIN BELL? NOT UNLESS JOANNA MENTIONED IT TO HIM. WHY—DO YOU SUSPECT HIM? I DON'T REALLY THINK HE'D EVER HARM JOANNA.
JUST COVERING THE BASES, MR. NEWTON. YOU MIND IF WE TAKE A DNA SAMPLE? TO HELP ELIMINATE YOU?

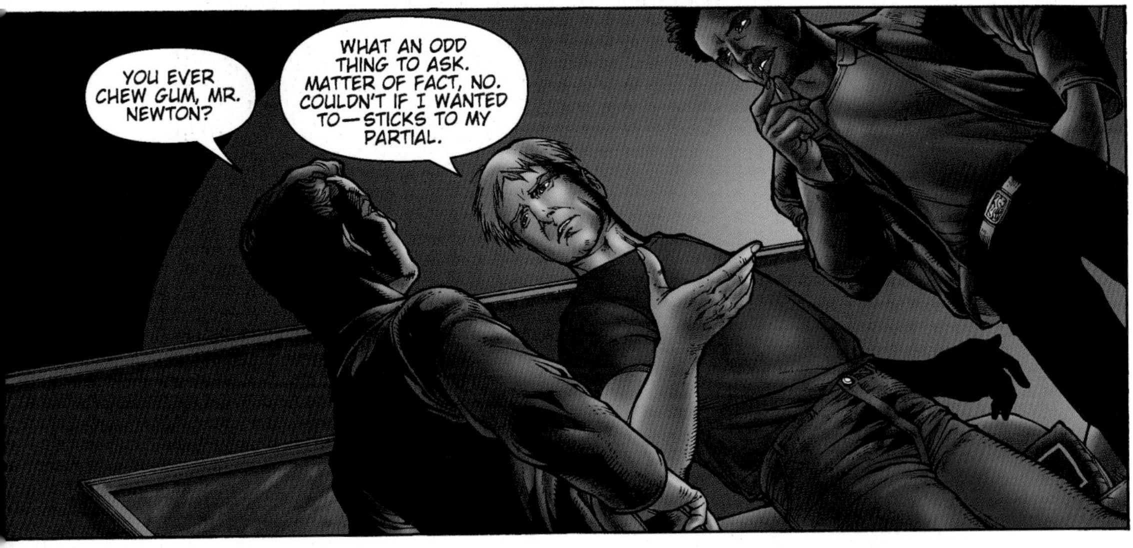
YOU EVER CHEW GUM, MR. NEWTON?
WHAT AN ODD THING TO ASK. MATTER OF FACT, NO. COULDN'T IF I WANTED TO—STICKS TO MY PARTIAL.

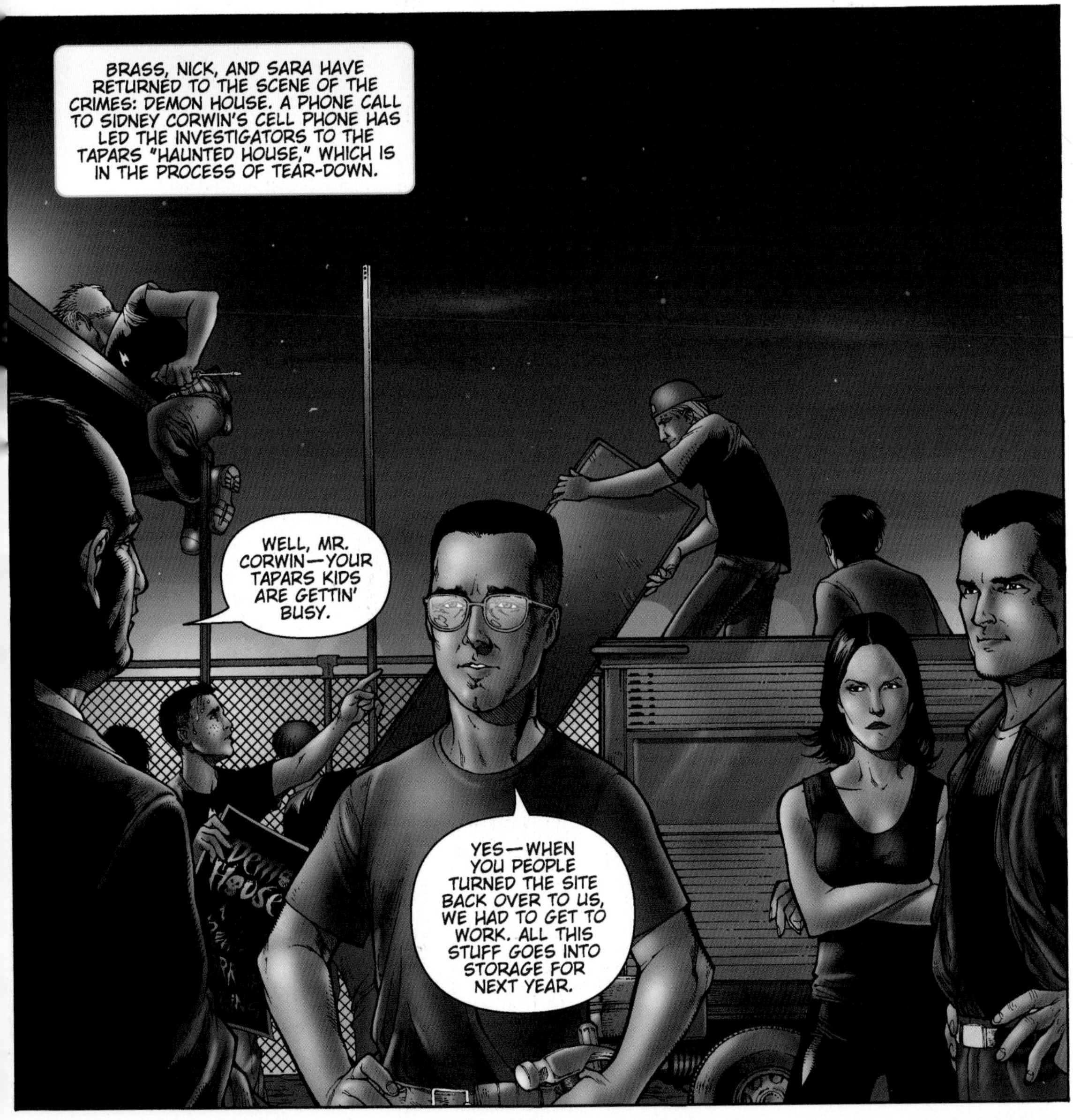
BRASS, NICK, AND SARA HAVE RETURNED TO THE SCENE OF THE CRIMES: DEMON HOUSE. A PHONE CALL TO SIDNEY CORWIN'S CELL PHONE HAS LED THE INVESTIGATORS TO THE TAPARS "HAUNTED HOUSE," WHICH IS IN THE PROCESS OF TEAR-DOWN.
WELL, MR. CORWIN—YOUR TAPARS KIDS ARE GETTIN' BUSY.
YES—WHEN YOU PEOPLE TURNED THE SITE BACK OVER TO US, WE HAD TO GET TO WORK. ALL THIS STUFF GOES INTO STORAGE FOR NEXT YEAR.

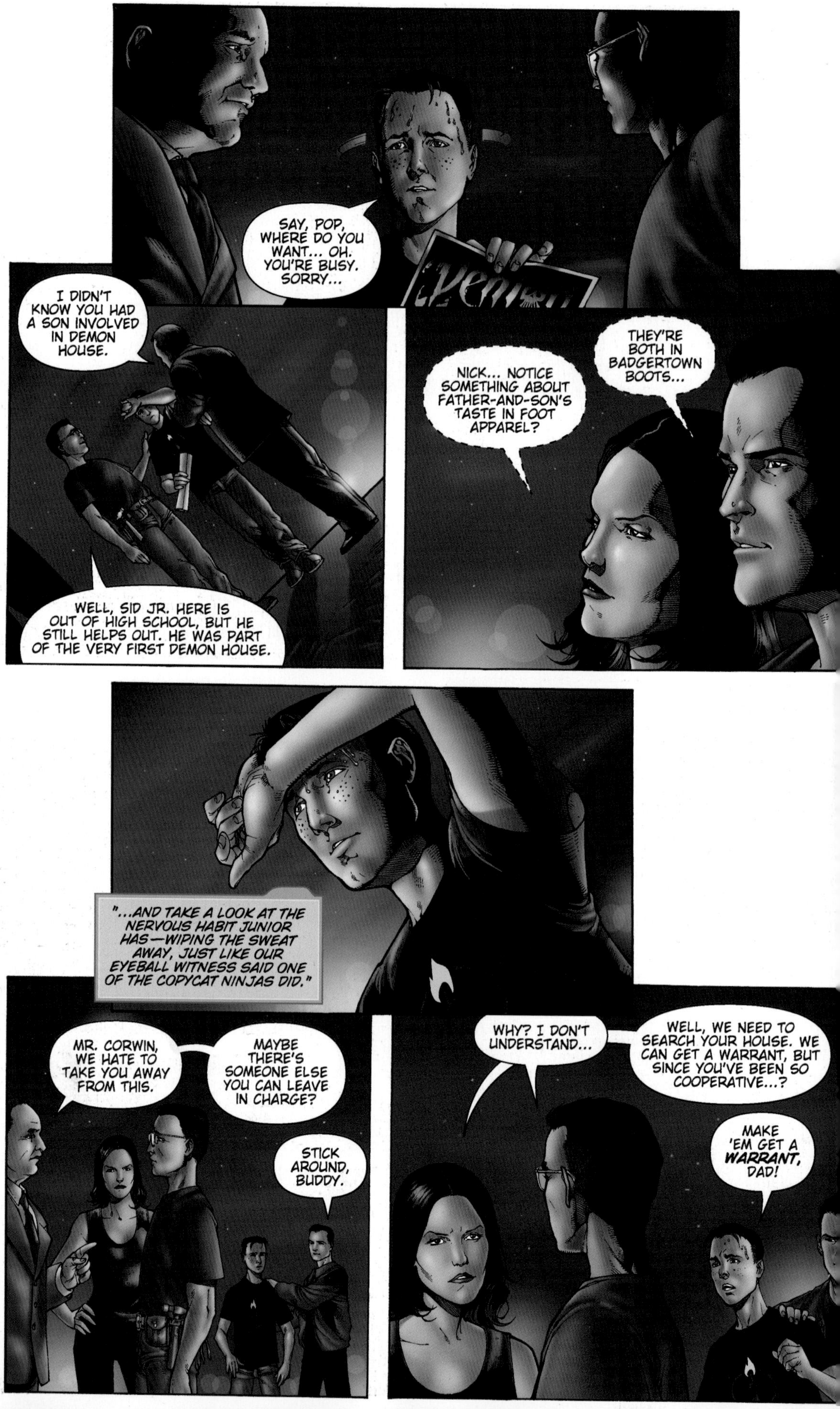
SAY, POP, WHERE DO YOU WANT... OH. YOU'RE BUSY. SORRY...
I DIDN'T KNOW YOU HAD A SON INVOLVED IN DEMON HOUSE.
WELL, SID JR. HERE IS OUT OF HIGH SCHOOL, BUT HE STILL HELPS OUT. HE WAS PART OF THE VERY FIRST DEMON HOUSE.
NICK... NOTICE SOMETHING ABOUT FATHER-AND-SON'S TASTE IN FOOT APPAREL?
THEY'RE BOTH IN BADGERTOWN BOOTS...
"...AND TAKE A LOOK AT THE NERVOUS HABIT JUNIOR HAS—WIPING THE SWEAT AWAY, JUST LIKE OUR EYEBALL WITNESS SAID ONE OF THE COPYCAT NINJAS DID."
MR. CORWIN, WE HATE TO TAKE YOU AWAY FROM THIS.
MAYBE THERE'S SOMEONE ELSE YOU CAN LEAVE IN CHARGE?
STICK AROUND, BUDDY.
WHY? I DON'T UNDERSTAND...
WELL, WE NEED TO SEARCH YOUR HOUSE. WE CAN GET A WARRANT, BUT SINCE YOU'VE BEEN SO COOPERATIVE...?
MAKE 'EM GET A WARRANT, DAD!

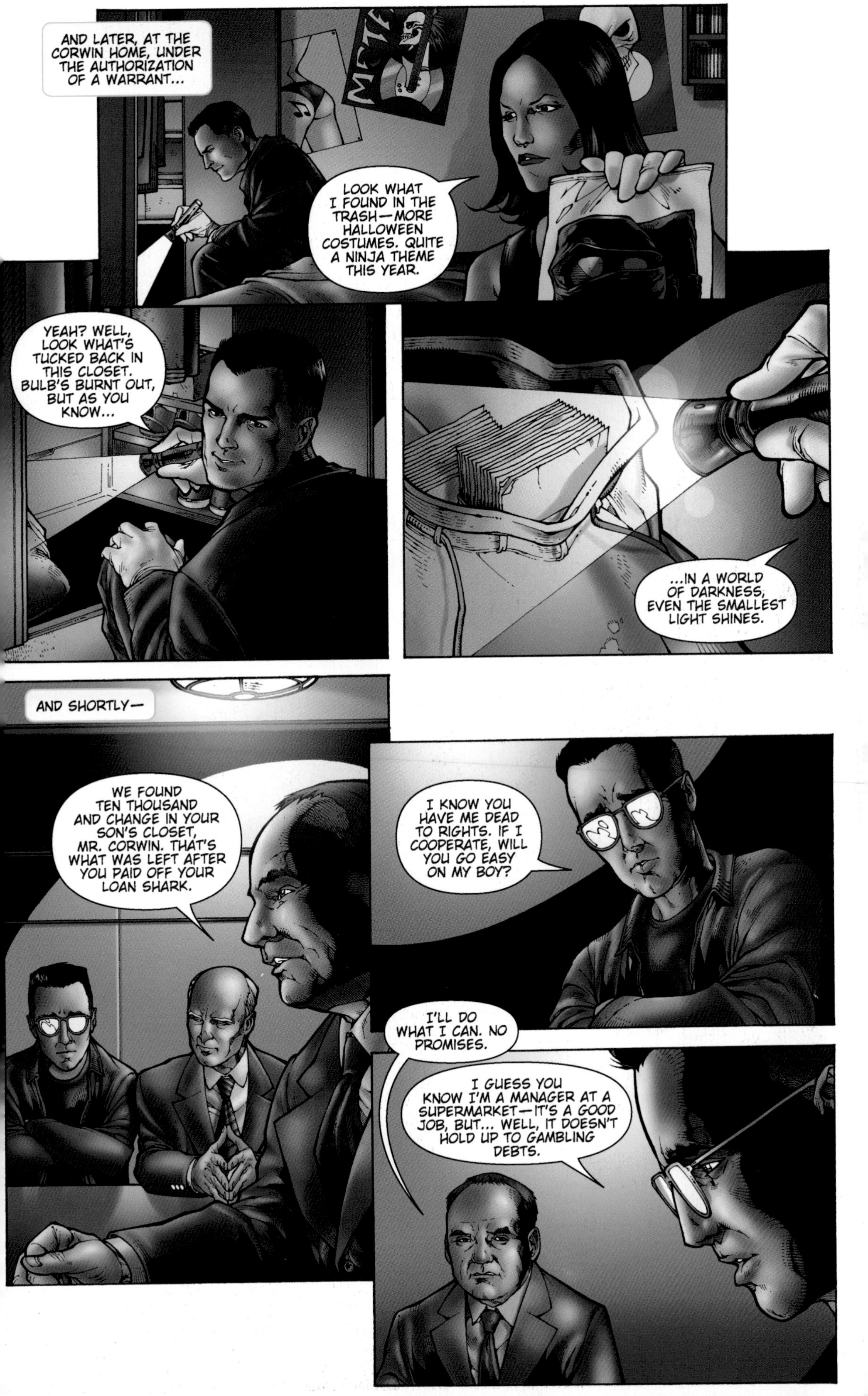
AND LATER, AT THE CORWIN HOME, UNDER THE AUTHORIZATION OF A WARRANT...
LOOK WHAT I FOUND IN THE TRASH—MORE HALLOWEEN COSTUMES. QUITE A NINJA THEME THIS YEAR.
YEAH? WELL, LOOK WHAT'S TUCKED BACK IN THIS CLOSET. BULB'S BURNT OUT, BUT AS YOU KNOW...
...IN A WORLD OF DARKNESS, EVEN THE SMALLEST LIGHT SHINES.
AND SHORTLY—
WE FOUND TEN THOUSAND AND CHANGE IN YOUR SON'S CLOSET, MR. CORWIN. THAT'S WHAT WAS LEFT AFTER YOU PAID OFF YOUR LOAN SHARK.
I KNOW YOU HAVE ME DEAD TO RIGHTS. IF I COOPERATE, WILL YOU GO EASY ON MY BOY?
I'LL DO WHAT I CAN. NO PROMISES.
I GUESS YOU KNOW I'M A MANAGER AT A SUPERMARKET—IT'S A GOOD JOB, BUT... WELL, IT DOESN'T HOLD UP TO GAMBLING DEBTS.

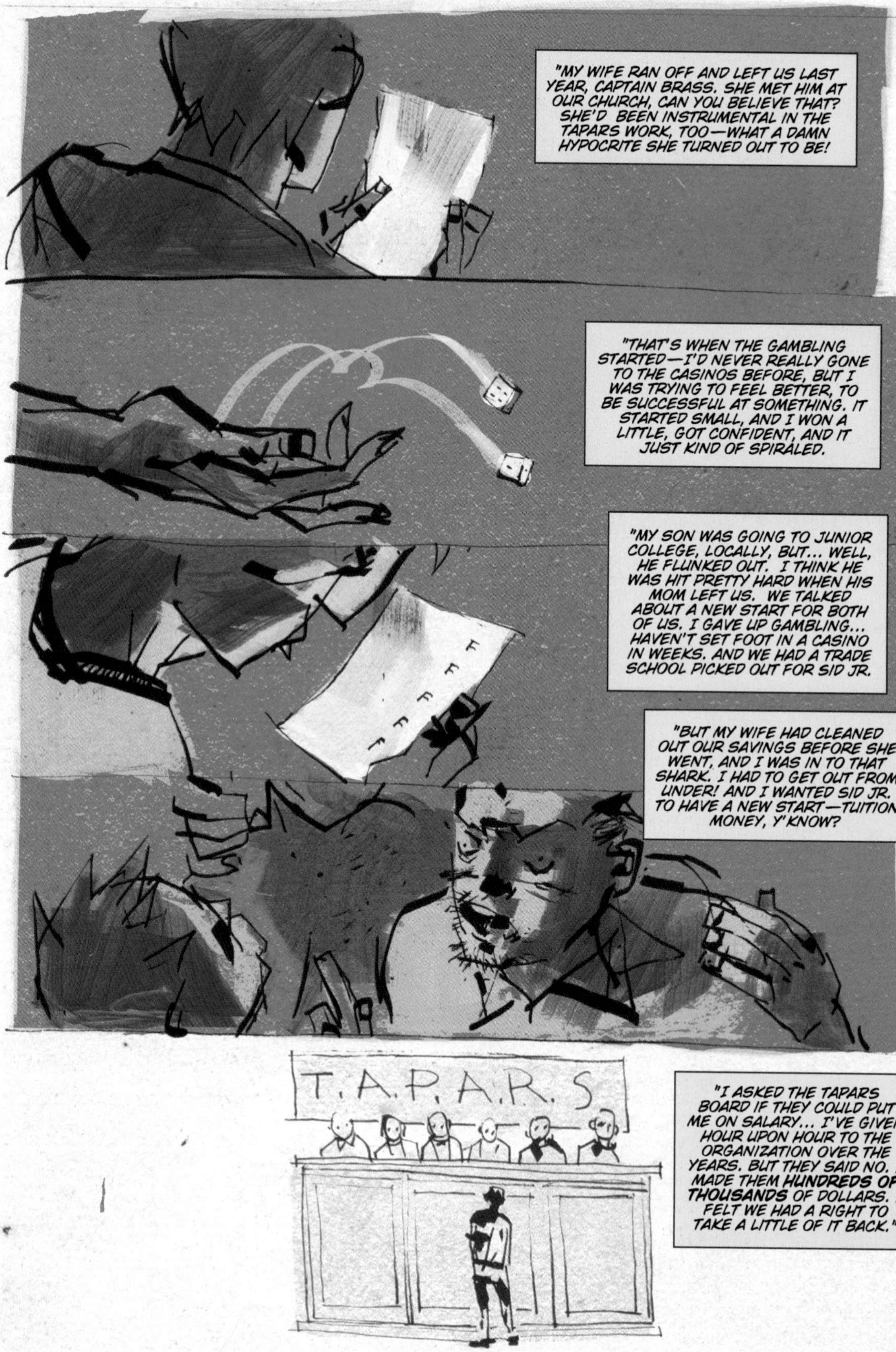
"MY WIFE RAN OFF AND LEFT US LAST YEAR, CAPTAIN BRASS. SHE MET HIM AT OUR CHURCH, CAN YOU BELIEVE THAT? SHE'D BEEN INSTRUMENTAL IN THE TAPARS WORK, TOO—WHAT A DAMN HYPOCRITE SHE TURNED OUT TO BE!
"THAT'S WHEN THE GAMBLING STARTED—I'D NEVER REALLY GONE TO THE CASINOS BEFORE, BUT I WAS TRYING TO FEEL BETTER, TO BE SUCCESSFUL AT SOMETHING. IT STARTED SMALL, AND I WON A LITTLE, GOT CONFIDENT, AND IT JUST KIND OF SPIRALED.
"MY SON WAS GOING TO JUNIOR COLLEGE, LOCALLY, BUT... WELL, HE FLUNKED OUT. I THINK HE WAS HIT PRETTY HARD WHEN HIS MOM LEFT US. WE TALKED ABOUT A NEW START FOR BOTH OF US. I GAVE UP GAMBLING... HAVEN'T SET FOOT IN A CASINO IN WEEKS. AND WE HAD A TRADE SCHOOL PICKED OUT FOR SID JR.
"BUT MY WIFE HAD CLEANED OUT OUR SAVINGS BEFORE SHE WENT, AND I WAS IN TO THAT SHARK. I HAD TO GET OUT FROM UNDER! AND I WANTED SID JR. TO HAVE A NEW START—TUITION MONEY, Y'KNOW?
T.A.P.A.R.S
"I ASKED THE TAPARS BOARD IF THEY COULD PUT ME ON SALARY... I'VE GIVEN HOUR UPON HOUR TO THE ORGANIZATION OVER THE YEARS. BUT THEY SAID NO. I MADE THEM **HUNDREDS OF THOUSANDS** OF DOLLARS. I FELT WE HAD A RIGHT TO TAKE A LITTLE OF IT BACK."

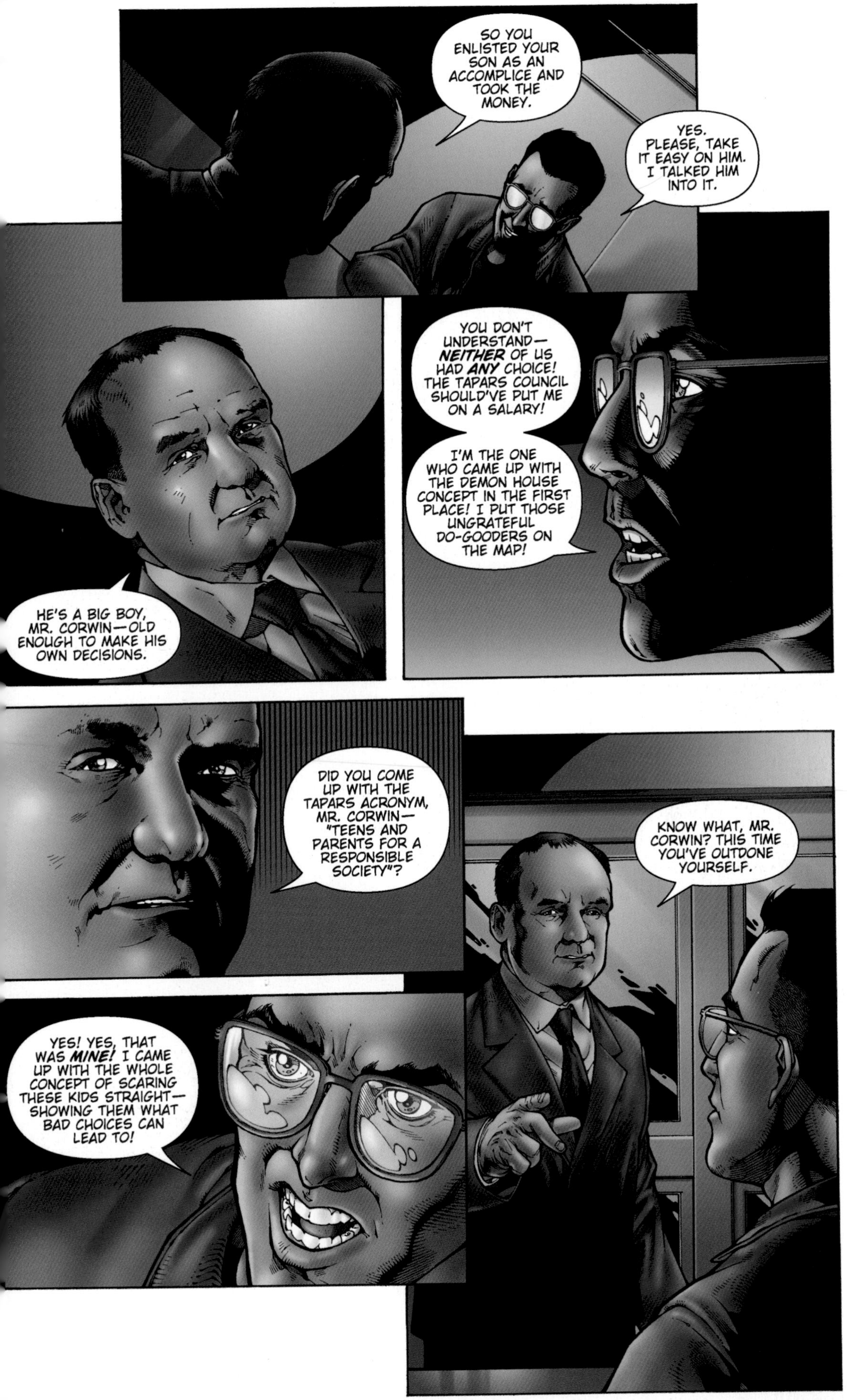
SO YOU ENLISTED YOUR SON AS AN ACCOMPLICE AND TOOK THE MONEY.
YES. PLEASE, TAKE IT EASY ON HIM. I TALKED HIM INTO IT.
HE'S A BIG BOY, MR. CORWIN—OLD ENOUGH TO MAKE HIS OWN DECISIONS.
YOU DON'T UNDERSTAND—**NEITHER** OF US HAD **ANY** CHOICE! THE TAPARS COUNCIL SHOULD'VE PUT ME ON A SALARY!
I'M THE ONE WHO CAME UP WITH THE DEMON HOUSE CONCEPT IN THE FIRST PLACE! I PUT THOSE UNGRATEFUL DO-GOODERS ON THE MAP!
DID YOU COME UP WITH THE TAPARS ACRONYM, MR. CORWIN—"TEENS AND PARENTS FOR A RESPONSIBLE SOCIETY"?
YES! YES, THAT WAS **MINE!** I CAME UP WITH THE WHOLE CONCEPT OF SCARING THESE KIDS STRAIGHT—SHOWING THEM WHAT BAD CHOICES CAN LEAD TO!
KNOW WHAT, MR. CORWIN? THIS TIME YOU'VE OUTDONE YOURSELF.

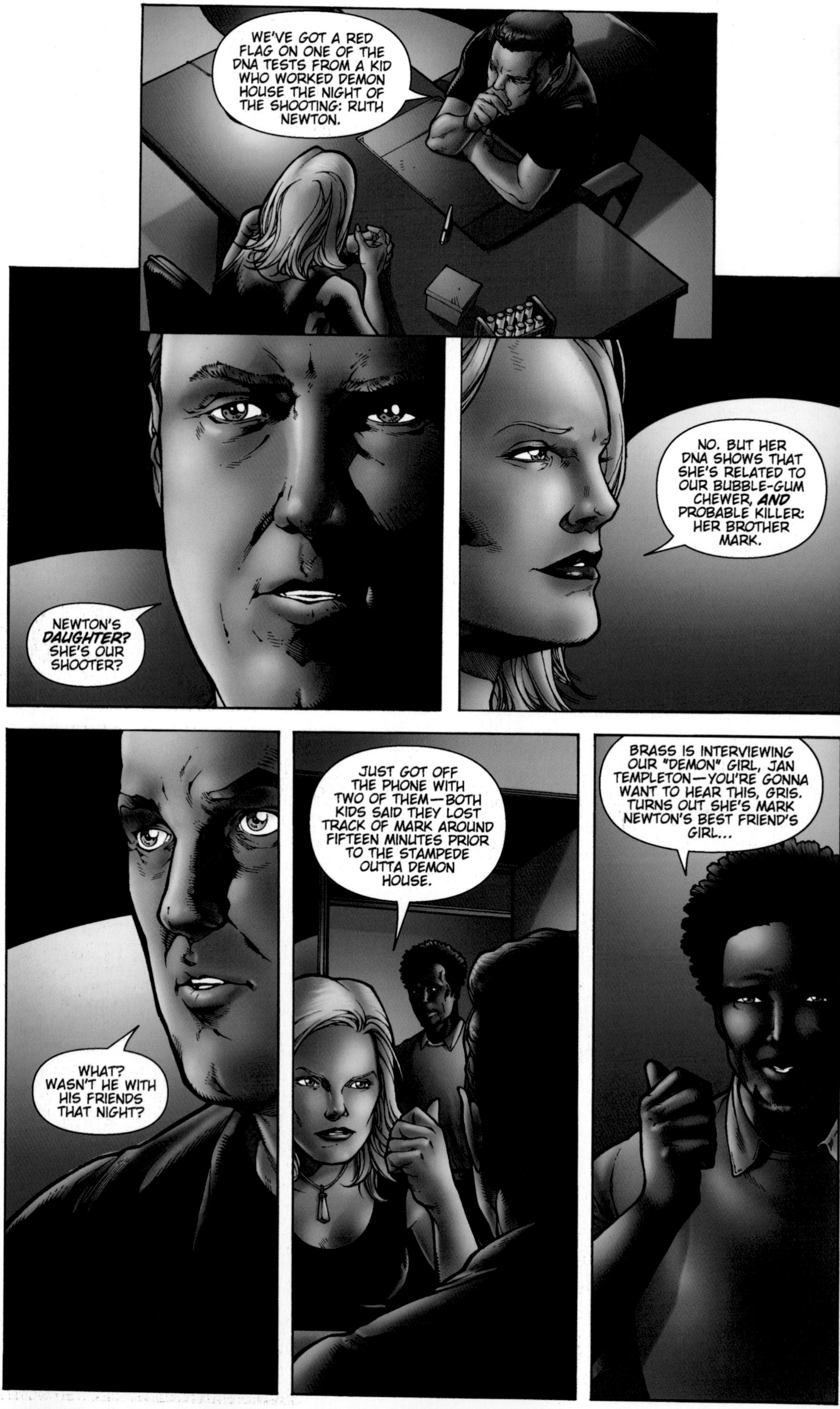
WE'VE GOT A RED FLAG ON ONE OF THE DNA TESTS FROM A KID WHO WORKED DEMON HOUSE THE NIGHT OF THE SHOOTING: RUTH NEWTON.
NEWTON'S DAUGHTER? SHE'S OUR SHOOTER?
NO. BUT HER DNA SHOWS THAT SHE'S RELATED TO OUR BUBBLE-GUM CHEWER, AND PROBABLE KILLER: HER BROTHER MARK.
WHAT? WASN'T HE WITH HIS FRIENDS THAT NIGHT?
JUST GOT OFF THE PHONE WITH TWO OF THEM—BOTH KIDS SAID THEY LOST TRACK OF MARK AROUND FIFTEEN MINUTES PRIOR TO THE STAMPEDE OUTTA DEMON HOUSE.
BRASS IS INTERVIEWING OUR "DEMON" GIRL, JAN TEMPLETON—YOU'RE GONNA WANT TO HEAR THIS, GRIS. TURNS OUT SHE'S MARK NEWTON'S BEST FRIEND'S GIRL...

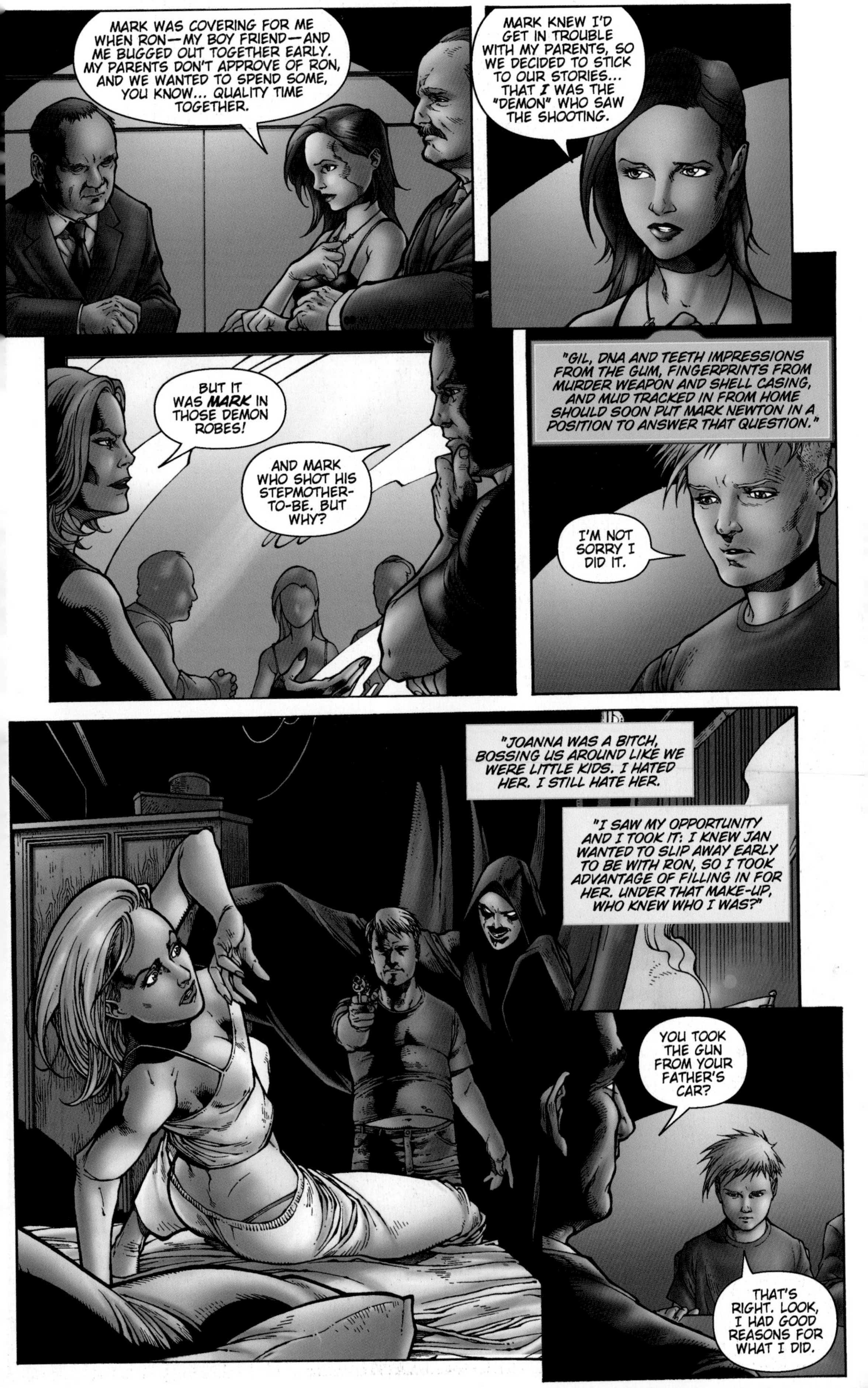
MARK WAS COVERING FOR ME WHEN RON—MY BOY FRIEND—AND ME BUGGED OUT TOGETHER EARLY. MY PARENTS DON'T APPROVE OF RON, AND WE WANTED TO SPEND SOME, YOU KNOW... QUALITY TIME TOGETHER.
MARK KNEW I'D GET IN TROUBLE WITH MY PARENTS, SO WE DECIDED TO STICK TO OUR STORIES... THAT *I* WAS THE "DEMON" WHO SAW THE SHOOTING.
BUT IT WAS ***MARK*** IN THOSE DEMON ROBES!
AND MARK WHO SHOT HIS STEPMOTHER-TO-BE. BUT WHY?
"GIL, DNA AND TEETH IMPRESSIONS FROM THE GUM, FINGERPRINTS FROM MURDER WEAPON AND SHELL CASING, AND MUD TRACKED IN FROM HOME SHOULD SOON PUT MARK NEWTON IN A POSITION TO ANSWER THAT QUESTION."
I'M NOT SORRY I DID IT.
"JOANNA WAS A BITCH, BOSSING US AROUND LIKE WE WERE LITTLE KIDS. I HATED HER. I STILL HATE HER.
"I SAW MY OPPORTUNITY AND I TOOK IT: I KNEW JAN WANTED TO SLIP AWAY EARLY TO BE WITH RON, SO I TOOK ADVANTAGE OF FILLING IN FOR HER. UNDER THAT MAKE-UP, WHO KNEW WHO I WAS?"
YOU TOOK THE GUN FROM YOUR FATHER'S CAR?
THAT'S RIGHT. LOOK, I HAD GOOD REASONS FOR WHAT I DID.

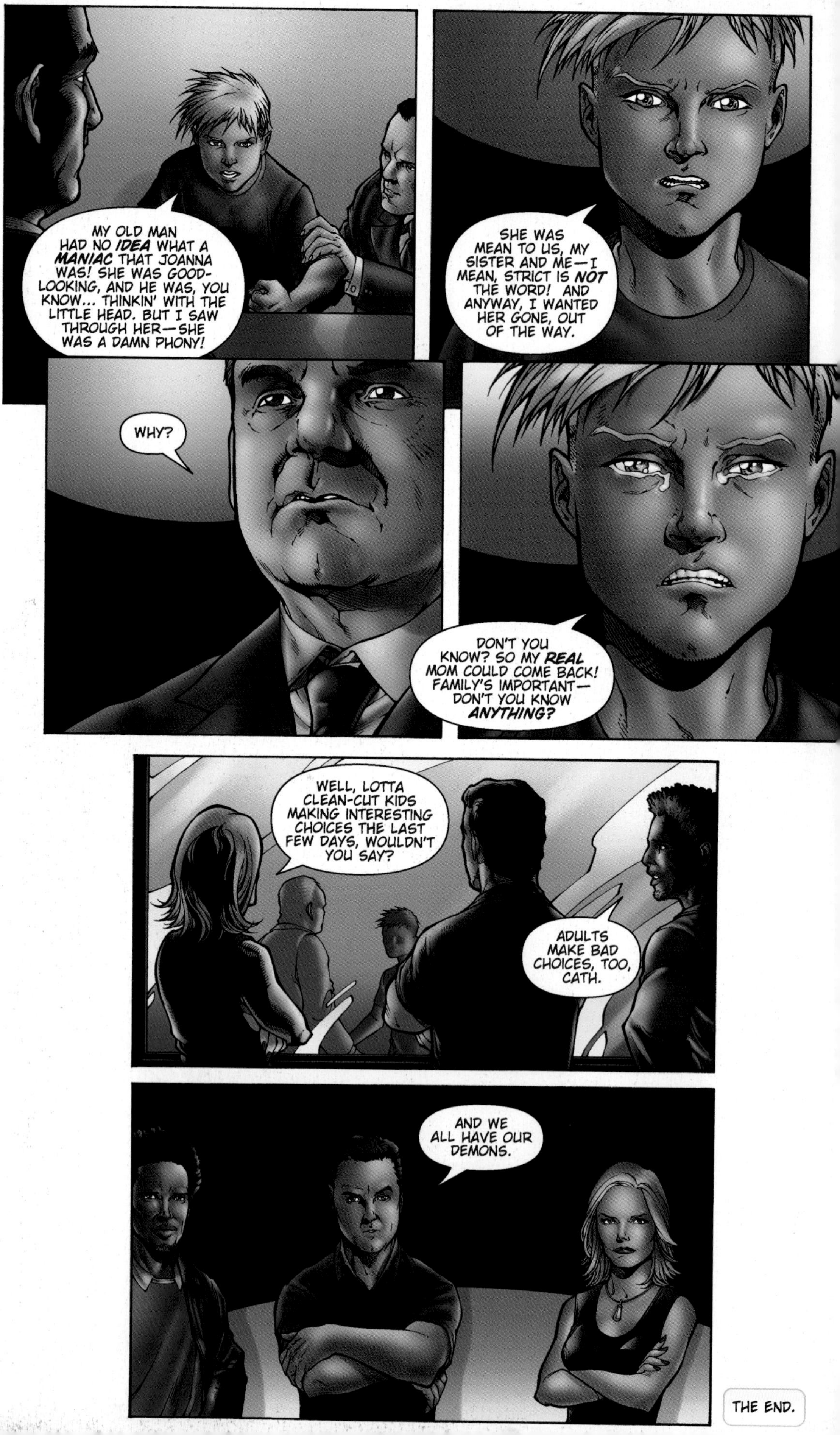
MY OLD MAN HAD NO IDEA WHAT A MANIAC THAT JOANNA WAS! SHE WAS GOOD-LOOKING, AND HE WAS, YOU KNOW... THINKIN' WITH THE LITTLE HEAD. BUT I SAW THROUGH HER—SHE WAS A DAMN PHONY!
SHE WAS MEAN TO US, MY SISTER AND ME—I MEAN, STRICT IS NOT THE WORD! AND ANYWAY, I WANTED HER GONE, OUT OF THE WAY.
WHY?
DON'T YOU KNOW? SO MY REAL MOM COULD COME BACK! FAMILY'S IMPORTANT—DON'T YOU KNOW ANYTHING?
WELL, LOTTA CLEAN-CUT KIDS MAKING INTERESTING CHOICES THE LAST FEW DAYS, WOULDN'T YOU SAY?
ADULTS MAKE BAD CHOICES, TOO, CATH.
AND WE ALL HAVE OUR DEMONS.
THE END.

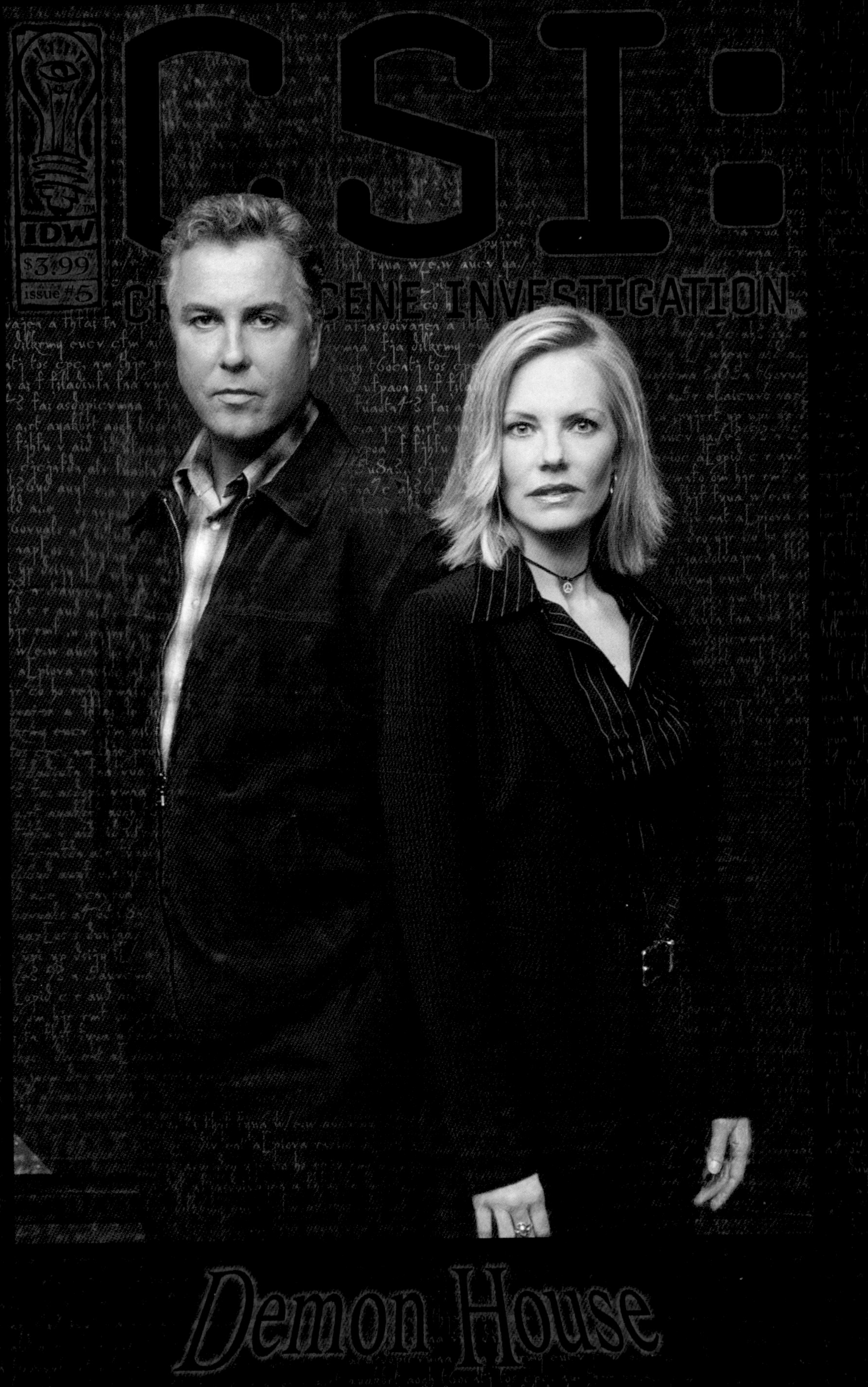
IDW
$3.99
ISSUE #5
CSI:
CRIME SCENE INVESTIGATION
Demon House

Greg Sanders Speaks!

An Interview with *CSI's* Eric Szmanda

How did you land the role of Greg Sanders?
I won a talent contest at the 4H County Fair back in Wisconsin. I sang '(C)luck be a Lady' to my pet hen, Esmerelda. The rest is history.

Your character has a definite love for chemistry. Were you a science geek growing up?

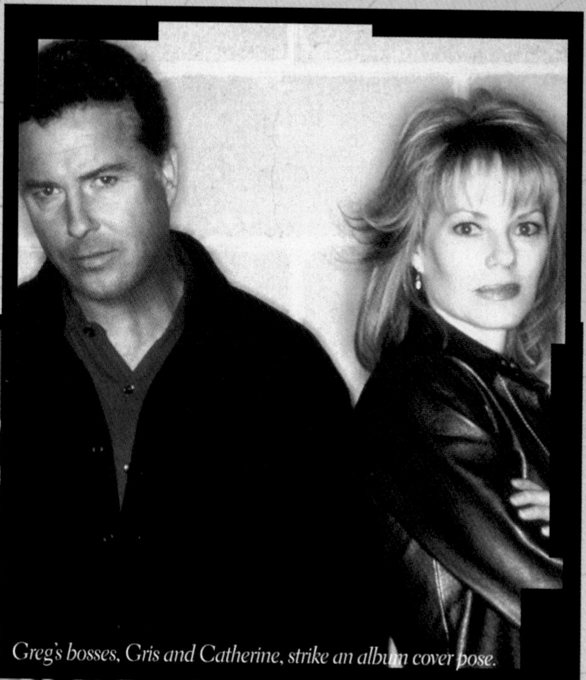

Greg's bosses, Gris and Catherine, strike an album cover pose.

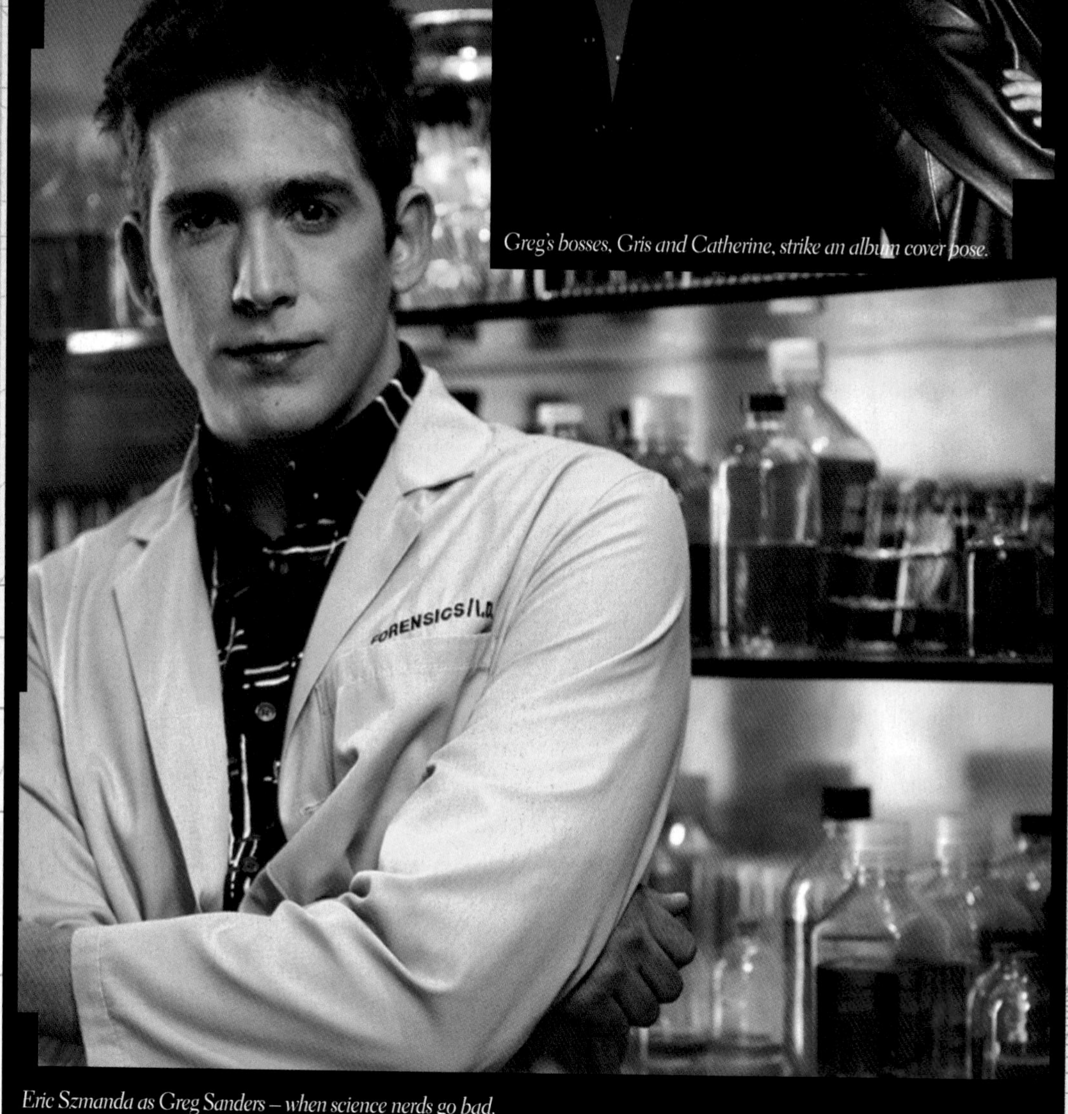
FORENSICS/L.D.

Eric Szmanda as Greg Sanders – when science nerds go bad.

Actually I used to build bombs for Libyan terrorists when I was in middle school. That helped me afford my first meth lab. But then it blew up. Ironic, huh?

Do you have any other character traits you share with Sanders?

Some say we have the same courageous and noble sense of commitment. But I see more resemblance in the perverse and twisted sense of humour.

Is preparation for your role particularly time-intensive?

If you mean, do I sit and wait the majority of the day, then yes. Do I expect anyone to feel sorry for me? No. I love sitting and waiting. It gives me the time to surf the net for really good porn in the privacy of my own trailer.

Have you visited actual crime labs to see how they function?

Only once. Years ago. But that's only because I was mistaken for a d.b. (dead body) I came to on the autopsy table, freaked out, and ran as fast as I could. I wasn't really interested in taking a tour at the time, but looking back I wish I had.

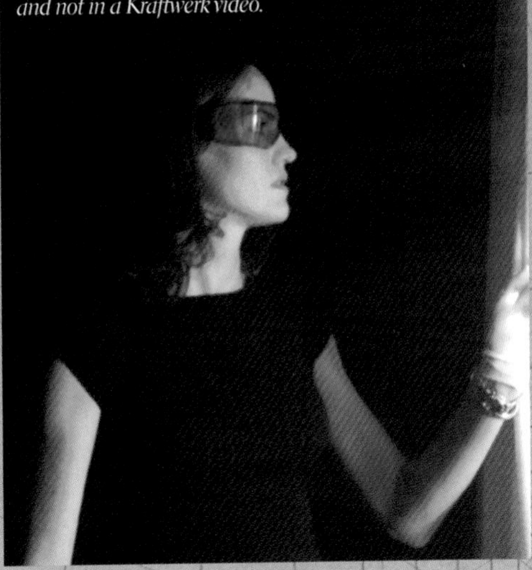

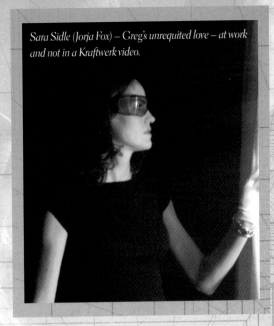

Sara Sidle (Jorja Fox) – Greg's unrequited love – at work and not in a Kraftwerk video.

How does if feel to see yourself in a video game?

Cool, but I wish I could kick my own ass. Or Grissom's! Unfortunately, the game doesn't allow you to fight.

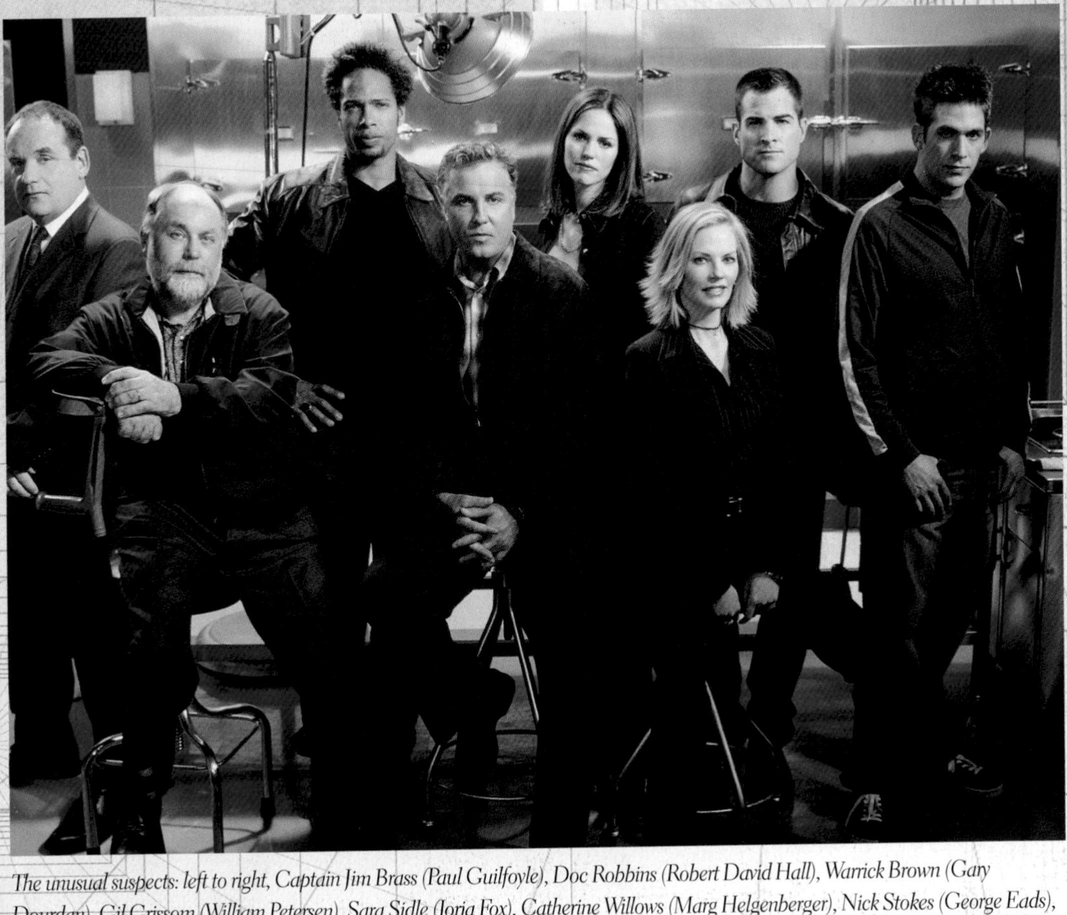

The unusual suspects: left to right, Captain Jim Brass (Paul Guilfoyle), Doc Robbins (Robert David Hall), Warrick Brown (Gary Dourdan), Gil Grissom (William Petersen), Sara Sidle (Jorja Fox), Catherine Willows (Marg Helgenberger), Nick Stokes (George Eads), and the junior member of the team…

Rich Catalani Speaks!

An Interview with *CSI*'s Technical Advisor **Rich Catalani**

As Technical Advisor on the show, you've had years of experience in forensics. In what areas do you specialise? What kind of education did you require to enter into the field?

I graduated from Cal State Northridge with a major in Biology and a minor in Chemistry. My speciality was in Medical Technology. This programme trains one in laboratory science in preparation for a Med Tech training programme following college. Med techs work in hospital or clinical labs where your blood, urine, etc. are sent for analysis when you go to the doctor's office or hospital for tests.

I graduated and was accepted into a training programme at Smith Kline Clinical Labs for Medical Technology training in the speciality license area of Toxicology, analysis of bodily fluids for drugs, poisons and heavy metals. I spent 12 months, 40 hours per week, training in clinical toxicology and analytical chemistry. Following the training, I had to take a comprehensive test for the state license, which I passed.

I worked a few years in the lab doing STAT and routine analysis of biological fluids for the lab. Then I saw an ad for a Toxicologist at the Los Angeles County Coroner's Office and applied. The Los Angeles

The man himself...

County Sheriff's Department also hired off the same list. I was hired 19 months later into the Toxicology Section at the Crime Lab. Once I got in the door, I discovered how interesting Forensic Sciences actually are and how science applies to the law. I was transferred around various sections in the lab, from Toxicology to the Narcotics section, then to the Serology section, and finally to the Firearms Identification section. The Narcotics section analyses solid dose drugs ranging from those taken in large

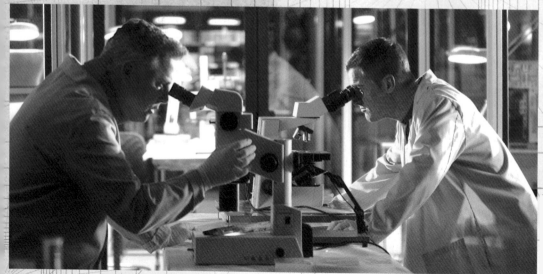

Toys for the boys. Gris (William Petersen) and Nick (George Eads) in the lab.

drug busts to small samples recovered from people's pockets. It was a really great application of my lab background. The Serology section analysed bodily fluids, attempting to attribute a source to blood or semen left at crime scenes. This is where I really developed my crime scene investigation techniques. It was extremely interesting and fulfilling to be involved in a case all the way from the crime scene to analysis and court testimony.

I was finally transferred to the Firearms Identification section, where I spent my last 10 or so years. This section analyses fired bullets and cartridge cases and compares them to suspected firearms. Many of the major crimes involve firearms and we're very busy. I was promoted to Section Supervisor in 1998 and spent four years supervising up to 17 sworn and civilian members.

How similar are the investigative portrayals on the show to what's actually done out in the field?

The forensic science we use on the show is well founded in reality and in our experiences. We have taken many of the real crimes we have investigated and woven them into the stories. Many times the area where we've 'cheated' is the time factor. For instance, I have been at a major crime scene for three days. We will condense the interesting aspects of that sort of investigation down into a few moments. Another area is our ability to consistently find evidence at scenes. In reality there are many times when evidence is not found at the scene or the evidence isn't as plentiful as we depict in the show. This lack of evidence is sometimes alluded to in the show. Sometimes this scarcity comes into play in a story. Overall, the techniques and science used in our show are the real deal.

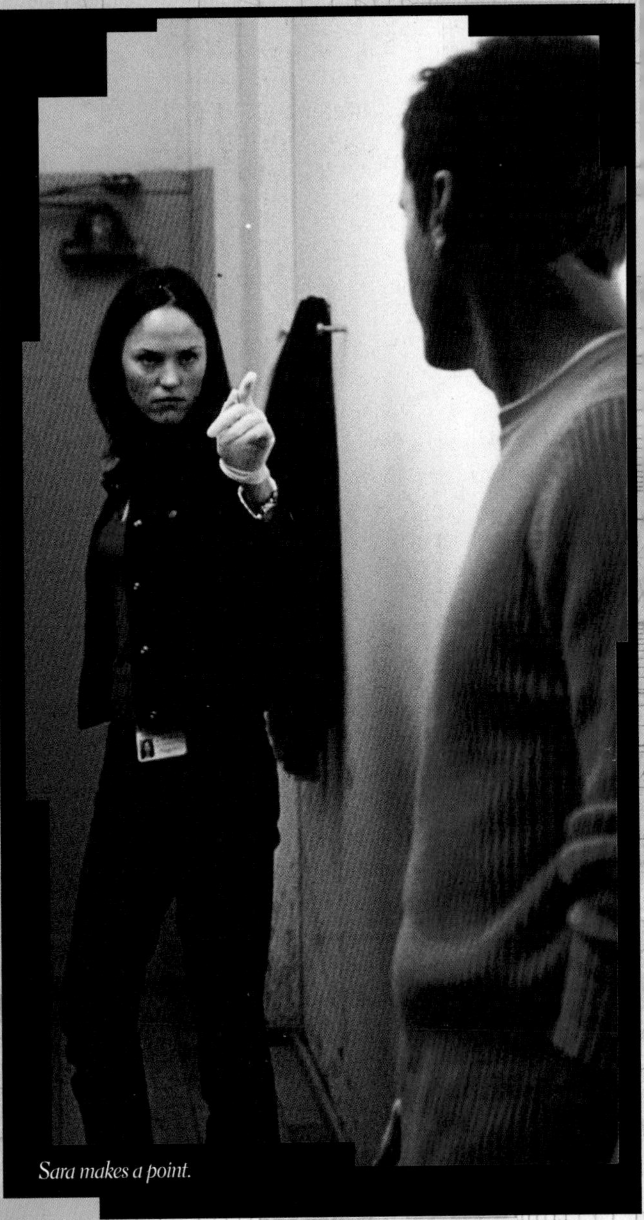

Sara makes a point.

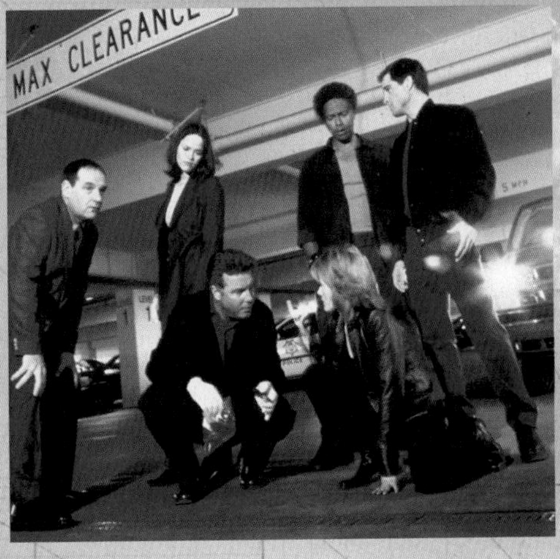
MAX CLEARANCE

The CSI team scouring for clues – or perhaps Catherine's earring?

So some cases from the show reflect real-life cases with which you've dealt?

Yes, I have experienced many of the scenarios we deal with in the show. One particular episode featured a mummified woman locked in an unplugged freezer for nine months. I am only sorry we can't relate the smell on TV.

How did crime-solving change from the time you began to the time you left? How did technology improve efficiency?

Just as technology is expanding and improving our everyday lives, it is improving the everyday lives of criminalists. DNA technology has improved vastly in the last few years. It can now be quickly done on samples that were too small only a few years ago. Computerised automation has made analysis of multiple samples simple. Modern digital photography techniques have made documentation and storage a breeze. The field of Firearms Identification has conducted analysis basically the same way since the early part of the 20th Century. Recently a computer system for screening fired bullets and cartridge cases has made national database comparisons a possibility. Technology has definitely improved the field of Criminalistics.

How were you selected to be the technical advisor for CSI?

My good friend Elizabeth Devine was the tech advisor prior to me. She has since advanced and was in need of a person to replace her. I had recently retired from the Los Angeles County Sheriff's Department and was available.

Gris and Catherine set to work, apparently in Sleepy Hollow...

Warrick Brown: "They were watching Gigli?!*"*

Do you prefer the behind-the-scenes work of television or the hands-on actual investigations?

I thoroughly enjoyed working as a forensic scientist. It is my opinion that it's the best job in the world for a 'science geek'. There are many disciplines in the field to keep one interested. The bureaucracy involved was what wore me down, but I really enjoyed the work and the people. I never imagined I would be working in the TV business. It is completely different from everything I have done before. I will miss the real-life investigations but for now, I am happy telling tales of my experiences and helping the actors portray forensic scientists.